# Celtic Lore

# Celtic Lore

The history of the Druids
and their timeless traditions

## Ward Rutherford

Aquarian/Thorsons
*An Imprint of* HarperCollins*Publishers*

Thorsons/Aquarian
An Imprint of HarperCollins*Publishers*
77-85 Fulham Palace Road,
Hammersmith, London W6 8JB

Published by Thorsons/Aquarian 1993
1  3  5  7  9  10  8  6  4  2

A catalogue record for this book
is available from the British Library

ISBN 1 85538 134 6

Typeset by Harper Phototypesetters Limited,
Northampton, England
Printed in Great Britain by
Hartnolls Ltd., Bodmin, Cornwall

# Contents

# Acknowledgements

This book could never have been completed but for the help of a number of people. They include the eminent Celticist Dr Anne Ross; David Keys, archaeological correspondent of the *Independent*; George Lambor, Editor of *Ancient* magazine; my good friend and fellow-author Eric Clark, who unearthed some of the books I needed; and, of course, my wife Marilyn, who patiently waded through the typescript, finding and correcting countless of my errors.

# Prologue: Laughter at Delphi

In 279 BC a Celtic force crossed the Alps from southern Gaul, passed through northern Italy and, sweeping all defence before it, marched through what was Yugoslavia and Albania into Greece. Still irresistible, by the late autumn it had scaled Mount Parnassus and was menacing the holiest place in the ancient world, the oracular shrine of Apollo at Delphi.

Before the end of the day it was in their hands and their commander took a conqueror's stroll through the sacred precinct, throwing open one after another the doors of the treasuries of the city states with mounting disbelief. He ended in the sanctuary itself where, according to Diodorus of Sicily (c. 40 BC), he was able to contain himself no longer and gave way to helpless laughter.

The cause of his mirth was two-fold. First, that mortals should make gifts to the gods, as the treasuries seemed to show that the Greeks had done; for, as he said, the gods had no need of gifts when 'they showered them so liberally on men'. Secondly, that they were so naïve as to conceive the divine as if it had human form and so create images in bronze and marble.

Standing legs astride, hands on hips, in the echoing, subterranean vault, he presented, as Diodorus tells us, not only a sacrilegious, but a bizarre and terrifying sight. Immensely tall in comparison with the Greeks and made more so by his horned helmet, his face was adorned with a flaring moustache and his costume consisted of breeches, a brightly coloured shirt and a tartan plaid cloak fastened with a heavy brooch.

No less bizarre and terrifying were his troops, a force historians have estimated at probably about 30,000 strong. In later conflicts Irish and Scottish troops struck such dread into their enemies that the Germans of the First World War dubbed the kilted Highlanders 'the ladies from Hell'. So, too, those who disrupted the sacred peace of Delphi must also have seemed to be not of this world. Its citizens can have heard nothing like the harsh Celtic war-shouts or the blood-chilling note of the carnyx, the long battle-trumpet; seen nothing like this horde of giants with their vicious, double-edged claymores and their shields as tall as they were. Or their spear-throwers who went into battle wearing only the torc, the thick, heavy, Celtic neck-ring. Or, most extraordinary of all, woman-warriors; fierce, strident-voiced Amazons.

Hearing that the Celts were on the march and apprehensive of the threat to the shrine, the Greeks had consulted the oracle. It had told them, with customary opacity, that it would be 'saved by the white virgins'. They took it to mean that its tutelary goddesses, Athena and Artemis, would intervene to destroy the impious barbarians, but the true meaning, or what was taken as the true meaning, shortly became clear. Winter set in early, bringing with it heavy snow-storms. A Greek army accustomed to fighting in such conditions – Mount Parnassus is a winter-sports centre – engaged the invaders at its foot. Unable to defend themselves against both their attackers and the snow flurries blowing in their faces, the Celts had to disengage and, with desperately over-stretched supply lines, start what was less a retreat than a rout. The 'white virgins' had fulfilled their promise.

The rise to power by which the Celts could challenge the classical world had been meteoric. The middle of the first millennium BC saw them burst from their original homelands round the source of the Danube in a series of waves[1]. Soon masters of great swathes of eastern Europe, Asia Minor and Spain, the whole of France, Belgium, Switzerland and finally the British Isles, the Greeks listed them as one of the three largest barbarian nations, with the Persians and the Scythians. (It has to be said at this point that the whole of the mass-migration of peoples has been thrown into the melting pot by Professor Colin Renfrew's theory, expounded in *Archaeology and Language*, that many of those cultural and even linguistic changes seen in particular areas are due less to the advent of new populations than to developments taking place among the existing populations. His thesis has yet to find general acceptance and as one lacking the competence to pronounce on it, I shall continue to treat the Celts and their history as it has been treated hitherto.)

Even the richest and most powerful of their neighbours found themselves vulnerable to what seemed like a remorseless Celtic floodtide. Moving into northern Italy, they pushed back the frontiers of the 500-year-old Etruscan civilisation and established what were to become the cities of Turin, Milan and Bergamo. A century before the march on Delphi a warrior force from what is now the city of Sens in Burgundy seized Rome, remained in occupation for seven months and withdrew only when paid an extortionate ransom. In the words of the Greek geographer, Strabo of Amasia (c. 64 BC-AD 19), the Celts were 'war-mad'. Besides those military adventures known to history, others of which we have only hints in legend took them across the Alps, into the valley of the Po and as far south as Sicily.

A reaction to their war-madness was, of course, inevitable. As Toynbee says of the Assyrians, they had rendered themselves intolerable to their neighbours. It was the Romans who shouldered the burden of subduing them and, after some reverses, succeeded in inflicting a series of decisive defeats. By ill chance for the Celts, these blows in the south came at a time when they were being squeezed by the advancing Germanic tribes in the east. Before the close of the millennium which had seen such extraordinary expansion the entire process had been thrown into reverse.

In *The New York Times* John Leonard, reviewing my book on the Druids, wrote that 'it has been downhill for the Celts for at least 2,500 years'. In many ways he was right.

But not quite. Despite their sudden emergence and equally sudden decline the Celts have left a heritage which prevents us from cataloguing them with all those other marauders – Huns, Goths, Saracens, Magyars, Vikings, Mongols – whose bloody incursions stain the pages of European history, but who remained a menace only until they had been comprehensively vanquished on the battlefield.

According to its mythical history Ireland was overrun by a succession of invaders, the last of whom, the Milesians, ancestors of the people we now call the Irish, found that their predecessors had left them four Gifts: a sword, a spear, a cauldron and a rough-hewn block of stone. What distinguished these objects from the ordinary run was that each had potent magical properties. Thus the stone could identify the rightful ruler of the country by emitting a loud cry. As the 'Stone of Destiny' it became the property of the early kings of Ireland who installed it at their stronghold on the Hill of Tara. There it provided their coronation seat and the throne from which they pronounced their edicts and meted out their justice.

Stones with supposed unusual powers are recurrent in myth worldwide, but none has as chequered a history as the Stone of

Destiny. In the sixth century AD Tara was abandoned. Thereafter Scottish and Irish myths, for once in accord, say it was taken to Scotland, which is where we next hear of it. Or, at least, of something very like it. What is today a modest Tayside village near Perth was, until the eighth century, the capital of the Pictish kingdom. This was Scone where its kings were crowned on a slab of stone which came to be called 'The Stone of Destiny'.

In the ninth century Pictish and Scottish thrones were united and their first king, Kenneth McAlpine, moved the stone to his own crowning place, at Dunstaffnage Castle, Perth. Two centuries later the English King Edward I, becoming entangled in a quarrel north of the border, used the opportunity to cart it off to Westminster where it has resided ever since. Built into the high-backed, gilded chair, it forms the seat on which British kings and queens have been crowned ever since[2]. (Its adventurous history has continued to modern times. Removed by Scottish Nationalists in 1950 it was recovered just in time for the coronation of the present queen, Elizabeth II, in 1952.)

Whether this is the original Stone of Destiny is debatable. Some scholars claim that the stone never left Ireland and that in 1798 it was moved from the Hill of Tara to mark the grave of a group of rebels who fought for Irish independence. All the same Scone has some claim as it was known to have been an important religious centre in pre-Christian times. In any event the English king's theft shows that he took it for the genuine article.

The three remaining Gifts were lost without trace – or almost. The Welsh tale of Peredur son of Evrawg abounds in mysterious incidents, but none is more so than the scene the ingenuous young knight witnesses during a visit to his uncle, the rich Fisher-King. Two youths enter his hall bearing a huge spear from which blood streams. They are followed by two maidens with a silver salver on which is a bleeding head. There is little doubt that both spear and dish were ritual objects carried over from pagan times. Despite its superficial dissimilarity, many scholars equate the salver with another of the Magic Gifts, namely the Cauldron.

The spear is certainly yet another, for it is said of the original that it dripped blood when held aloft. An Irish text records that sparks 'as big as eggs' fell from it when it was brandished and Jean Marx suggests that it may in fact symbolise the lightning shaft or possibly the thunderbolt, frequently represented as a divine spear. Nonetheless, once christianised it became the Spear of Longinus, the centurion said to have used it to pierce the side of Jesus as he hung on the cross.

Like the 'The Stone of Destiny', the Spear of Longinus had a physical existence, not as one but at least two objects, each claiming to be the original and each with its own history. The first, possessed of healing properties, like the spear of Celtic mythology, was venerated in the basilica of Constantine from about AD 530, only to vanish during the Arab invasions. It was recovered by Crusaders who captured Antioch in 1098 and the momentous news was proclaimed by Pope Urban II, though thereafter little was heard of it.

The second, which appears to have had a less adventurous career, turned up in the sixth century at the monastery of St-Maurice d'Agaune in Burgundy where it became an object of pilgrimage. Such was its reputation that, two hundred years later, the first Holy Roman Emperor, Charlemagne, was said to have carried it in battle. Not only did it ensure victory, it also endowed him with clairvoyant powers and, like the Stone, it was prefixed with the word 'destiny' and became known as the 'Spear of Destiny'. Such a vital part of the Holy Roman imperial regalia did it become that its mere possession carried the right to the throne, so that by seizing it, in 1002, Henry II of Germany made himself emperor.

In the fifteenth century, when the title of Holy Roman Emperor became hereditary to the Austrian royal house of Habsburg, the Spear passed into their custody. Down the centuries its supposed occult qualities continued to exert a fascination for many, among them the composer Richard Wagner and an ardent admirer of his music named Adolf Hitler. He so convinced himself that his own fate and that of the Spear were linked that in 1938, when as Chancellor and Führer of Germany, he annexed Austria to his Greater Reich, among his first actions was to order that the Spear should be brought from Vienna to Nürnberg. (After the war it was returned to Austria and is now in the Künsthistorisches Museum in Vienna.)

Its authenticity, either as one of the original Gifts to the people of Ireland or as the Spear of Longinus, is even more doubtful than that of the Stone of Destiny. There is to begin with no scriptural sanction for the name Longinus. The gospels simply state that Christ was pierced in the side by a soldier present at his execution without recording his name. A centurion called Longinus first appears, in a quite different context, in the *Acta Pilati*, or Acts of Pilate, part of the apocryphal gospel of Nicodemus. At about the same time the story that the soldier responsible for piercing Christ's side had converted was current among the early fathers. The two legends obviously became fused and the soldier became the centurion Longinus.

Nor is it even certain that the Habsburg spear had ever been a weapon. Some antiquarians have suggested it was probably a monastic bread knife mounted on a long shaft!

There was, of course, a second weapon among the Gifts: the sword. In its ability, where it did not kill outright, to inflict wounds from which the sufferer never recovered, it bears an obvious similarity to what is perhaps the best known of all mythical swords – Arthur's Excalibur. There is no doubt of Excalibur's Irish origins. It is Caladbolg, the sword of the legendary king of Ulster Fergus mac Roech which later becomes the Caledfwlch of the early Welsh tales.

As the properties of the Gifts indicate, their donors were no mere mortals. They were a race of gods, the Tuatha De Danann or People of Dana, migrants from the 'islands of the north of the world' according to the ancient texts, who came to Irish shores bringing with them, besides their Gifts, 'science, magic, wisdom, art and Druidism'. With such a combination they were invulnerable to all enemies, until the arrival of the Milesians. Forced to cede their land to them, some of the Tuatha returned to their northerly islands, while others took up residence in the prehistoric tumuli, the *sidhs*.

The blood which flowed through the veins of the legendary Milesians, the blood of the Celtic race, also flows through others, notably the Scots, Welsh, Cornish and Bretons. But it is also found in various admixtures and dilutions in many European peoples, among them the French.

From the sixteenth century France was ruled by the House of Bourbon, which also provided Spain, Naples and Sicily with their kings during the eighteenth and nineteenth centuries. The name derives from that of the god Borvo, whose cult was popular in the Loire and Rhône valleys as well as in Provence and the Alps, in all of which places the word Bourbon or Bourbonne occurs as part of a place-name. Thus, while British monarchs were maintaining one Celtic custom, those of their traditional enemies, the French, were maintaining another – that of deriving the foundation of a ruling dynasty from a god.

But it is not only among royalty that such traces of a distant past survive. Most of us touch wood, kiss under the Christmas mistletoe or refrain from bringing maythorn into our homes, unmindful of the fact that these acts are the relics of a complex system of Celtic tree lore. We talk glibly of 'things happening in threes' and so keep alive their belief in the sacred triad. We celebrate November the Fifth or May Day with their unmistakable echoes of the festivals celebrated by our pagan ancestors.

One might dismiss all these as chance atavistic survivals were it not for countless Celtic attitudes which have penetrated the psyche to exert their influence upon history. Many will be discussed in these pages, but one will serve here.

The Celts were not only war mad, they waged it as a game with strict rules of which one was the *fír fer* (literally 'men's truth'). By mutual agreement, the clash of contending armies was converted into a fight between a champion from each side, the single combats which figure so prominently in literature from Irish epics like the *Tain Bo Cualnge* (The Cattle Raid of Cooley) down to Medieval Arthurian legend. By this means, for a time at least, war became effectively a trial by combat in which he who had right on his side was expected to triumph.

It was such rules, jealously maintained throughout the Middle Ages, that governed the conduct of European chivalry. Typical was an incident during the Hundred Years' War. In 1359, Thomas of Canterbury, an English knight, violated a truce by seizing a French knight, Olivier du Guesclin, who happened to be walking the streets of the Breton town of Dinan, then in English hands.

Olivier was the brother of the great Breton soldier, Bertrand du Guesclin, who complained of the outrage to the English commander-in-chief, the Duke of Lancaster. The duke ordered Olivier's captor to meet Bertrand in single combat. After a hard-fought duel with lance and sword, a smashing blow to the face from du Guesclin's mailed fist overcame his opponent. As he was dragged from the field the Breton knight apologised for his own violence, to be told by the English commander that Thomas's fate was 'no more than he deserved'. He had broken the rules.

# PART 1
# THE WEB OF BELIEF

# Chapter 1
# The Celtic Civilisation

It was not only their adversaries across the battlefield who recorded a profound culture shock on first encountering the Celts. The Roman historian Tacitus and the poet Lucan are among those who express their abhorrence for the Celtic practice of human sacrifice. The Greek geographer and philosopher Posidonius of Apamea (135–51 BC), who travelled extensively in the Celtic lands, had difficulty overcoming his nausea the first time he saw warriors returning from the fray with the blood-dripping heads of decapitated enemies – 'the crop of warfare', as they were called – dangling like a string of oversized onions from their saddle-bows, though he admits that familiarity accustomed him to the sight.

But besides horror, there was also astonishment. Astonishment, for example, at their immense appetites especially for roast boar, their unslakable thirst for wine or their uninhibitedly public sexual displays. Julius Caesar, in *The Conquest of Gaul*, mentions the British custom of sharing one woman among groups of ten to twelve men 'especially among brothers and among brothers and sons'. Dio Cassio (AD 150–225) records an exchange between Julia Domna, the wife of the emperor Severus (AD 193–211) and an unnamed Caledonian woman. The sedate patrician chaffs her interlocutor about the freedom with which she and her sisters extended what the Celts euphemistically called 'the friendship of the thighs'. She answered with some asperity that her own people's ways were vastly superior to Roman ones. Since everything was frank and open, they were able to consort unashamedly with the finest of men. Roman matrons, on the other hand, with the secrecy their false standards of respectability imposed on them, could find lovers only among those prepared to indulge in hole-and-corner liaisons. In fact, one reason why Celtic succession was matrilinear was probably because, amid such general promiscuity, it was difficult to be sure exactly who the father of a particular child had been.

Yet, sharp as were the contrasts between their respective ways of

life, the Celts, as we are now beginning to appreciate, were not
barbarians by any accepted usage of the word.

It is true that Celtic society was very differently organised from that
of the Greek city states or imperial Rome. In place of their centralised
authority, a system of interlocking political entities enjoyed a wide
measure of individual autonomy and took decisions through its own
public assembly. The smallest of these, the family, belonged to the
clan or *fine* (the word means, roughly, 'kindred'), which possessed
considerable independence and continued to do so in Scotland until
the rebellion of the Young Pretender, 'Bonnie Prince Charlie', in 1745.
Clan ties were strong and most duties and responsibilities applied
to its members as a whole rather than to any individual. Thus the
clan was effectively the common owner of all land, while each
member of it was liable for his share of fines or other dues. A similar
form of social organisation, stressing the interests of kindred rather
than of the individual, is also to be found in India in one of its many
parallels with Celtic society.

The *fine* was itself part of the *tuath*, a word which means 'people'
or 'tribe', though later it was extended to include the territory it
occupied which was ruled by a king or *rí*.

Society was rooted in the land and archaeology has shown Celtic
farms to be equal and often superior to those found elsewhere.
Cereals and pulses were grown; pigs, cattle, sheep and horses reared.
In Ireland there is even evidence of selective breeding. Farm
buildings included granaries for seedcorn, racks on which corn and
hay could be dried, husking and winnowing areas, storage pits for
the grain as well as livestock enclosures. Among rural crafts were
cloth weaving and pottery throwing.

Nor were they technologically backward. Before their time grain
had been ground in so-called saddle querns in which one large flat
stone was rubbed laboriously to and fro against another. The Celts
introduced the rotary quern whereby grinding could be carried out
with a more efficient rotary movement. Experts in dry-stone
building, they also built roads and bridges unsurpassed until the
coming of the Romans. From a bronze-working people, they were
among the first iron users, increasing their agricultural productivity
with the iron-shod plough, besides using the metal in a number of
other innovations such as scissors.[1]

Standards of craftsmanship were high and often well in advance
of their time. Four-wheeled wagons found in burials are of elegant

design and ran on wheels whose precise spokes of hornbeam were mortised into oak hubs which themselves turned on ingenious wooden roller-bearings. The design is so similar wherever the wheels are found that Professor Piggott suggests there was a common Celtic tradition in the wheelwright's craft. This is supported by the existence of what is almost a standard gauge between wheels of 4'8".

This is not the only instance of standardisation. It seems also to have applied to weights, while metal ingots were of consistent size. Salt was in standard sized cakes and the storage pits mentioned earlier were so dug as to take a pre-determined quantity of grain.

If gargantuan appetites struck their observers, high standards of farming bespeak a taste for good food well cooked. This is borne out, not only by other things we know about the Celtic life, but by evidence that cheese and other dairy products were made on farms. It is equally plain that they enjoyed sharing life's pleasures. They were great party givers and party goers. Standards of hospitality were proverbially high and all comers, irrespective of origin, were fed before any inquiry was made as to their business.

Such was the importance of hospitality that it was expected even of the gods. Bress, who falls short in this respect, ends by losing his kingdom. On the other hand, In Dagda, the Good God, merits the epithet on account of his cauldron from which no one leaves hungry. In the Irish *Adventure of Art son of Conn*, the hero arrives at an Otherworld palace where laden tables appear before him as if by magic, and the ability to feed large numbers was, of course, one possessed by the Holy Grail. In the anonymously-written *Quest of the Holy Grail*, the grail circuits King Arthur's hall at the time the assembled company is gathered for its evening repast, setting before each place 'the food its occupant desired'.

Caesar may or may not be right in condemning the life of the plebeians as little better than that of slaves, but travellers were impressed by Celtic cleanliness, a concern for which is emphasised in one of the Welsh stories where the central character expresses disgust at the squalor of a guest-house in which he is compelled to pass a night.

From Celtic burials we know, too, that the upper classes, at any rate, lived in some elegance and luxury with successful farming producing sufficient surpluses of cereal and other crops for them to trade for the finest works of art and craftsmanship from all over the world. Shards of Greek black-figure ware are frequent on Celtic sites and a sixth century BC burial chamber at Höhmichele, near Heuneberg in Austria, is even hung with draperies which include Chinese silk thread.

Not that the Celtic magnates despised their native artists. Indeed, a status close to that of the aristocracy was enjoyed by the intellectual and artistic elite, to which the Irish gave the name of *aes dana*, the folk of art, and among whom they numbered artists, poets, historians, lawyers and doctors. The *aes dana* even possessed a privilege not always available to the aristocracy – that of crossing the tribal frontiers without let.

It was their craftsmen who were responsible for the magnificent Celtic jewelry, including the gold torcs. Their invention of enamelling on metal provided a means of decorating scabbards, shields, helmets and sword hilts as well as domestic and other objects, many of which can be seen still with jewel-like colours aglow. Celtic art reached its zenith from what is usually known as the La Téne period. La Téne is at the shallow north-eastern end of Lake Neuchâtel in Switzerland and it was here in 1856 that a large collection of Celtic objects including swords, spears, fibulae, tools and other objects dated to the fourth and fifth centuries BC was found. What was most striking about them was their decoration of s-shapes, spirals, patterns of symmetrical rounds, of twisting tendrils and, in some cases, of highly stylised but elegant animals. Nothing like them had been seen in previous Celtic discoveries so that the term La Téne came to be used for artefacts in the same style and of the same quality found all over the Celtic culture-province. It has been characterised as the 'most significant artistic achievement north of the Alps since the Ice Age'.

As the Empress Julia Domna's exchange with the Caledonian woman shows, the attitude to women in the Celtic world was in marked contradistinction to that of the classical.

This went well beyond sexual licence. A well-known painting portrays Socrates surrounded by friends and disciples in the hours before he quaffed the hemlock. His wife, Xantippe, a shadowy figure so lost in the background as to be almost invisible, reflects the position of the Greek woman who, on marriage, surrendered to her husband all her possessions and, while expected to be housekeeper and cook, was kept well out of sight when he entertained cronies. If she left the house at all it was for some religious festival or to attend a performance of the drama, itself a quasi-religious activity. And no matter whither her destination, she was accompanied by a slave-chaperon.

The lot of the Roman wife was better, though she was expected to embody what were seen as the feminine virtues. 'Caesar's wife must be above suspicion', Plutarch declares, referring to the dictator's divorce of Pompeia on the mere suspicion of adultery. The wife's place was as moral supporter to her husband and, by breeding, to perpetuate his name. Julius Caesar first appears in Shakespeare's play of the same name during the fertility festival of Lupercalia when, desperate for an heir, he tries to manoeuvre his third wife Calpurnia into the path of the Luperci, the youths whose goat's-hide whips were believed to cure sterility.

By contrast the Celtic women could inherit property and, though on marriage an equitable division of the goods of both partners was devised, this did not affect either partner's legal ownership, so that she was able to dispose of her possessions freely. That she could be extremely wealthy is shown by lavish grave goods. A burial chamber found in 1953 in the hillfort at Vix, near Châtillon-sur-Seine in Burgundy, contained the skeleton of a Sequanian princess. Her body lies adorned with bracelets and pearl necklaces and crowned with a gold diadem amid the remains of a funerary chariot. Surrounding her were goods imported from as far afield as the Baltic in the north and the Mediterranean in the south, while in one corner stood an enormous Greek-made bronze vase or *krater*, weighing four hundredweight and large enough to accommodate five adults.

Wealth went hand in hand with authority and if the wife happened to be the wealthier she was accepted as family head and hence as the dominant partner in the marriage. Cartimandua, Queen of the Brigantes, demonstrated this by her treatment of her husband, the warrior Venutius, whom she discarded in favour of one of his knights, Vellocatus. We know of the woman-warrior from the raid on Delphi and other classical references, but women could also hold military command. Among heroines of British history is Boadicea or, properly, Boudicca – the name means 'Victory' – queen and commander of the British Iceni. Huge of frame, with spear grasped in ample fist, a heavy torc round her neck and knee-length red hair billowing like a flag, she ploughed the ranks of the Roman IX Legion in her sickle-hubbed chariot. She is not an isolated example. Weapons and armour have been found among the grave goods in female burials from many parts of the Celtic world and, as Nora Chadwick reminds us, women warriors were to be found in the Celtic lands until the ninth century when enactments banning them were passed.

Besides their warrior role women also appear to have had another martial one as instructors in arms. We are told how the Ulster hero Cu Chulainn was trained by the Amazon Scáthach, and Nora Chadwick points to hints of something similar in the Welsh story of Peredur. When the hero tries to defend the castle in which he is lodging against the witches attacking it, one of them recognises him and tells him that under her he will receive his weapon-training. For three weeks he is a guest of the witch and her sister crones, receiving at the end a horse and arms.

One is reminded by these ladies of another aspect of Celtic womanhood – the ferocious harridan, as portrayed by Ammianus Marcellinus (AD 330–95). Quick to turn an argument into physical violence, he tells us how, with 'swelling neck, gnashing teeth, and brandishing sallow arms of enormous size . . .' she would 'strike blows mingled with kicks, as if they were missiles from a catapult.' He has linguistic support. An old Celtic root *wraki* was corrupted by the Gauls into *virago*, a word borrowed by the Romans and, in due course, ourselves.

Yet it would be a mistake to suppose that the harridan or the sexual antics which scandalised Julia Domna meant that the Celts were unacquainted with the tenderer shores of love. The aesthetic sensibility they displayed in other areas extended to standards of both male and female beauty. For the latter, figure, deportment and dress were important and the Celtic woman cared for her complexion as assiduously as many of her contemporary descendants, using special soaps and complexion lotions and adding to her charms with perfume. Thus Étain is described in *Da Derga's Hostel*:

> She wore a purple cloak with a good fleece, held with silver brooches chased with gold, and a smock of green silk with gold embroidery. There were wonderful ornaments of animal design in gold and silver on her breast and shoulders . . . The colour of her hair was like pure polished gold. She was loosing her hair to wash, her dress falling free of her arms. White as the snow of night's fall were her hands. Soft and even her cheeks and red as mountain foxglove. Beetle-black, her eyebrows. A shower of pearls, her teeth. Blue as hyacinth, her eyes.

Red as Parthian leather, her lips. High, smooth, and white her
shoulders, clear white her long fingers. Her hands were long, white
as the foam of a wave was her side, long and slender, yielding, smooth,
soft as wool. Her thighs were warm and smooth and white. The
blushing light of the moon was in her noble face, a lofty pride in her
smooth brow. The radiance of love was in her eyes; the flush of
pleasure in her cheek. There was a gentle dignity in her voice. Her
step was firm and graceful. She had the walk of a queen. She was the
fairest, loveliest, finest that men's eyes had seen of all the women of
the world.

Such beauties, as Julia Domna's Caledonian informant made
explicit, expected as consorts 'the finest of men'. They were required
to be so irresistibly handsome that women flocked from their houses
just to look at them, as they did when the Ulster hero Cu Chulainn,
with his red-gold hair, dimpled cheeks, bright eyes and white breast
walked the streets of Emain Macha.

None but the brave deserving the fair, when he catches a glimpse
of the lovely Emer's breasts over her dress and comments, 'I see a
sweet country where I could rest my weapon', she warns him, 'No
man will travel this country until he has killed a hundred men at
every ford from Scenmenn to the river Ailbine . . .Until he has struck
down three groups of nine men with a single stroke, leaving the
middle man of each nine unharmed.' As she multiplies her tests, one
might wonder whether a pair of pretty breasts was ever won so hardly.

These descriptions are drawn from a mythological literature which
could well be credited with introducing Europe to the romantic ideal.

Some of us are acquainted with it through retellings of the Irish
myths, such as those of Deirdre or Ossian by writers like W.B. Yeats,
or perhaps through the Welsh *Mabinogion*. For an overwhelming
majority, however, they are known from the stories of King Arthur
and the Round Table and it is a tribute to their literary qualities that
all down the centuries writers of all nationalities and of all languages
have been retelling them.

# Note

1 The scanning electron microscope has shown that something akin to
shears or scissors had been used only a day or two before death to trim
the moustache of the Iron Age man whose body was found at Lindow
Moss, Cheshire, in 1982.

# Chapter 2
# The Druids

The mythologies with which most of us are best acquainted, those of the Greek and Romans, have come down to us as a collection of written stories. Despite often quite wide variations of detail between versions, they still possess enough unity for, say, the story of Oedipus to be immediately recognisable. Celtic mythology has a totally different ancestry. Despite the size of the original Celtic territories it has survived only in Ireland and Britain and it comes from an assortment of oral sources. The Irish Matter did not achieve written form until about the seventh century of our era; the British probably not until about three centuries later.

In both cases this was after the conversion and the transcribers are likely to have been monks who, viewing this blatantly pagan matter through Christian eyes, censored where they thought necessary. There is a possible instance of this in *Tristan and Isoult*. That a couple, travelling together, should become lovers would have seemed quite normal to the Celts. To Christian ears it was shocking and so the detail of the aphrodisiac-philtre which they accidentally drink and which causes them to become enamoured of one another was added to make them seem morally blameless.

For the student of Celtic mythology there is an added complication in that by this time a separation had taken place between the form of Celtic spoken in Gaul and Britain on the one hand, and that spoken in Ireland and Scotland on the other. The two are now respectively identified by scholars as Brythonic or 'P Celtic' and Goidelic or 'Q Celtic'. By the time of the Christian conversion the two forms had long since been incomprehensible to each other with the result that their respective literatures had evolved along divergent lines. An example occurs in a Welsh and a Scottish version of the same basic incident. In the first, *Pwyll Lord of Dyved*, a boy-child is stolen. His nurses, fearful they will be blamed for his disappearance, kill a pup and smear his mother's sleeping face with its blood to make it appear she has killed the child. The incident is paralleled by another in the same story in which newborn foals are repeatedly stolen from a stable by an enormous hand which comes in through a window. In the Scottish variant the two incidents are combined and a thieving hand takes the newborn child instead of the foal, while the nurses try to pin blame on a tame – and innocent – household wolf rather than on the mother.

When considering any body of myths one thing must be kept constantly in mind: that they always originate as hierophanies, fables – always transmitted orally – which explain the origins of the world, human race and the gods and frequently lay down the parameters of human behaviour toward them. Their originators must therefore have been those who dominated the religion of pagan Celtic society. However, by the time the stories were recorded they had ceased to be the property of any religious body and had become that of storytellers and bards. These people embellished them to make them more entertaining to their audiences and stressed those elements they found popular, often losing much of the sacred element in the process.

In Britain there was the added complication of four hundred years of Roman occupation. Many in the educated urban classes, encouraged by the occupiers, tended to dismiss the past and all its works as a barbaric Dark Age which had produced nothing worth preserving. In the countryside, because their matter was so tied to much in everyday life such as the seasonal cycle, the stories continued as part of the repertoire of the storytellers down to late times. In Ireland and Cornwall, indeed, the itinerant storyteller was a professional enjoying high status in his society. Nonetheless, the stories became further corrupted and confused. Incidents from one narrative would be mixed up with those of another. Thus, in the Welsh *Math son of Mathonwy*, when Blodeuwedd asks her husband the god Lleu (one of the Welsh forms of Lugh) how he can be killed, he answers: 'I cannot be slain within a house, nor without. I cannot be slain on horseback nor on foot.' In a Scottish version of the story of *Diarmait and Grainme*, Diarmait uses the same formula in a different context to make his elopement with Grainme, which he wishes to avoid, seem impossible. 'I will not take thee within doors, and I will not take thee without', he tells her. 'I will not take thee on horseback, neither will I take thee on foot.' Even climaxes were changed: if the storyteller had forgotten an original ending he simply invented or tagged on one from another tale.

Undergoing such ravages, the amazing thing is not that the stories survived at all, but that they preserved matter whose antiquity is attested by archaeology[1]. (Their origins are discussed at greater length in my *Celtic Mythology*.)

Like most of the peoples of Europe, the Celts are Indo-Europeans. The earliest hint of those we can identify with confidence as belonging to this ethnic group go back to about 1500 BC, but even then cultural separation had taken place so long before that the various population groups were speaking languages as different as Spanish and Russian are today. The Indo-European groups known to history must therefore have migrated much earlier. Indeed such is the remoteness of the epoch when there was a unitary Indo-European people inhabiting a single homeland that we do not know with certainty where it was.

Nonetheless, a comparison of Celtic mythology with that of others of the same ethnic origin reveals countless parallels. For instance, magic apples like those of the Greek Garden of Hesperides occur in the Irish stories. Dillon points out that the incident in the *Tain Bo Cualnge* in which Fergus, king of Ulster, is persuaded by his wife Nessa to abdicate in favour of his son is matched by one in the Hindu epic, *The Ramayana*, where Kaikeyi persuades her husband, Dasfaratha to make the same sacrifice. Cu Chulainn's inadvertent killing of his own son also occurs in the German *Hildebrandslied*. Other examples are the linking of the horse and agricultural gods, discussed more fully later; the Cattle Raid Myth, central to the Irish Cu Chulainn cycle. The Irish Second Battle of Mag Tured or Moytura may well derive from the myth of the Final Battle which occurs, *inter alia* in the Norse *Ragnorok* and the Hindu epic *The Mahabharata*. There are also the numerous relics in the British Matter for which parallels are found in Indian, Iranian, Greek, Roman, German and Hittite contexts.

As we shall see, such examples are capable of infinite multiplication and go to prove that the Celts brought with them as they spread a mythology and beliefs whose roots went back to a past before the Indo-European migrations, and hence long before they themselves had emerged as a separate and identifiable people.

The religious leaders who created Celtic myth were the Druids as is shown by the fact that they figure prominently in the Irish stories and, though never so titled, in the British. For a number of reasons, some of their own deliberate making, they have remained a profound mystery. For one thing, as Caesar tells us, they refused to commit their teachings to writing.

Celtic society has been described as non- or pre-literate. This is not strictly accurate. The Greek alphabet was used for public and private accounts and we find on Celtic coinage combinations of letters obviously intended to represent sounds outside the range of Greek phonetics. This is echoed in the way that we combine the P and H of our own Roman alphabet in words like 'photograph' because it does not contain the Greek letter Φ. Such niceties are necessary only where someone, on receiving the money, will want to know what is on it and is able to read it. In Ireland there was, besides, a form of script, somewhat akin to the Norse runes, called *ogam*, which was in use until the eighth century AD, although by this late date it was found principally on tombstones. Its name may derive from the god Ogmios, the Celtic Hercules credited with the invention of writing, and prompting the suggestion, on little solid evidence, that ogam was originally a means of cryptographic communication among the Druids.

Nevertheless there is a Welsh tradition of something which sounds very like *ogam*. This is a forty-four letter alphabet called the *Coelbrenn* used by the bards. It was written on bars of wood, square or triangular in section, with a sharp instrument, the *bwyell* or axe, originally of flint but later of metal, the bars being bound together in a frame called a *peithynen*. The bard Llawdden, winner of an eisteddfod held at Carmarthen in 1451, was awarded a *bwyell* of gold. He was known thenceforward as Llawdden of the Golden Axe, and any work of exceptional merit was said to bear the mark of 'Llawden's Axe'.

The Druids must have had other reasons for maintaining their traditions orally. Partly it may have been because, in the words of Lévy Bruhl, sacred matter once made available in written form 'would become profane and lose its mystic value'. But Caesar is no doubt right in suggesting that it was also to prevent their pupils from neglecting their memories by reliance on the written word[1].

To further impede attempts to broaden our knowledge of the Druids, almost all the major studies of the early Celts by their contemporaries, such as those by Aristotle (384–22 BC), Timagenes (c. 100 BC), Titus Livy (59 BC-AD 17) and – a key document – *The Histories* of Posidonius of Apamea, are lost and known to us solely from references in other authors. Of surviving sources, there is the well-known chapter in Caesar's *Conquest of Gaul* from which quotation has been made, as well as the Elder Pliny's *Natural History*.

With so little to go on, our picture of Druidism has to be pieced together much as a criminal investigator might piece together a crime from a scattering of clues. They include such items as bent swords dredged from a lake, a corpse preserved in a bog, a clutch of worn manuscripts in Old Irish and Old Welsh – which is to say, the surviving versions of the myths, fragmentary quotations by ancient authors from works now lost.

The most trustworthy clues are those from archaeology, though only where we can be certain about the date and provenance of a particular find, and unfortunately this is far from invariably the case. Two of the most informative artefacts (a cauldron from a ritual deposit at Gundestrup, Denmark, on whose panels are shown what are taken to be gods and ritual scenes, and a five by three foot bronze calendar found at Coligny near Bourg-en-Bresse in the last century) are generally, though not unanimously, accepted as Celtic. In fact, Robert Graves suggests that the Coligny calendar is Gallo-Roman and it has been suggested that the Gundestrup Cauldron may even be Indian.

There are, of course, other clues, such as our knowledge of the Indo-Europeans; the effects of cross-fertilisation from peoples with whom the Celts came into contact; and by drawing cautious analogies with other societies at a similar state of development. And, perhaps, we have one last clue: namely folklore and custom, which, if incapable of providing hard and fast data, frequently offer useful pointers. For example, Frazer mentions that the inhabitants of Lacaune in southern France used mistletoe as an antidote to poison which chimes with Pliny's description of its use by the Druids.

When we are lucky, data from one area may be backed up by that from another. For example, we learn in the myths of four major festivals and these are found on the Coligny calendar. There is even better support for the Celtic practice of head-hunting. Besides allusions in the myths, Strabo quotes Posidonius on the subject and there is further confirmation from a number of excavation sites. Among the most impressive is a sanctuary at Entremont in Provence where fifteen adult male skulls were found. Some were still pierced by the iron nails used to fix them perhaps to a door lintel, confirming Posidonius who mentions the practice.

However, where there is no collateral support, which is often the case, we must accept or reject a particular statement on the balance of probabilities.

Thus, there is no backing for Caesar's account of the annual Druidic synod, held in what we regarded as the centre of Gaul, at which an archdruid was elected. The very existence of an archdruid is often dismissed as improbable because of the loose tribal structure of their society and the Celts' ingrained aversion to centralised authority. On the other hand, the territory of the Carnutes, where it was supposed to take place, includes what is today called the 'Beauce', the fertile plain, north of the Loire often referred to as 'the heart of France'. Between the third and first centuries BC the Carnutes established their capital in the *oppidum* or hill-top town at what is now Chartres, site of Europe's premier Gothic cathedral, Nôtre Dame de Chartres. It was usual for the early missionary fathers to build churches on pagan sacred sites, often using the same stones, and the cathedral's scale and grandeur suggest a need to affirm the dominance of the new religion and that the area had been a very important one in the past.

The presence of a well dedicated to the Virgin in the sanctuary is taken by the French Celticist Jean Markale as further evidence, Celtic sites often being associated with wells or springs. As a consequence an increasing number of scholars are inclined to accept Caesar's statement.

If there ever was such an election of the type Caesar describes it is likely that it involved only the Druids of Gaul, though Jan de Vries, on the basis of a statement in the *Life of St Patrick*, believes there may have been a similar one in Ireland and that the Druids of Britain were at least hierarchically organised even if they held no regular synods.

We must still be on our guard about swallowing Caesar's story whole. His chapter headed 'The Customs and Institutions of the Gauls' was undoubtedly intended to serve a propagandist purpose: that of showing that he came less as conqueror than as torchbearer of Roman enlightenment. He is, nevertheless, the best informant on the Druids we have. He tells us that they enjoyed such privileges as exemption from military service and taxation, that they were 'held in great honour by the people', ranking them equal to knights on the social scale. Given their prestige and fringe benefits it was hardly surprising if, as he goes on to tell us, 'large numbers of young men flocked for instruction' in Druidism. This is supported by one of the epics where we find the Ulster Druid, Cathbad, teaching a hundred pupils, and the hero Cu Chulainn is said to have had a Druidic education. However, rather than novice-Druids, Cathbad's pupils – and probably the majority of Caesar's young men – were likely to have been receiving a general education much as in later times a group of boys might receive theirs from a Christian priest.

If we are to believe Caesar the curriculum included subjects in the categories of metaphysics and high theology, but it is probable that more basic ones such as the three Rs were also inculcated.

As to the Druidic novitiate proper, the Jesuit seminarian's seven years pales by comparison, for we are told that it lasted twenty years, most of it spent in learning great numbers of verses by heart. This was the lore of Druidism, for, as Dillon points out, a distinction was drawn between verse and poetry. Druidic doctrine being transmitted orally, the former was used as an aide memoire in keeping genealogies, the often complex liturgies, prayers and hymns, even the law, for as Caesar also tells us the Druids were lawyers and judges. We ourselves still speak of someone being 'well versed' in a particular subject.

His information on Druidic training is amplified by the statement of Pomponius Mela that it took place in remote caves and forest sanctuaries. For all that Pomponius, who flourished about 43 AD, is a fairly late writer, the link between the Druids and forest sanctuaries is too persistent to be disregarded and has become one of the stereotype images of Druidism down the ages. In his *Pharsalia* the Roman poet Lucan refers to the gloomy and sinister woodland groves where the Druids lived and we have examples in the myths of forest-dwelling Druids. And it is against such a sylvan background that Pliny sets his description of the mistletoe-gathering ceremony, our sole first-hand account of Druidism in action. He tells us how, on the sixth day of the moon, a white-robed Druid climbed an oak tree on which mistletoe was growing and cut down the plant. This was caught in a white cloth by those below – according to Nicholas Culpeper's *Complete Herbal*, published in 1653, mistletoe lost its efficacity if it touched the ground. Then two white bulls, which had been brought to the spot, were sacrificed.

Again caution is needed. Pliny's account, like Caesar's, comes from Gaul and without licence it is risky to apply it to the Celtic world at large. There is, besides, the trap of extrapolation into which so many have fallen, making two features of the account – the mistletoe and the white robes of the Druids – into another stereotype. As Pliny's text makes clear, white applied to a specific ritual. The bulls were white, as was the cloth in which the cut branch was caught. So, too, are the berries of mistletoe. And such uniformity is wholly consistent with ritual practices of the kind in question.

Whether there was anything like a regular Druidic canonical dress we cannot be sure, though crowns and headdresses found at Hockwold, Norfolk and Cavenham, Suffolk, have been interpreted as ritual garments. That metal face masks found in Bath and at Tarbes in southern France served such a function is entirely plausible. The Druids performed sacrifice, including human sacrifice, and the wearing of masks by sacrificers is known in other cultures. Presumably the purpose, as with the masks worn by public executioners, was to conceal identity.

However, as to the mistletoe, the discovery of what appeared to be its remains, with oak branches, in a coffin exhumed at Gristhorpe near Scarborough in 1834, and of its pollen in the stomach-contents of the male body found at Lindow Moss, Cheshire in 1982 tend to corroborate Pliny's statement about the importance the Druids placed upon it.

For all the persistence of the sacred grove it is not necessarily true that all religious practice took place in such an environment. Hecateus of Abdera (c. 500 BC), Livy and Polybius (c. 202–120 BC) mention temples at various locations. The remains of temple-like buildings which have been found, such as the one on the site of London Airport at Heathrow, support this and mean that worship may also have been conducted in formal surroundings. There is also increasing evidence of very early wooden temples of which an example was found at Frilford, Oxfordshire.

We might also question Pomponius's assertion about Druidic studies taking place in cave and forest for then, as now, the climate of most of the Celtic countries can hardly have been reliable enough for extended al fresco activities. Cave and forest may well have entered into training, but probably as the setting for an initiatory rite of the kind which will be explored in the next chapter.

In any case we have evidence of more conventional training establishments. One somewhat tenuous indication that the Stone of Destiny appropriated by Edward I may have been the original is that, according to early writers, up till the twelfth century, when it was taken over by Augustinian monks, Scone was the home of a community of Culdees. The Culdees emerged as an exclusively Scottish and Irish religious order in about the eighth century and were widely regarded as Christian heirs to Druidic knowledge. At the same time the ritual significance of the Scone area from prehistoric times is proved by the abundance of remains there.

In addition we have the two Bangors, one in Northern Ireland and the other in Gwynedd, North Wales. 'Bangor' (or Banchor) means 'college' and Markale believes they were the sites of Druidic training colleges which later became the locations of sixth century monasteries internationally famous as seats of learning. Furthermore, that at Gwynedd overlooked the Menai Straits, the narrow strip of water dividing the Welsh mainland from the isle of Anglesey or Môn. This was arguably the most important of Druidic centres in the entire Celtic world, as we know not only from the trouble the Romans took to obliterate it and annihilate its occupants, but also from the fanaticism with which it was defended and from the artefacts found there.

Geoffrey of Monmouth mentions a 'college of astronomers' at Caerleon-on-Usk, consulted by King Arthur. In view of other finds there (they include antefixae with the spoked-wheel sun-symbol often connected with the god Taranis) his information may be more reliable here than elsewhere. Furthermore, there was a school of rhetoric, for which the Celts were famous, at Bordeaux, which was still functioning in the fourth century AD, and was said to have been founded by the Druids from Armorica, probably as a training college.

Another possible way of increasing our knowledge of Druidism is to compare the Celts with other Indo-European peoples. One particularly fruitful area is Hindu Brahminism where the correspondences are so numerous that it is impossible to list more than a handful of examples. The Brahmins occupied the same place in the social hierarchy as the Druids and served their societies in similar ways. As Druidic doctrine was transmitted orally, so from prehistoric times until comparatively recently were the texts of the *Vedas*. Brahminic students, the *brahmacarin*, were taught, in schools set up deep in the forest, a corpus of doctrine whose tenets included the reincarnation of the soul which the earliest authorities claim that the Druids also promulgated.

However, parallels are to be found elsewhere. The most recent studies, such as Mallory's, reveal numerous linguistic affinities between Proto-Indo-European and Celtic words. Thus, the word *tuatha*, folk or people, is close to *teuta*, root of 'teutonic' and 'Deutsch', which have the same meaning. The Gaulish *Ario-Manus* and the Irish *Airem* Mallory believes to be cognates of the word Aryan which may have been what the Indo-Europeans actually called themselves. It is even suggested that Eire, which comes from *Eriu* (the more common *Erin* is the dative form), derives from a similar radical.

The last example is interesting. Eriu is one of a trio of mythological goddesses, the others being Fotla and Banba who, according to the *Lebor Gabála Erenn* manuscript, opposed the invading Milesians by raising a magical army of peat sods. However, when powerful Druidic spells were cast against them, they gave in and welcomed the newcomers setting the one condition that the country should be given their name. The Milesians may well have been the first Indo-European arrivals, so that the use of a form of the word Aryan in the name would be appropriate.

Another Indo-European root, *dyeus peter*, interpreted as 'father god', yields 'Jupiter' as well as 'Dispater' whom Caesar declares to have been the most important of the Celtic gods. The fosterage mentioned by the same author and confirmed in the myths may also have been a surviving Indo-European custom.

In fact, as is often found with Celtic goddesses, Eriu, Fotla and Banba were probably a single deity of triple aspect since three was the Druidic sacred number and this is yet another example of a surviving Indo-European belief. Georges Dumézil believes tripartition to be found in all the Indo-European pantheons corresponding with the tripartite structure of society itself.

Lastly, we must also take account of the effects of encounters with other cultures. Among the earliest they had contact with were the Scythians who shared a border in their original homeland. It was the Scythians who taught the Celts how to dye and weave wool in tartan patterns. The earliest art of the Celts is clearly imitative of Scythian and it was no doubt in the same spirit of emulation that the Celts adopted the custom of growing moustaches so big they were said to act as strainers for their drinks. No less significantly, it was from the Scythians that they acquired much of their horse lore.

Herodotus says the Scythians were given to decapitating and scalping enemies. It might be inferred from this that they initiated the Celts into the practice, though it is actually characteristic of most nomadic peoples. What is certain is the Scythian effect on Celtic burial custom. The wagon or chariot burials found throughout the Celtic world were plainly the continuance of Scythian practice known from their burial sites. Echoes can even be found in mythology. Awakened by a scream in the night, Cu Chulainn rushes outside and comes upon a woman in a chariot at whose side walks a man driving a cow. When the hero, guardian of the cattle of the province, seeks an explanation he is answered in riddles. When he tries to leap on the chariot, it vanishes leaving a dark and empty landscape. One of many strange elements in the passage is that the chariot is drawn by a one-legged horse held up by means of the chariot-pole which passes through its body and is kept in place by a peg in the middle of its forehead. This is an emulation of the custom whereby, when a Scythian chieftain was buried, his horse was killed, stuffed and coupled to the battle-wagon in which the body rested, being kept upright in the shafts by a similar means.

Scythian mediation on the Celtic view of the supernatural is harder to estimate largely because both peoples were heirs of an Indo-European heritage and it is not easy to separate what is unique to either. Though their *enarees* have been compared with the Druids, there is at least one fundamental difference – the *enarees* were probably eunuchs. Their name is translated as 'man-woman' and they dressed and spoke as women, supposedly in punishment for their desecration of the shrine of the Great Earth Mother. Celtic myth, on the other hand, presents us with married Druids like Cathbad, who were also fathers – in his case of King Conchobhar of Ulster.

Among the earliest of the cultures with which the Celts were brought into contact through their migrations was the Etruscan around 400 BC. Their considerable trade relations are proved by Etruscan goods in Celtic burials. It was from this time, too, that the Celts began tentatively sculpting human representations of their gods, where hitherto they had been satisfied with the rough hewn shapes from tree-trunks of which Lucan writes disparagingly.

After the migrations which took them into what was to become known as Gaul, the Celts entered into trade relations with the Greeks via Massilia, which became a principal source for Greek wine imports. The upshot of these contacts was that the Celts were spoken of as 'more Greek than the Greeks'. Their building and town-planning ideas were so transformed that Strabo uses the Greek word *polis*, city, to describe the capital of the Saluvii tribe while Celtic coinage plainly copied Greek models.

What was perhaps the most important of all the by-products of migration was that it brought the Celts, originally nomadic pastoralists, into contact with economies based on sedentary agriculture. Though the Indo-Europeans probably practised agriculture on at least a limited scale, linguistic evidence suggests that animal husbandry was more important, for among the most common words traceable to Indo-European roots are those referring to it, including, as Mallory points out, cow, ox and steer.

That this retained its importance is shown by the example of Ireland where the economy remained largely dependent upon it. Nevertheless, with their settlement among the Neolithic farmers of the arable plains of Europe, cereal-growing began to take on an increasing role. One may well suppose that it was during this period that, besides adopting – and improving – the farming techniques they found, there would also have occurred modifications in belief.

But it may well have been that the greatest of these, amounting to revolution, took place when they came into contact with the Neolithic farmers of Britain. Caesar writes that 'the Druidic doctrine is believed to have been found existing in Britain and thence imported into Gaul', adding that 'even today those who want to make a profound study of it generally go to Britain for the purpose'. There is some support in the vernacular literature, but more important is the existence in Britain of a number of major sites which, even before the Celts arrived in the country, must have been known if only from the trading contacts.

These are the uniquely British cursuses and henges of which there are at least 900 and, according to Aubrey Burl, well over a thousand. Of those now known to us, Avebury and Stonehenge are obviously the most impressive, but that recently discovered at Godmanchester near Cambridge may have had an equal or possibly greater claim. The evidence that all are astronomically aligned is now generally accepted, with some disagreement about the degree of sophistication involved. Hecateus describes a huge circular temple usually taken to be Stonehenge. Dedicated to the solar god Apollo, it is of such sanctity that the god himself visits it every nineteen years. This is roughly the period between eclipses, times when the sun appeared to be absent from the sky, a phenomenon explicable if a sun-god was celebrating with his British worshippers. The fact that they were honoured in this way would lend them and their temple an unusual cachet. Hecateus seems to have known something of both the Celts and Druidism, and as he was an extensive traveller, he may well have heard the story in Gaul.

But, as Piggott points out, there is also some archaeological support for the belief that Britain was of special significance to Druidism. Some of the continental Celtic sites, such as the large circular earthwork at Goloring, near Coblenz, were constructed in the style of the Neolithic British cursuses, as though a past already distant were being imitated deliberately.

There are similar parallels for the ritual shafts found all over the Celtic world. Some of the earliest examples are to be found in Britain and are well pre-Celtic. Wooden artefacts found in those at Wilsford and Swanwick were carbon dated to around 1400 BC. Both the pre-Celtic and the much later shafts have been found to contain human remains probably from sacrifice and, in several cases, a wooden stake or tree trunk. The scene on one of the plates of the Gundestrup Cauldron, among the most important of Celtic artefacts, in which a large figure, assumed to be a god, is about to immerse a much smaller one into some kind of vat, has usually been taken as illustrating ritual drowning. However, the fact that a troop of warriors in the panel appear to be carrying a treetrunk on the points of their spears has led some to interpret it as the deposition of a human victim and the tree trunk in a ritual shaft.

Also carried over from pre-Celtic times is the custom of burying a body, particularly that of a youth or child, in the foundations of a new building of which examples occur at both Stonehenge and Avebury.

On this whole question one can only summon in support Nora Chadwick. 'Any appreciation of Celtic culture,' she writes in *The Celts*, 'is to be gained most adequately from a recognition of the continuity extending from the pre-Iron Age past . . . It is not without interest that some Neolithic chambered tombs, such as New Grange, are mentioned frequently in early Irish literature.'

Those words were written over two decades ago, when a great deal of scepticism surrounded such ideas. More recent studies, among them those of Professor Colin Renfrew and Dr Anne Ross, have largely transformed the picture and thus help to corroborate Nora Chadwick.

# Note

1 There are still peoples who retain an oral tradition and possess memories which are, to us, startling. An example of this is the Navajo Indians. A writer in the *Independent Magazine* in August 1990 records a visit to a restaurant in Navajo country. The waitress went from packed table to packed table taking orders without the benefit of written notes, then returned with laden trays bearing the correct dishes.

# Chapter 3
# The Nature of Druidism

Caesar says of the Druids that they 'officiated at the worship of the gods, regulated public and private sacrifices, and gave rulings on all religious questions', a description many writers have interpreted as meaning that they were a priesthood. If they were it is surely strange that Caesar, not normally given to prolixity, did not simply call them that. In fact, the earliest author so to describe them is Dio Chrysostum who, writing in the first century AD, brackets them with the priesthoods of Persia, Egypt and India. However, he is comparing them, not in terms of sacerdotal function, but of arcane knowledge.

In any case, even if the Druids could be said to have fulfilled some of the functions associated with a priesthood there must also have been other people in Celtic life similarly engaged for, though the Romans banished the Druids by a series of edicts issued soon after their occupation, they allowed the worship of the gods to continue, one might almost say to flourish. One has, therefore, to assume the existence of a body which officiated. Two other names actually occur. One is that of *gutuater*, mentioned by Caesar; the other is *semnotheoi* mentioned by Diogenes Laertius (AD 200-50). *Gutuater* has been translated as 'Father of prayer' (or 'invocation'), but we have no indication as to his role, though Jan de Vries points to a Germanic priest called a *gudja*. Diogenes couples his *semnotheoi* with the Druids and describes both as 'seers', but we have no other reference to them and the word itself has defied translation.

Possibly the clearest hint of the Druids' true role in pre-Roman Celtic life comes from Pliny. In a passage on magic in *Natural History*, he writes that, though it originated in Persia, the British of his day were so fascinated by it that it was if they had taught the Persians rather than the other way round. His Persian originators were the Magi, the Wise Men of the Gospel, from whom the word 'magic' derives. This explains why Dio Chrysostum brackets the Druids with Persian, Hindu and Egyptian priesthoods, all of whom are credited with magical powers.

Priest and magician can obviously be combined in the same person, as with the Egyptians, but their functions are quite different. In the view of the French sociologist Emile Durkheim the magician is distinguished from the priest by the fact that, where the latter has a congregation, the former has a clientele. That the Druids had a clientele is plain, among other things, from Caesar's statement that those about to be exposed to the dangers of war or who were suffering from serious illness employed them to offer propitiatory human sacrifices. Often, too, when they are serving as advisers to kings their royal patrons could be said to be clients.

The Druids were credited with other typical magical gifts. They could cast spells and control the elements. Tuathan Druids raised fog and storm in an attempt to prevent the Milesian invaders from landing. In the Medieval Welsh *Gereint and Enide*, a hedge of mist concealed the enclosure where magical games were held. A battle-mist hid the advancing Ulster army in the *Tain Bo Cualnge*. The Druid Tadg used fog to prevent Cumhail, father of Finn, from finding his magic weapons.

They could change their own shapes and that of others. The Druids of Caín Bile, who appear in the *Tain*, when taken for enemy spies, transformed themselves into deer to escape pursuit. Merlin acted like a Druid when he obliged Uther Pendragon by changing him into a simulacrum of the Duke of Cornwall, so that he could sleep with the Duke's wife and beget the future King Arthur upon her.

Merlin could be described as a court magician. The Magi were also court magicians. So too were Dio Chrysostum's Egyptian and Indian priests. The second were, of course, the Brahmins, some of whose similarities with the Druids have been noted. Among our earliest informants on the Brahmins is Strabo who specifically couples them with shamans, possibly the earliest use of the word. Can a similar coupling be made in the case of the Druids?

Thanks to a whole host of studies over the past fifty years we now know a great deal about shamans. We are reasonably certain they emerged in the hunting phase for they are plainly recognisable in cave paintings dated to around 30,000 BC where they are shown among groups of hunters. Their function was two-fold: that of finding the richest hunting grounds and, thereafter, of acting as go-between and conciliator with the spirits whom the hunters' activities had ejected from their bodies. The dangers arising from this were summarised by an Arctic shaman to the Danish explorer Knud

Rasmussen in the 1920s: 'All the creatures that we have to kill and eat, all those that we have to strike down and destroy to make clothes for ourselves, have souls . . . which must therefore be pacified lest they should avenge themselves on us for taking away their bodies.'

The shaman is able to act as pacifier because of his unique gift: in trance he can leave his own body and in this discarnate state visit the Otherworld home of the spirits. To identify himself to those he seeks, he adopts the guise of its species, dressing, for instance, in its hide.

The ability to make the journey is a gift the spirits themselves grant, but only to chosen individuals. And they must prove themselves through appalling ordeals. To those selected the summons will come in the form of illness or recurrent nightmare and the person who experiences them knows the choice lies between obedience to the call or madness and death. If he does obey, he must abandon family, friends and familiar surroundings to take himself into the wilderness, endure hunger, thirst, possibly cold or intolerable heat and, in their train, hallucinations in which he will be tormented by hideous beings who, in the end, destroy him. That is the instant of enlightenment from which he will awaken reborn, ready to return to the living to be initiated into the secret lore of shamanism by one of its elders. His teachings will be conveyed solely by word of mouth.

Now accepted by the Otherworld, his journeys thence to act as his people's mediator will always be fraught with hazards he must negotiate and enemies whose malice he must overcome or outwit. Often he will have to cross a body of water, the archetype of countless mythical rivers, from the biblical Jordan to the Greek Styx. The sole means of negotiating it is often a bridge whose slender and precarious span traverses an angry torrent, the 'razor's edge' of the Hindu *Katha Upanishad* which must be crossed to attain spiritual enlightenment.

For all that the Otherworld is the home of the spirits, it often has entrances in our world. A particular cave, a fissure in rock or earth, a burial place – the last indicative of the element of ancestor-worship in most shamanistic systems – all of which can be entered freely by the shaman himself, are to be shunned by lesser mortals. Some places are more powerful than others. In particular there is the Great Centre which may have a geometrical or geographical connotation, but is a centre primarily by virtue of the intense concentration of spiritual forces within it. Hence, every holy place is a centre. Just as the Delphic sanctuary was the omphalos or navel of the world, so too was the Sumerian Nippur or the Rock of Jerusalem, while the Romans had the *mundus* which represented the junction of the lower regions and the terrestrial world.

Not all centres have their axis in our world – the Norse World Tree, Yggdrasil, for example. Indeed, the Otherworld is less a location than another plane of existence, what we might call an 'alternative state of consciousness'.

Nonetheless, though in some ways it resembles our world, in others it is quite different. As Mircea Eliade tells us, it is a mirror image with not only top and bottom and right and left, but also night and day, reversed. Space and time are different from ours. As in dreams, movement from one location to another, even the most distant one, can take place in a moment. And what seems like a few hours in the Otherworld can prove, on return to this one, to have been centuries, which is one reason why ordinary mortals are exhorted to resist all temptation to visit it. The shaman, however, can go through centuries there in a matter of earthly moments.

Its time differs from ours in other ways, too. It is cyclical. Hence, the great festivals are not the commemorative enactment of a past mythological event, they are that event itself, a point to which we regularly and constantly return, a circuit with its known landmarks. There is a similar concept in the Catholic Mass which is not the commemoration, but the actual Last Supper and Passion itself.

Through repeated Otherworld visits, the shaman forges a close relationship between himself and one or other of its inhabitants who thereafter shows special favour to himself and his people[1]. In gratitude, they will adopt the animal it represents as totem, the common parent from whom all descend and whose name the tribe may take. It then becomes taboo to hunt or to eat members of its species except at the sacred feasts held in its honour.

As the permanent link between his fellows and these powerful and dangerous beings, the shaman becomes interpreter of their will. He serves his people, not only as mediator, but as prophet, augur, healer, teacher and law-giver. He is also its mythologue, for he alone has been vouchsafed the histories of the spirits and instructed by them in their relationship with mortals.

Like our own, the Otherworld has its social strata at the apex of which are those who rule nature and its phenomena and whose realm is in the highest, most inaccessible reaches of the spirit world. At the lowest are those others, animal and human, who, deprived of bodies, roam the earth in search of new habitation.

How much of this is to be found in Druidism?

Among the first things that strike one is the Druidic insistence on the transmission of doctrine by word of mouth. Water sources of all kinds were certainly regarded as junctions with the Otherworld. So, too, were the prehistoric tumuli, the Irish *sidhs*. The suffix *-shee*, which reflects the accepted pronunciation, occurs in Scottish place-names, such as Glenshee in Perthshire.

As is consistent with their hunting ancestry, shamans are invariably shown in cave paintings in hunting scenes. Though the Celts had long since abandoned such a precarious basis for their economy, the importance of the hunt and especially the boar hunt is attested by hundreds of artefacts, often of superb artistic quality, from all over the Celtic world. Boars are found as decoration on shields and on coinage. A bronze votive model from Merida in Spain, now in the Musée des Antiquités Nationales at St-Germain-en-Laye, even shows a boar hunt in progress with mounted, spear-carrying huntsman, accompanied by baying hound. The areas to which the Celts migrated during their period of expansion were ones whose great oak forests were the habitat of large numbers wild boar – and they are still hunted, of course, in the forests of Spain and south western France. However, the Merida model could represent one of the several Otherworld boar hunts such as that for the terrible Twrch Trwyth which is recorded in the Welsh *Mabinogion* story of *Kulhwych and Olwen*.

The master of the hunt is King Arthur, whose credentials in this respect are well established, for a courtly hunt is the starting point of a number of the Medieval romances. Nonetheless, the same story contains hints of a second hunter. Among those named in an interminable list of Arthurian warriors is Gwynn son of Nudd. That Gwynn comes from the underworld is proved by two pieces of evidence. One is a subsequent reference to him as one 'in whom God has set the energy of the demons of Annwvyn' (literally 'not world'), that is to say the underworld which later became the Welsh word for Hell. The other is a dialogue poem in *The Black Book of Carmarthen*. Here Gwynn establishes himself as a hunter, who on his pale horse and with his hound 'Death's Door' at his side, is present wherever there is slaughter: in Squire's words, a hunter 'not of deer, but of men's souls'.

There is, in fact, still a third hunter, though his markedly underworld characteristics may mean that he is another form of Gwynn. In another *Mabinogion* story, the thirteenth century *Owein* or *The Countess of the Fountain*, the hero, while passing through an enchanted forest, is waylaid by a black giant armed with a club. Hideously ugly, he has only one foot and one eye. Ugliness is an aspect Celtic gods frequently take on when they wish to impress mortals with their power, and the one-legged, one-eyed stance is that of the magician. (When collecting folklore in Ireland in the early years of the century Evans Wentz was told of a boatman whose passengers had once included two Otherworld beings. He discovered he could see them through only one of his eyes. When both were open they became invisible.)

Owein has been warned that the giant is the 'keeper of the forest' and, when he meets him, asks what power he has over the animals. By way of reply the giant strikes a stag with his club and its crying brings every forest creature, including 'serpents and vipers' to him.

A Gallo-Roman stela from Reims shows the horned god, Cernunnos, seated in the so-called 'buddhic' posture of the Celts. Apart from the distinctly classical style of his portrayal, in most respects he matches the best-known representation of Cernunnos, that on the Gundestrup Cauldron. In both he wears the torc round his neck and is surrounded by animals, evoking the scene in *Owein*. Other representations of him occur in northern Italy, Romania, Germany, Spain and France and what has been interpreted as a relief of a horned god has been found on a stone pillar at Tara, a place replete with potent associations with Irish Druidism.

Cernunnos must be the 'Dispater' from whom, if Caesar is to be credited, 'all the Gauls claimed descent by a tradition preserved by the Druids'. On the Reims stela he is flanked by Apollo and Mercury, two of the other gods mentioned by Caesar, but Cernunnos, seated on a throne, occupies the dominant position.

The alternative name of the Roman Dispater was Pluto who, as wealth-bestower, has been absorbed into our word 'plutocracy', meaning rule by the rich. The wealth he bestowed was the metals, precious and utilitarian, derived from his kingdom beneath the earth. On the stela Cernunnos is shown with a bag on his lap pouring coins in Plutonic profusion. The Gundestrup Cernunnos grasps a torc in one hand, and in the other, not a money bag, but a snake, at once an underworld creature and the guardian of treasure.

The horned god is an archaic and universal figure. Wooden statuettes of horned men have been unearthed from as far afield as a burial ground in Hunan Province, China, and in *The Bacchae* of Euripides the newborn Dionysus is addressed as 'the bull-horned'. The designation of Owein's giant as 'keeper of the forest' identifies him as of the same lineage: the Lord of the Animals, master of the hunting grounds. His affinity with shamanism is shown by numerous cave paintings, among them the famous 'Sorcerer of Trois Frères', which portrays a horn-wearing shaman. Horns have also been found attached to skulls in Mesolithic burials in Brittany and many Siberian shamans wear antlers during their séances[2].

That the Celtic Cernunnos is a hunter is proved by a carved relief on a small altar found near Carlisle where he is shown armed and equipped for the chase.

Cernunnos does not appear to have been the only deity associated with the hunt. The Greek writer Flavius Arrian (c. AD 95–175) tells us that on 'Artemis's birthday' the Celts sacrificed an animal bought out of fines paid for every creature hunted during the year and we have examples of goddesses participating in the hunt as Rhiannon does in the Welsh *Manawydan*. Nonetheless, on the whole, the chase was an exclusively male preserve. Many societies had taboos which kept women, particularly menstruating women, away even from the hunters' weapons. In the same way the calling of shaman was closed to women and such 'shamanesses' as are to be found were exceptions; a male exclusiveness which Druidism appears largely to have retained. There are some late references to 'Druidesses'. One was supposed to have given a young Roman subaltern named Diocletian the unlikely information that one day he would be emperor. There is also a Breton belief that the corrigans, or fairies, were formerly Druidesses who were particularly hostile to Christian priests, and the nine virgin prophetesses who lived on the île de Sein, off Ushant, are also sometimes so described.

In his blood-curdling account of the seizure of Môn, Tacitus clearly distinguishes between the 'black-robed women with dishevelled hair like Furies, brandishing torches' and the Druids. There are no Druidesses in the myths and any association between women and Druidism seems to have been fortuitous. The villainess Fuamnach in *The Wooing of Étain* is said to have been 'versed in the knowledge of the Tuatha de Danann' having been reared by the Druid, Breasail.

In most societies, while their men were on hunting expeditions, the women had tasks of their own. Before ways of making fire were discovered and reliance had to be placed on naturally occurring sources, tending and maintaining the tribal hearth was one of the foremost. There was, in addition, the gathering of the wild fruit, nuts and roots which helped to extend the diet.

By the time hunting had developed into cattle breeding and gathering had developed into agriculture, each sex had evolved its own exclusive mystery with its own distinct mythology. So closely did each sex guard its secrets that any attempt on the part of one to learn those of the other could result in his or her death.

As the shaman's proto-myth is that of the hunt and its magic quarry, the agriculturist's tells of the young god, personification of both the sun and the dormant seed, who dies, descends to the Underworld, to be found and brought back to life through the agency of a woman, the Great Earth Mother. This is the so-called vegetation myth, symbolising the cycle from the planting of the 'dead' seed in the ground to its germination, ripening and harvesting. Unlike the shaman's animal totems, from very earliest times the Great Mother was portrayed in human terms as the naked, often pregnant 'Venuses', such as those of Lespugue or Willendorf. Her pregnancy is significant. It is not only the increase of the soil that comes from her bounteous womb. The male role yet unrecognised – it was not, in point of fact, recognised until comparatively late times – all new life was the product of a magical conspiracy between mortal woman and the Great Mother. Hence, every woman was the possessor of formidable powers challenging the shaman's.

A profound terror inspired by these powers and the impotence of male magic to combat them is found in most archaic societies, and Markale is undoubtedly right in believing the Celts shared this. The beautiful woman, visible only to him, who tempts Connle the Red, son of Con of the Hundred Battles, to accompany her to her land across the seas, is more powerful than the king's Druid whose attempts to counter her spells fail as the couple sail off in her glass boat. When circumstances enable Viviane to wheedle magic knowledge from Merlin, he is incapable of saving himself.

To the shaman, it was a threat so overwhelming that he took the only course open to him: he denied the instrumentation of the Great

Mother in the central mystery of birth. We have those instances where the male actually becomes the child-bearer. Zeus brings forth Athena from his head, Dionysus from his thigh. Similar examples occur among the American Indians and in Hindu myth we come across the *ayonija*, that is those born without uterine gestation.

But there is also the notion of the wandering spirit of the dead which takes up lodging in the body of a woman in order to be reborn. Recurrent in the Indo-European mythologies, its wider distribution is shown by its presence among the non-Indo-European Finns. In the *Kalevala* the virgin, Marjatta, gives birth to the son who will be King of Karelia after eating a cranberry. Bronislaw Malinowski, sometimes called the 'father of social anthropology', came upon a similar belief during field researches in Oceania early this century[3].

The Welsh Cerridwen bears the bard Taliesin through eating a grain of wheat which is really the spirit of Gwyon Bach. After swallowing a drink given her by the Druid Cathbad, Nessa becomes the mother of King Conchobhar of Ulster. Dechtine, his daughter and charioteer, gives birth to Cu Chulainn as a result of quaffing a drink, this time one given her by the god Lugh. In some versions she is said to have swallowed a mayfly which had fallen into it. In the *Wooing of Étain*, Etar, wife of the Ulster chieftain, finds herself pregnant by accidentally swallowing a fly which has landed in her cup. Even the Brown Bull of Cualnge, the cause of the war between Ulster and Connaught, owes its conception to the maggot swallowed by a cow drinking from a river. It is a logical corollary that in Breton folk belief the soul should leave the body at death as a gnat or a fly.

Underlying this notion of disembodied spirits seeking a means of rebirth it is possible to see a primitive form of the doctrine of reincarnation with which the Druids were credited.

However vigorous the attempts to exclude her may have been, traces of the Great Mother can still be found in Celtic literature, though the ease with which she shifts from human to animal forms show how close is her kinship with the tribal totems. This may be due, if not to Druidic, at least to shamanic intervention. Totemism is also suggested by the animal or bird names adopted by some of the Celtic tribes, such as the Taurini, the People of the Bull, or the Bodiocasses, the Crow Warriors, and by the innumerable animal figurines found in votive deposits.

Caesar mentions a Gaulish ban on eating goose reminiscent of the taboo on eating the totemic creature, and similar proscriptions are frequently found in the myths. The Irish High King Conare was to avoid eating bird flesh because, we are told, his father was a bird. Cu Chulainn, whose name means 'hound of Chulainn', is similarly tabooed from eating dog flesh.

But what of other shamanistic concepts, such as the Great Centre, supernatural time or the Otherworld as a mirror image of our own? And can it be said that the Druid served his society as the shaman served his?

Caesar, of course, tells us that the annual Druidic convention took place at what was regarded as the 'centre of Gaul'. The *Mabinogion* story of *Llud and Llevelys* is a thoroughly confused hotchpotch of fragments from some earlier lost myth. The original must have involved two gods and the important Celtic festival of Beltaine or May Day is mentioned in the story. The storyteller has tried to give these elements narrative coherence, but what is particularly significant is that the story turns on the need to discover the true centre of Britain.

There is further evidence for centres of special sanctity in place names. The Milan derives from the Celtic Mediolanum, roughly the 'sacred enclosure at the centre' (the suffix -*lanum* survives as the *llan* repeatedly found in Welsh place names and in the Breton *lan* and *lam*, both now often signifying a church). Early records allude to a Medionemeton, 'the sacred grove at the centre' in Scotland. In the twelfth century *The History and Topography of Ireland*, Gerald of Wales writes of ancient Ireland having been divided up among themselves by five chieftains, the boundaries of their domains meeting at a stone near the castle of Kildare. He goes on: 'This stone is said to be the navel of Ireland, as it were, placed right in the middle of the land.' The text goes on to make clear that the area in question is Meath, a word which itself means centre. The place must be Tara and the stone, therefore, the 'Stone of Destiny'.

For Druidic Otherworld time concepts we are mainly dependent on references in the magical voyage stories, the Irish *imramma*, in which, as in the *Adventure of Bran mac Febail*, the hero imprudently accepts the invitation of an Otherworld woman to sojourn in her paradise only to find, when he leaves it, that what has seemed such a short time has been many centuries.

The reversal characteristic of the shaman's Otherworld can also be found in that of the Druids. Caesar tells us that it was on account of the chthonic origins of their Dispater that the Gauls measured time by nights rather than days – a relic is our own 'fortnight' or 'fourteen nights' – so that the principal festivals took place during the hours of darkness. Jan de Vries believes that this was only one of the reversals to be found in the Druidic Otherworld and has at least circumstantial support. Robert Graves, in *The White Goddess*, mentions a bas relief discovered in Nôtre Dame Cathedral, Paris, in 1711, which shows a Celtic god cutting a branch from a willow tree with, as the author puts it, his 'left hand where his right hand should be'. We also have the statement from Pliny that the Druids gathered a plant he calls *selago* with the left hand.

Lastly, there is the question of the role played by the Druids in Celtic society and how far this corresponded with that of the shaman in his. Certainly the Druid, too, was prophet, augur, healer and teacher. Caesar tells us he was also the giver and interpreter of the law in Gaulish society. The *brehons*, a class of travelling jurists, whose legal knowledge was entirely in their head, survived in Ireland until the English persecutions under Elizabeth. The Isle of Man's 'Breast Law', which has been orally transmitted down the centuries, is still regarded as no less binding than the written statute.

As others might draw legal precedents from their various scriptures, the shaman draws his from the tribal myths of which he is revealer and custodian. Strabo, Diodorus of Sicily and the later Ammianus Marcellinus, associate the Druids with two other groups said to be 'held in high honour' – the Vates and the bards. The Vates, root of the word 'vaticination' and cognate with the Irish *faithi*, are as the name suggests, seers. Strabo tells us that 'they interpreted sacrifice', that is to say sacrifice offered for divinatory purposes. Originally the Celtic bards were more than mere epic-singers. They were the custodians of myth, and throughout their existence possessed the quasi-magical power of chanting the *glam dicin*, a satire so potent it could lead to the madness or death of its target and was so feared even by heroes like Cu Chulainn that he was willing to surrender his weapons rather than risk exposure to it.

The division into Druids, Vates and Bards must have been a late development, for a confusion between bard and Druid was evident at the time the Irish myths were being put into writing. Sometimes the two words are used interchangeably and in the *Tain* we are told that the 'sweet-mouth harpers of Caín Bile' were 'Druids of great knowledge'.

Something very much akin to the shaman's perilous Otherworld journey is made by Owain in the pilgrimage discussed later. He achieves his objective only after braving a bridge as narrow and sharp as a sword blade which crosses an abyss, just as Chrétien's *Lancelot* has to cross the Sword Bridge to reach the Isle of Glass where Guinevere is imprisoned.

In *The Frenzy of Suibne*, dated in its existing form to the twelfth century but likely to be much older, the main character, Suibne, King of Dalriada, who is also a poet, goes mad after the Battle of Mag Rath (AD 642) and spends the rest of his life as a wanderer of the wilds. In fact, his state may be nearer to that of shaman than madman for at one point he is said to have ascended from the tree in which he was hiding from pursuers 'towards the rain clouds of the firmament, over the summits of every place and the ridge pole of every land', terminology closely approximating that frequently found in the descriptions of shamanic spirit flights.

Possessed of this ability the shaman could and did use it for what can only be called 'secular' purposes, in other words, to observe others under a cloak of invisibility. Of a Druid indulging in just such a practice there is one persuasive piece of evidence. It comes from the Irish myths. Anxious to know what is afoot among their Ulster enemies, the king and queen of Connaught seek the help of the Druid, Mag Roth. He dons his bull hide costume, highly appropriate since the epic in which he figures revolves round the fate of an Otherworld bull, and hovers invisibly over the massing forces to observe their strength and disposition. Particularly significant is the fact that he is said to have 'risen up with the smoke from the fire'. Once again the terminology coincides with innumerable accounts of Siberian shamanising down to recent times where the shaman's temporarily disembodied spirit is invariably said to ascend through the smoke hole of the yurt or tent.

The novice-shaman emerges from his wilderness ordeal intimately united with the natural environment. Rasmussen's Eskimo informant described the overwhelming moment of union at the climax of solitary and terrifying weeks spent in the icy wastes. He had gained, he says, the shaman's light of brain and body by which he 'could see through the darkness of life' and was 'visible to all the spirits of earth and sky and sea'. Thus, for the shaman, not only animate creation, but those things we should regard as inanimate, pulsate with a sentient life with which he, through his special gifts, can communicate. He speaks the language of the animals, birds, trees, and it is among them that he will now take up his dwelling. Like Lucan's forest-dwelling Druids, like King Suibne of Dalriada, he is the archetypal wild man of the woods.

If there is nothing in what we know of the training of the Druid to suggest the wilderness ordeal of the novice-shaman, history provides several examples of what might be called a ritualised shamanic initiation. Typical is the case of Orphism, a quasi-religious system supposedly derived from the teachings of the pre-Homeric musician-prophet Orpheus. He was almost certainly a *kapnobatai*, one of the Thracian shamans who induced trance by smoking, possibly hemp. What were thought to be his teachings, which included reincarnation, were taken up in the sixth century BC by Greek intellectuals. Among them was the Greek philosopher Pythagoras who, because of his supposed ability to leave his body in trance, E.R. Dodds rightly designates as a 'Greek shaman'[4].

Closely linked with Orphism was the Cretan cult of the Idaean Zeus into which Pythagoras was allegedly initiated. Preparatory rites involved nine days of solitary meditation in one of the caves on Mount Ida, where the infant Zeus was supposed to have been concealed from his father Chronos who was seeking to kill him for fear he might supplant him just as he had supplanted his own father, Ouranos. This was followed by the symbolical enactment of the initiate's death and rebirth, mirroring the death-and-rebirth climax of the shaman's wilderness experience.

Such practices have a much more extended ancestry than was hitherto thought. As Mark Patton says in *Jersey in Prehistory* the fact that so few human remains have actually been found in the so-called passage-graves has led to a reassessment of their primary function. There is now a tendency to regard them less as burial places than as ritual sites in which humans were sometimes interred as they were later interred in the naves of Christian churches. Bradley points out a number of characteristics of the earliest passage-graves which support this. Several contain what he calls 'trance imagery', abstract patterns cut into the stone which, like certain types of optical illusion, appear to move as though alive when one gazes at them fixedly. This sense of movement would be increased in some cases, as in the graves round the Gulf of Morbihan in Brittany, where the trance imagery is so placed that no natural light can reach it. In other words, those visiting them would have needed flickering artificial light to see them at all.

Meditation in such an environment makes sense of Pomponius Mela's statement that Druidic training took place in 'remote caves and forest sanctuaries'. The Irish word *uamh*, usually translated as 'cave', was also used to designate the vaulted inner chamber of a tumulus – the *sidh* – with its Otherworld connotations. It may well have been that the trainee Druid had to undergo a period of meditation in a *sidh* which culminated in his ritualised rebirth and was much akin to that of Orphic initiates on Mount Ida.

Evans Wentz came across legends of rites supposedly conducted in pagan times at the most impressive of all the *sidhs*, the 5,000 year-old passage grave at New Grange, County Meath, where the god In Dagda was supposed to have taken up residence after the human invaders had driven the Tuathan gods into exile. Suppliants were said to immure themselves in them for three days and three nights, fasting throughout. Stokes, in his *Tripartite Life of Patrick*, mentions that early Irish Christians would retire to caves for periods of fasting and meditation, a custom which also seems to have been practised in Britain and Scotland.

Still more illuminating is a rite which took place on an island, known as 'St Patrick's Purgatory', in Lough Derg, County Donegal. Locals claim that it was the last stronghold of the Irish Druids whom the saint extirpated, a victory symbolised by the legend of his expulsion of the serpents (his own name may mean 'snake destroyer'). They were supposedly drowned in the lough.

The rite, with its unmistakably pagan echoes, was one regarded as so perilous that every effort was made to dissuade a penitent from undertaking it. If he remained adamant, he spent fifteen days in fasting and prayer at the nearby monastery at the end of which he was absolved, given communion and asperged with holy water before one final attempt was made to dissuade him.

Only if he still persisted was he blessed and let into the cave, its entrance door then being locked and not reopened until next morning. If the penitent were there, he was led amid great jubilation to the church and after a further fifteen days of watching and praying allowed to go on his way. If he was not, he was regarded as having perished on his pilgrimage, the door was closed and he was never again mentioned.

Among the more august pilgrims, if we are to believe a story by the sixteenth-century French writer Estienne Forcatulus, was King Arthur. However, our knowledge of what actually took place in the cave comes from an account of the experience of the knight Owain, a pilgrim who obviously survived the ordeal, as it is recorded in the poem *Owain Miles*.

As he begins to penetrate the cave's depths, he has a little light which, as in the Morbihan caves, dwindles till he is in total darkness. Then in an eerie twilight he finds himself in the presence of fifteen men dressed in white and with the shaven heads of monks, who warn him of the unclean spirits about to assail him and instruct him how he can prevail over them[5].

No sooner has the white company dissolved than demons drag him through the prefigured torments. At last he comes to a narrow bridge, but as he reaches its centre the fiends scream so horribly he nearly falls into the raging abyss below. He succeeds in gaining the far shore nevertheless and finds himself in a splendid city where he is made so welcome that all previous pain is obliterated. Though the desire to return to the everyday world is gone, he is told it is his duty to live out his mortal life and he returns by a safe pleasant way, meeting again en route the fifteen white-clad figures who reveal the future to him.

Rites such as those connected with New Grange and St Patrick's Purgatory resemble not only the initiations of cults like that of the Idaean Zeus, but also those of the Mystery Religions which often took place in cavernous subterranean chambers, either natural or man-made.

Evans Wentz points to another curious similarity: that between the Breton pardons and the Mystery initiations. In particular he compares the three-day Pardon of St Anne d'Auray with the Eleusinian Mysteries of Demeter and Persephone. In addition, besides a torchlight procession, it involved purificatory rites carried out at the holy fountain of St Anne. These rites are very like those conducted on the seashore by initiates of both the Eleusinian and the Isis Mysteries which, borrowed from the Egyptians by the Greeks, spread to Rome.

The growth of the Mystery Religions came at a time when a growing dissatisfaction with the bland official cults of the gods caused first the Greeks and, centuries later, the Romans to look for religious inspiration toward the beliefs of peoples previously regarded as barbarian. The vast area over which the Greeks traded included the Celtic countries, among them the British Isles, and in this way ideas from Druidism could well have been absorbed into the Mystery Religions, though the source was not necessarily acknowledged.

# Notes

1 Animal spirits are important even in contemporary shamanism. Thus Michael Harner writes in *The Way of the Shaman*: 'The connectedness between the human and animal world is very basic to shamanism . . . Through his guardian spirit or power animal, the shaman connects with the power of the animal world, the mammals, birds, fish and other beings.'

2 The Lord of the Animals as shamanistic proto-god is discussed in more detail in my *Shamanism* where, inter alia, I point out his survival as the 'Green Man', popular as a pub name, and on whose signs he is often portrayed complete with horns.

3 Malinovsky does not suggest that the Oceanians of his day were under such a delusion. Mythology invariably reflects the beliefs of the past.

4 According to some accounts, Pythagoras was converted to a belief in reincarnation by Druids and one explanation of the Pythagorean taboo on eating beans was because the bean was one of the disguises adopted by spirits seeking rebirth.

5 The tonsure and white habits, as well as their number – fifteen or thrice five – makes them sound less like monks than Druids.

# Chapter 4

# Gods – The Bountiful and Blood-thirsty

One thing the outburst in the sanctuary of Apollo demonstrates is the breadth of the gulf separating the Celtic view of the supernatural from that of their contemporaries. In one cryptic reference Lucan writes of the Druids that 'to them alone is granted knowledge – or ignorance, it may be – of the gods and celestial powers' (Book I, lines 445–63). As the editor of the Loeb edition of the *Pharsalia* rightly points out, what he means is that their beliefs were so unlike anyone else's, that if they are right, then all the rest were wrong.

The oracle was internationally respected as one of the most sacred places in the ancient world. It proclaimed itself, not just as a centre, but as the omphalos of the world. Foreigners, worshippers of other gods, made long and arduous journeys to seek the judgement of Apollo. The Celts were well aware of all this and manifestly unimpressed.

The Greek religion might share the same ancestry as theirs, but they were never in any doubt which lay closer to the pure, primitive fount. Their gods, like the Old Testament Jehovah, were the true ones. This conviction of religious rectitude, maintained into later times, was one which frequently led them into bigotry and the scene in the sanctuary reminds one of the kind of reaction one might expect from some dour old Scots Wee Free finding himself amid the ornate magnificence of the Sistine Chapel. Seen from their respective viewpoints the reaction of each of them is not totally without justification. The Greek Apollo was a god of many functions. Besides the oracle through which he, virtually alone of the Olympians, communicated directly with mortals, he was best known for two others: as Phoebus, he was a sun god; and as Alexikakos, he was the healer, particularly through his sacred springs. In each of these the Celts had their own equivalents. Among healer-gods is Borvo, whose connection with the French royal house has been mentioned. He, too, is associated with curative springs.

Another healer is Nuada, the king of the Tuatha De Danann, to whom as Nodens, one of the British variants of his name, the immense temple complex discovered by Sir Mortimer Wheeler at Lydney Park on the banks of the Severn was dedicated. Having lost a hand in battle, Nuada had it replaced by a silver prosthesis made by the divine physician, Diancecht, and a small votive arm has indeed been found on the temple site.

The temple's construction, at the close of the fourth century AD, demonstrates that he was the focus of a cult which may by this time have spread beyond the native population. As Llud, another British variant of his name, he is taken by Geoffrey of Monmouth for an early king, responsible for the rebuilding of the city of Trinovantum (from *Troia Nova* or New Troy) which he renamed Caerludd or 'Ludd's town'. This city ultimately became London. The same dubious source tells us that at his death he was buried at its principal gate known, until the Anglo-Saxons made it Ludgate, as Porthludd.

However, it is symptomatic of the complexity of the Celtic gods and the difficulty of slipping them into the neatly labelled pigeonholes that in Latin inscriptions Nodens is equated with Mars, which is consistent with the Irish Nuada's participation in battle and his ownership of the sword which was one of the Four Gifts of Tuatha. At the same time, while he has several underworld associations, a bronze plaque from Lydney shows him as a young man with a sun-like halo, giving him a similarity to Apollo.

But to further bedevil the issue, Caesar's Gaulish Apollo is generally taken to be Belenos (Belinus in Britain). Apollo is actually a mysterious latecomer to the Greek pantheon and one of a variety of theories about his origins is that he was adopted from the Celts. Hence a sort of proprietorial interest in its tutelary deity has been advanced as the motive for the Celtic raid on Delphi. Markale suggests that, aware that Apollo's sacred utterances were being distorted to serve the needs of state, the march on the sanctuary was part of an attempt to guide it back to its true destiny – an objective frustrated by fate.

It is true that, over the centuries, the oracle had degenerated into a political instrument and certainly, if it was the raid for booty it has been often been assumed to be, it was singularly unsuccessful. A hoard of 45,000 kilograms of gold and 50,000 kilograms of silver bullion plundered by the Roman general Caepio, who came upon it two centuries later in the Lake Toulouse area, was said to have come from this source. Although the Volcae Tectosages, who formed the vanguard of the expedition, came from this region, it is unlikely that Caepio's loot represented the Delphic treasure. Most of this had been plundered by earlier raiders and, while the Celts might have taken what was left, their withdrawal was so precipitate that most of the baggage had to be burned and the wounded – according to Greek sources, including the commander of the expedition himself – slaughtered. Even then the long march to the safety of their native lands was dogged by such misfortune that little could have survived. Thus there is reason to suppose that the Delphic raid was actuated by other motives, though it is far from clear what these were.

Attempts to show that the Greeks stole Belinus and renamed him 'Apollo' seem to me to be based on shaky ground. It is true that Belinus, like Apollo, is a god of sacred springs. The miraculous Fountain of Barenton, which lies on the edge of the Breton Forest of Paimpont, the Arthurian Brocéliande, derives its name from him as is indicated by the thirteenth-century *Ordinances of the Count of Laval* in which it is called the Fountain of Belenton.

According to one version of the Greek god's myth, as an infant he was borne on a dolphin's back across the sea from his birthplace on the island of Delos to Mount Parnassus where he appropriated the oracular sanctuary of the Great Earth Mother. Dolphins are fairly common in Celtic art. A minor figure on a panel of the Gundestrup Cauldron is shown riding one in the manner of Apollo, while the same motif occurs on the sceptre from Willingham Fen, Cambridgeshire. However, myth yields nothing remotely comparable.

Markale has sought to derive the name 'Apollo' from the Celtic word for 'apple', *aval*, but this too seems to me forced and inconclusive.

Belinus is commemorated in a number of place names. British examples include Billingshurst in Sussex and Billingsgate in London. In Geoffrey of Monmouth Belinus is an early British king who, returning from successfully campaigning on the Continent, raised a city named after himself on the banks of the Thames. Though his account is plainly specious, one may be justified in assuming that Billingsgate was once a cult centre of Belinus.

A number of places in France also bear his name. A striking instance is the high rocky islet off the Normandy coast formerly called Tombelaine which, in the slightly altered form of Les Tombelènes, is also the name of a reef off Jersey's north coast. In yet another of his pieces of bogus etymology Geoffrey makes the Norman Tombelaine into 'The Tomb of Elaine', she being a young girl killed by a serpent, subsequently itself killed by Arthur. The serpent slayer traditionally associated with the rock is the warrior-archangel St Michael, whose legend makes no mention of a maiden. It was on account of his killing of the serpent that Tombelaine was renamed Mont-St-Michel and has become one of France's two most visited tourist sites. (The other is Carcassonne.) The role of serpent slayer is also, of course, one played by Apollo. No known similar story is attached to Belinus, though the introduction to the location of Arthur, who possesses some of the characteristics of the god, makes it possible that Geoffrey has garbled a lost myth in which it actually is Belinus who is the slayer and 'St Michael' his Christian alias.

Belinus is not the only god so treated. Down to late times Scottish churchmen were deploring the popularity of stories about the Tuatha De Danann and condemning the subterfuges used to disguise Lugh's name behind that of St Michael.

Lugh, whom Caesar calls 'Mercury', is said to be the god 'most reverenced' in Gaul. He is undoubtedly right. His name, which means Light, is commemorated in the name of Carlisle in northern England and possibly Lewes in southern England, as well as Leyden in Holland and Lyons in France and a number of other places. It is indicative of the ubiquity of his cult that claims of a special association with him are to be found in many of the Celtic lands. Stories from the Isle of Man speak of his spending his childhood there with his foster-father Mananann mac Lir. In Wales his foster-father is said to be the magician Gwyddion, who some scholars take to be an alternative form of Lugh himself. In Ireland, the emphasis is on foster-mother rather than father, who is the goddess Tailtiu.

Like Mercury, Lugh was patron of commerce, invention and art, all of which he was supposed to have inaugurated. He figures repeatedly in the Irish stories, and is divine progenitor of the hero Cu Chulainn. In Wales, where his name is given as Llwch and Lleu, he was associated with shoemakers, which just might connect him with the Irish leprechaun, the shoemaker in old-fashioned clothes who guards a treasure. In both places his name is frequently augmented with the cognomen the 'Many Skilled' or the 'Skilful Handed' and he is the owner of the highly destructive spear which in due time becomes the Spear of Longinus. Since, in the Welsh form, his name can also mean 'lion' (*llew* in modern Welsh), Graves, following Lady Charlotte Guest's nineteenth-century translation, renders *Lleu Law Gaffes* as 'the lion with the steady hand'. He may well be the ultimate source of the Lions, Red, White and Blue, so frequently found in British pub names.

There was another significant difference between the classical attitude to the supernatural and that of the Celts. Their gods have none of the aloof impassivity of the Olympians. Like the shaman's Otherworld, theirs is an alternative state of consciousness. The central male character of a story can find himself whisked off to *Tir na nOg*, the Land of Youth, or *Tir Tairngirē*, the Land of Promise. In any case, as Markale says, to reach it 'one has only to cross a wood, a hill, a river, a stretch of sea'. In the *Mabinogion* tale of *Manawydan Son of Llyr*, Pryderi and Rhiannon chase a boar into a magic castle in which they become prisoners as it vanishes in the mist. Lancelot crosses into the Otherworld via the Sword Bridge when he goes in pursuit of the abducted Guinevere; so does Owein, when he pours water from the Fountain of Barenton over the magic stone.

It is a frontier which can be crossed from both directions. The goddess Macha crosses it to come into the life of the widower Crunniuc mac Agnomain. Establishing herself in his lonely mountain home, in the words of the *Tain*, 'she began working at once, as though she were well used to the house and when night came, put everything in order without being asked. Then she slept with Crunniuc'.

The gods are active participants in many human endeavours. There is no better example than in the Delphic adventure itself. The descriptions of it by Greek and Latin historians are a concoction of the actual and the mythological. The desecration of the holy place brings down the wrath of the gods in the forms, not only of snowstorms, but of earthquakes and thunderbolts. Ancient heroes rise from the grave to appear in the heavens.

Most telling of all is the name 'Brennus', ascribed to the commander of the Celtic forces. It is, to begin with, the same name as that of the commander of the attack on Rome. Yet in that instance the forces came mainly from what is now Burgundy. Those who marched on Greece were from far to the south, the area round what is now Toulouse. In other words, we have the coincidence of two operations, separated by nearly a century, led by different tribes, both having leaders of the same name.

The likely answer is that 'Brennus' is a latinisation of the godname Bran. Bran means 'raven', the bird which, as scavenger of carrion, haunts the battlefield, its hard beak stretching scarlet shreds from the corpses of the freshly dead. Bran is the subject of a eulogy in which he is called 'harsh spear', 'sun of warriors' and, especially relevant, 'fierce raider'. Large scale military enterprises, while dominated by one tribe, were often drawn from several and a commander, who was given the title of 'war leader', was chosen by the joint consent of all. At the same time, to further cement unity, it was customary to ascribe command-in-chief, not to any mortal, but to a war god who was common to all the tribes.

This must be the case with 'Brennus' and added force is lent to the argument by the account of his death during the retreat from Parnassus as related by Pausanias, Justinus and Diodorus of Sicily. All agree he killed himself, but ascribe two different motives to the deed. One is remorse at the disaster he brought down on his troops; the other, the unbearable pain from a wound he had sustained. Diodorus adds another detail: that before dealing the death blow to himself, he urged members of his entourage to kill him.

In the Welsh *Branwen Daughter of Llyr*, Bran is leader of a struggle against Irish enemies which involves a magic cauldron. A terrible battle takes place and only seven of his companions survive. Bran is not only defeated, he has been wounded with a poisoned spear. Though, according to the text, this was in the foot, it was more probably in the testicles, thereby depriving him not only of sexual powers but, according to Celtic belief, all authority. It is for this reason that he ordered his companions cut off his head.

In *Branwen* a further strange adventure follows the decapitation, for Bran bids them carry his head to White Hill in London for burial. So long as it remained there, Britain would be free of invaders. However, their journey was to be a prolonged one. First there was a seven-year feast over which the head presided. Then, still with it for companion, they were to spend a further eighty years in Pembroke, a place which in its Welsh form of Penvro means the 'The place (or vale) of the Head'. During this time they were strictly enjoined not to 'open the door to the Bristol Channel on the side facing Cornwall'. Should they do so, corruption would overtake the head and they would have to hurry to London to bury it.

All eventuated as foretold until curiosity about what lay behind the forbidden door became irresistible and one of the companions opened it. Instantly joy turned to sorrow as the head decayed before their eyes and they hastened to perform their last duty. White Hill has been identified with Ludgate Hill, thus associating Bran with Nuada/Llud, though there is nothing else to associate them. It is more usually regarded as Tower Hill, site of the Tower of London. It is here that a flock of tame ravens has been kept in perpetuity by the Crown and guarded by Beefeaters. The link with Bran the raven god seems inescapable. According to legend the kingdom is safe from conquest so long as they are present, just as Bran prophesied that his head would ward off invasion. During the Blitz in 1940 when the ravens, like many of London's other citizens, took flight to somewhere safer, the government kept the news from the people because of the effect it might have on morale and replaced the birds as quickly as possible. Merrifield even mentions seeing coins including silver dropped into the birds' drinking bowl, in the manner of votive offerings, as late as the 1960s.

Bran the raven god demonstrates yet another of the profound differences between the Celtic and the classical gods: the proximity of the former to the totems. In the Fenian cycle Oisin (Ossian) is the son of the stag goddess Sadv, probably the prototype of the white deer who appear in the Arthurian stories. Sow and bear goddesses are to be found both in artefact and, sometimes half-disguised, in literature. One example is Goleudydd, mother of Kulwych (Pig-Run), who gives birth to him in a sty.

Caer Ibormeith, object of the hopeless infatuation of Oengus mac Oc, turns into a swan every alternate year and, during this phase, she and her thrice fifty companions are coupled together in pairs with a chain. Models of swans, some with the remains of the chains, others with rings for them under their beaks, are particularly associated with the La Tène figurines found in central Europe and suggest a link with the swan maidens of Russian folk stories and the German swan knight, Lohengrin.

But the creature which takes precedence is the horse.

Among the gifts of Crunniuc mac Agnomain's mistress-housekeeper, Macha, is her fleetness of foot. Though far gone in pregnancy she accompanies him to a fair and is coerced into running in a race. She wins, but expires in the effort, in her death throes giving birth to twins and punishing the heartless Ulstermen with the curse which renders them powerless with pangs akin to those of birth at the very moment their land is in its greatest crisis. The incident reveals her equine aspect, for her opponent in the race is the king's chariot, whose horses, it was said, nothing could beat.

In British literature the horse goddess is represented by Rhiannon. In the Welsh story that takes his name Pwyll, Lord of Dyved, visits Gorsedd Arberth. *Gorsedd* means both a throne and a mound and so is cognate with the Irish *sidh*. This particular one has a similar property to the Hill of Tara in that whenever anyone of royal blood sits on it a marvel will occur. The marvel Pwyll sees is a mysterious woman on a grey horse. She proves to be Rhiannon who becomes his wife. When later her infant son – whose birth is linked with the foaling of a mare – vanishes, she is accused of murdering him and made to stand at the mounting-block outside her husband's court to bring visitors to it on her back. In *Manawydan* she tries to rescue her son, Pryderi, from the mysterious Castle of the Golden Bowl and is made a prisoner with him. When the two are delivered through the intervention of Manawydan (the Irish Mananann) it is reported that Rhiannon had been forced to wear 'the collars of asses after they have been carrying hay'.

The Golden Bowl incident shows plain traces of the vegetation myth. The bowl itself must stand for the sun, especially as Rhiannon and Pryderi are led into the Castle while hunting a shining white boar, and its solar nature is further confirmed by the fact that, while Pwyll and Rhiannon are missing, Manawydan's cornfields are repeatedly devoured by mice, in other words rendered barren, the typical state of the land while the Young God is immured in the Underworld. However, what must be a variant of the same myth is found in another story. *Kulhwych and Olwen* contains references to a 'Mabon ap Modron', the Son of Mother or the Young Son, who has been a prisoner from infancy. He must have been the object of a cult in northern Britain as the name 'Maponus' appears on an altar at Corbridge, Northumberland, where he is equated with the Roman Apollo. In addition he is commemorated in the Dumfriesshire village of Lochmaben and in a stone near Annan known as Clochmabenstane. He also occurs in Chrétien de Troyes's *Erec* as the Little King Mabonagrain, a participant in the strange games which form the story's climax. The same incident recurs in *Gereint and Enide*, though here without the Little King being named, and he must also be the 'Mabuz' linked with the hero of the twelfth-century High German *Lanzelet*. Tolstoy identifies him as the youthful Lugh, and Lochmaben and the Clochmabenstane are in an area whose Middle Welsh name was Lleudinyawn, roughly the place of Lleu's stronghold. Chrétien's epithet 'Little' may therefore have less to do with stature than age. In other words, the cult of Mabon involved the invocation of Lugh as a child just as the Orphics invoked Dionysus as child god. This means the unidentified Modron is Rhiannon which in its turn makes Pryderi an alias for Lugh. Though this may seem to be contradicted in *Math son of Mathonwy*, where young Lleu's mother is named as Arianrhod, in No 124 of *The Triads of the Isle of Britain* she is actually called Rhiannon.

The equine aspect of Macha and Rhiannon distinguished them from the wholly anthropomorphic Great Mothers of many cultures and is one they share with the continental horse goddess Epona who, in the Gallo-Roman sculpture at Lezoux, near Puy-de-Dôme, is shown with her mount and an overflowing cornucopia, a typical symbol of the Great Mother's all-providing womb. In a bronze figure from Wiltshire the seated Epona has a pony on either side of her and a *patera* or dish which is spilling corn on her lap.

The horse was of paramount importance in both Britain and Ireland – horse-breeding is, of course, still a significant part of the Irish economy – but the fact that the young Arvernian king, Vercingetorix, had his horses secreted to a safe place when besieged by Caesar at Alésia (now Alise-Sainte-Reine in Burgundy) shows that reverence for it extended into Gaul.

Throughout the British Isles it is attested archaeologically by the presence of horses' heads, apparently deposited for apotropaic reasons, in grain silos. There is also their representation in the hillside figures, such as the Uffington White Horse. Of these there were once a great many, the majority having grown over. Near the Bratton Down white horse in Wiltshire, aerial photography has revealed the faint outline in the turf of another and T.C. Lethbridge's researches at Wandlebury brought to light a stylised representation of a horse-riding goddess.

In the Irish vernacular literature one of the titles of the powerful In Dagda is Eochaid Ollathair, meaning 'Great Horse Father'. Among the lovers of the Connaught queen, Mebd, is Fergus mac Roech, 'Fergus son of Great Horse'.

However, as a solar symbol the horse was important to all the Indo-

European peoples. In the official state pantheon the Roman gods were equated with Greek ones. Hence, Diana was equated with the Greek Artemis, sister of Apollo. In fact, she actually had a long and quite separate history of her own demonstrated by the oldest of her known cults, that of Diana Nemorensis. Its centre was the sacred grove at Aricia in the Alban Hills where she was jointly worshipped with Virbius, an alias for the Greek Hippolytus killed when his horses took fright at the sight of Poseidon's bull and flung him from his chariot. As in the typical vegetation myth, he is brought back from the dead through the good offices of a woman, in this case Artemis/Diana. His name, which means 'he of the wild horses', was inherited from his mother, Hippolyta, plainly a horse goddess. (Jan de Vries points out that the Arcadians, who claimed to be the oldest people in Greece and whose land had many associations with mythology, represented Demeter as a horse.)

Besides their common horse nature Rhiannon resembles Macha in another way. The name comes from Rigatona, the 'great queen' as does Morrigan, one of the alternate names of Macha. Frightening and powerful, the Morrigan is said to have mated with In Dagda with one foot on either bank of the River Unius, but is often represented in the triple form typical of many Celtic deities. Besides Macha, the trio includes Nemain and Babd, names which reveal their sinister natures, for Nemain means 'Frenzy' and Babd or Babd Catha 'Battle Raven'. Cormac glosses Macha as 'crow' and writes of the Mesrad Machae, the mast of Macha, being the forest acorns and beech nuts much favoured as food by pigs. Here it stands as a metaphor for the heads of enemies taken in war, but her crow-form shows her ability to take on other shapes besides that of the horse and we know she could metamorphose at will into a deer. As might be expected of so sinister a trio, their favoured haunt is the battlefield where they influence the outcome by the terror their presence inspires. (Their triple nature brings to mind the Three Weird Sisters in Shakespeare's *Macbeth* who make their first appearance after a bloody battle.) Cu Chulainn has several encounters with her, the last just before his death when she appears as a woman washing blood-stained clothes and armour at a ford. Asked whose they are she tells him they are his. Though less blatantly, Rhiannon, too, shows this Kali-like destructive streak. The incident in which Gwawl, Pwyll's rival to her hand, is trapped in a bag and treated like a football echoes a method of torture mentioned in Scottish Highland contexts in which the

victim was tied so his feet were brought up to his ears, in other words
so he resembled a ball, and then kicked 'over the rafters'.

Beneath this one detects the Evil Witch against whose terrible
powers the shaman and Druid are in ceaseless conflict and it is
significant that the word *cailleach*, 'hag', incorporates connotations
of the divinity. She haunts the myths as a figure of stomach-turning
horror. The *cailleach* whom the five sons of Eochaid, King of Ireland,
come upon while hunting is bleary-eyed, fang-toothed, snotty-nosed
and has a boil-encrusted body. Equally nauseous is she who turns
up at Finn's hall. Both make exorbitant sexual demands of the men
present. It is only the youngest – Niall in the first, Diarmait in the
second – who can bring themselves to accede and, by so doing,
transform them into rare young beauties.

For all the power of love these two examples illustrate, the virago
and hag are indicative of a deep suspicion, at times of hostility,
toward woman wholly of a piece with the attitude of the shaman. In
these circumstances it is at least a matter for conjecture whether
Celtic males granted their women the privileges they enjoyed out of
generosity or fear.

Even at her most desirable she is all too liable to turn out to be
a snare. In two of the Irish *imramma*, or voyage tales, the heroes find
themselves in the Land of Promise, inhabited by ravishing sexually-
accommodating creatures. In the end a life given over to eating,
drinking and love-making palls and the yearning to hear again the
laughing voices of old companions grows unendurable. It is then
they find they are not guests, but prisoners, and when, with the
utmost difficulty, they escape, it is, of course, only to discover a
terrible truth: long since dead are the old companions; weed-grown
ruins the haunts of youth.

Women had yet another power over men through the *geis*. This is
sometimes interpreted as a taboo, but where most forms of taboo are
binding on a specific, defined group, the *geis* is a magical
proscription laid on a single individual, usually a hero or king.

It is frequently a woman who will force the man to break it. At his
accession King Conare was bound by a whole list of *gessa*, one of
which prohibits him from admitting a single woman to his presence
after sunset. Having inadvertently broken all save one, he is finally
made to break even this by the Otherworld woman who arrives after
nightfall and demands admission to the hostel where he is staying,
thereby bringing destruction on his head.

But a woman can impose a *geis* and is liable to do so if her sexual desires are engaged. 'In Celtic literature,' writes Jean Marx, 'it is the woman who chooses, conquers, binds and enchains the man, often against his wishes and inclinations.' When Uathach, daughter of Scáthach, climbs into Cu Chulainn's bed he pushes her out. She responds by placing him under a *geis* to allow her to stay. It is in this way, too, that Grainme, daughter of King Cormac of Leinster, binds the handsome young warrior Diarmait. She places him under *geis* to elope with her on the very night of her marriage to his beloved chief, Finn mac Cumhail. The advice of his companions is that he cannot resist, though by his compliance he brings down perils ending in his death.

Even Merlin, 'wisest of men', is impotent. Falling for Viviane in his dotage, she demands his magical secrets. While recognising the folly of his actions, he has no option but to accede. She, for her part, uses one of his own spells to make him prisoner and confine him in a glass castle, thereby ridding herself of his aged and unwelcome advances.

Nonetheless, witch-like in their cruelty, rapacity and cunning as the goddesses may be, they are nothing if not as changeable as the breeze. When Cu Chulainn rejects the Morrigan's advances she avenges the snub by thrice impeding him at critical moments in his life-and-death struggle against the men of Connaught. Then when, with the greatest difficulty, he succeeds in inflicting such injuries upon her she has to give up, she tricks him into tending her. When the chariot and one-legged horse of his nightmare vanish, the only living thing in the desolate landscape is the Babd in bird form. As three crones cooking a dog-meat meal by the wayside, she shames him into breaking his *geis* against eating dog-flesh by reproaching him for eating the food of the great, but spurning that of the poor. She it is who forces Conare to break his last *geis*. Yet, having done her utmost to bring about Cu Chulainn's defeat and death, she later comes to his aid by appearing as Nemain causing many of his enemies to die of terror or heartbreak.

According to legend, just as she manifested herself to Cu Chulainn as the Washer-at-the-Ford warning of his impending death, she also showed herself to the High King Cormac (c. 227–66) just before he was killed in battle. Nonetheless, by raising up the water, she enabled him, with his whole army, to cross dry-shod the very river in which she was scouring the blood from his armour.

She is no less ambivalent in her later epiphany as the Morgan le Fée (or Fairy) of the Arthurian stories. Malory accuses her of trying, at one stage, to kill her royal half-brother, but later she is among the queens who bear him off to Avalon in her barge to cure him of his wounds, and her skill as healer is mentioned by Chrétien de Troyes.

That Malory mentions that the barge contained three queens further helps to identify Morgan le Fée as the triple Morrigan, the Great Queen. But in her association with water she also resembles the wave-born Aphrodite, since another etymology of her name gives Morgenos, Born of the Sea. In addition, there is little doubt that she is ruler of the Islands of Women visited by Bran mac Febail and Mael Duin and of which Avalon is a latterday example. In the Finistère area of Brittany Morgan, or sometimes Mari Morgan, plays the role of siren enticing sailors with her charmingly plaintive singing. If they yield, their ships will strike rocks and founder and they will join her in her underwater realm. In many places she is equated with Dahut, daughter of Gradlon, King of Ker-Ys, the most famous of the Breton underwater cities which tradition has always set in the Bay of Douarnenez. Beautiful but lascivious, Dahut gives a lover the key which opens the sluicegates. The seas rush in and Gradlon tries to escape on horseback with Dahut as pillion. When the rising waters threaten to overwhelm them, the king's confessor, St Guénolé, who has accompanied them, warns Gradlon to cast off the she-devil. At that moment Dahut falls with a shriek into the sea whence, like the Finistère siren, she continues to lure sailors and fishermen to their doom. Such stories were said to have been carried by twelfth-century Breton sailors to Sicily where the mirages sometimes seen off the coast came to be called the 'Fata Morgana'. Folk stories of these underwater cities, supposedly of glittering brilliance (although where the stories have been christianised they become places of licentiousness), are also to be found in Wales and Ireland where a drunken peasant can find himself in a fairy palace often beneath the waters.

# Chapter 5
# The Lord of the Grove

Lucan's description of the sacred grove of the Druids presents us with images the producer of a horror film would be hard put to surpass and is worth giving in full:

> A grove there was, untouched by men's hands from ancient times, whose interlacing boughs enclosed a space of darkness and cold shade, and banished the sunlight far above. No rural Pan dwelt there, nor Silvanus, ruler of the woods, no Nymphs; but gods were worshipped there with savage rites, the altars were heaped with hideous offerings, and every tree was sprinkled with human gore. On these boughs, if antiquity, reverential of the gods, deserves any credit, birds feared to perch; in those coverts wild beast did not lie down; no wind ever bore down upon that wood, nor thunderbolt hurled from black clouds; the trees, even when they spread their leaves to no breeze, rustled among themselves. Water also fell there in abundance from dark springs. The images of gods, grim and rude, were uncouth formed of felled tree-trunks. Legend also told that often the subterranean hollows quaked and bellowed, that yew-trees fell down and rose again, that the glare of conflagration came from trees that were not on fire, and that serpents twined and glided down the stems. The people never resorted thither to worship at close-quarters, but left the place to the gods. When the sun is in mid-heaven or dark night fills the sky, the priest himself dreads their approach and fears to surprise the Lord of the Grove.

> *(Book III, lines 390–425)*

Miranda Green is of the opinion that Lucan had not travelled in Gaul and that his principal source was Livy's now lost book. However, the Phocaean Greeks had established a system of trading posts along the Mediterranean seaboard, one of which was at Massilia, the present-day Marseilles, and Lucan may well have visited it. His

Druidic grove is certainly the one near the Greek city and later cut down on the orders of Caesar, for Lucan describes the event. He tells us that 'the solemnity and terror of the place' struck such awe into the labourers that Caesar himself had to seize an axe and drive it into the trunk of an oak, crying, 'Believe that I am guilty of the sacrilege and henceforth none of you need fear to cut down the trees.' Thereafter, the labourers, having 'weighed Caesar's wrath against the wrath of heaven', decided the immediacy of the first was to be the more feared than the second and set to work. Meanwhile the Gauls watched the proceedings with perverse satisfaction, convinced the gods would not stand idly by in the face of such profanation and that their foes were thus bringing doom upon themselves (Book III, lines 426–40).

Lucan was a patriotic Roman and it was his intention, consciously or unconsciously, to present the religion which his countrymen were in the process of extirpating as a cruel and wanton superstition. Yet, and despite the eerie, stagnant silence pervading it, his image of the sacred grove is not without substance and even hints at some acquaintance with Druidism. His reference to 'the glare of conflagration from trees that were not on fire' brings to mind an incident in the *Mabinogion* story of *Peredur* in which the young knight comes to a wooded valley divided by a river. At its brink stands a tree, one side of which is aflame from roots to crown, while the other is green with thriving foliage.

Notwithstanding such traces of Celtic temples as archaeology has uncovered, there is no doubt of the importance to Druidism of the kind of setting he depicts. The Celtic root *nemeton*, literally 'sacred grove', occurs in place names like Medionemeton in Scotland, Vernemeton near Lincoln, Nemetobriga in Spain, while Nanterre in southern France derives its name from Nemetodurum, and Drunemeton in what was Galatia (now Anatolia, Turkey) may mean 'the sacred grove of the Druids'. An alternative reading would be 'the sacred oak grove' and has been taken as further evidence that the tree, featured in Pliny's description, was of special significance to the Druids, whose own name has been held to mean the 'wise men of the oak'. Though this is now largely discounted, it would seem to me to run counter to a cloud of witnesses to fail to recognise that among the doctrines of Druidism was an elaborate system of tree lore.

Trees occur in most mythologies, of course, including the Chinese and Semitic (the Hebrew *Minorah* or seven-branched candlestick has sometimes been interpreted as a symbol of the Tree of Life which stood in the Garden of Eden). Hints of tree lore are to be found in the Finnish *Kalevala* so that the magician-hero Väinömöinen, in search of the magic formula which will enable him to finish the ship he is building, visits the giant, Antero Vipunen. He discovers him 'lying under the earth with . . . the poplar growing from his shoulders, the birch from his temples, the alder from his cheeks, the willow from his beard, the fir from his forehead, the wild pine from his teeth'. Among the most famous of mythical trees must certainly be the Norse evergreen ash Yggdrasil on which Odin hung for nine days and nine nights to acquire the secrets of magic. Like Delphi or the Hill of Tara, it is a Great Centre uniting the three worlds, the celestial, our own and the underworld.

Trees also seem to have served as centres for the Celts. The Irish word *bile* denoted a sacred tree, the habitation of a spirit or god who is sometimes actually named, so that *Bile Meidbe* was sacred to the Ulster goddess Mebd. In later times a *bile* was often a hawthorn or may tree and was regarded as one of the dwelling places of the Tuatha De Danann. It was therefore courting their wrath to damage it, accounting for the surviving taboo on bringing may blossom into a house. Even now local authorities in Ireland think twice before demolishing a hawthorn standing on the intended route of a new road or some other project.

When chanting the potent *glam dicin*, a bard would go with six companions to a hawthorn bush. All stood with their backs to it and, with a slingshot in one hand and a branch of the bush in the other, sang the *glam*, finally leaving their branches by the hawthorn's roots.

Later the *bile* came to be associated with kingly rule so that a branch of the tree provided his sceptre. For their subjects the cutting of branches or plucking of fruit from such royal trees was an act of *lèse-majesté* carrying drastic punishments. In Ireland the word *bile* is still attached to any tree with an historical significance or to one of extreme age or unusual shape, especially if it grows in the precincts of a fort or near a well. People will sometimes pray or leave offerings at it and many have acquired their reputation through a supposed association with a saint or because a miracle was said to have taken place in its shade. That the word itself – and one must assume the concept of the sacred tree – was known beyond Ireland is shown by the place names Bilum in Denmark and Bilem in France.

The importance of trees in general to the Celts is attested archaeologically by the presence of trunks in ritual shafts as in one at St Bernard in the Vendée. A panel of the Gundestrup Cauldron shows a procession of marching warriors carrying a tree trunk. (See chapter 2, page 38.)

In addition there are the Jupiter Columns, the tall stone plinths of which 150 are recorded in eastern France and Rhineland Germany, while the small number outside this main area include two in Britain – at Circencester and Chichester. They are usually topped by a figure, often grasping a spoked wheel. This matches the wheel-holding figure on the Gundestrup Cauldron, interpreted as the thunder god Taranis and, because of this similarity of function, equated by the Romans with their own Jupiter to whom, like Taranis, the oak tree was sacred. Besides the animal names assumed by tribes, there was also a penchant for tree names. The Eburovices were the people of yew; the Arverni, the people from the Land of the Alder; the Lemnovices, the people of the elm and so on. Besides its usual interpretation as 'raven', Bran can also mean 'alder', and he was identified with both, while the god Fagus or Beech Tree occurs in the Pyrenees.

The oak tree and mistletoe, whose association with Druidism in the popular imagination emanates from Pliny, is largely confirmed by the Gristhorpe and Lindow Moss finds. Since the Greek counterpart for the Roman Jupiter is Zeus, the statement by the second century Maximus of Tyre that the Celts represented their Zeus as a high oak tree supports Powell's contention that the original Jupiter Columns were of wood and, it seems likely, oak wood. In Wales oak sticks were rubbed together to light the May Day fires.

That oak worship survived into late times is proved by royal edicts against it in both Gaul and England, as well as attempts to christianise individual trees by dedicating them to the Virgin Mary as 'Our Lady of the Oaks'. Merlin's habit of working his spells under an oak tree may well echo Druidic custom. Unlike other oaks, relics of the one claimed to be his still exist. For years, as a dead stump secured with bands of iron, embedded in concrete and railed off, it stood in the middle of Priory Street, Carmarthen. The reason for this careful conservation is a rhyme warning that:

When Merlin's oak shall tumble down,
Then shall fall Carmarthen town.

Defying this monition the local authorities finally decided it was a traffic hazard and had it removed in the 1970s. Part is now in Carmarthen Museum and part in St Peter's Civic Centre. So far Carmarthen has survived. Sadly for the romantics, though, the oak is actually only about 150 years old and both its planting and the composition of the rhyme may have been part of a Victorian publicity drive to bring tourists to Carmarthen, whose connections with Merlin are, in any case, extremely dubious.

As Peredur's burning one illustrates, trees occur frequently in the myths. In the story of *Diarmait and Grainme*, the fugitive lovers hide in the branches of a rowan or mountain ash which grows near a spring. The tree has magical properties and the couple are forbidden to eat its berries, a prohibition they defy with tragic results. The juxtaposition of tree and spring is a typically shamanistic one – Yggdrasil grew by the Well of Mimir and the combination recurs in the final episode of *Math son of Mathonwy*, where Lleu manifests himself as an eagle perched in the topmost branches of an oak tree which grows between two lakes.

That the rowan possessed special properties for the Druids is shown by a story in which, by burning its wood, they raise a magical mist covering an entire area. In Scottish folklore a rowan twig is the means of guarding oneself against the malice of fairies. The need for protection of this kind may be the reason why it was one of the two trees which, according to Markale, the Druids chose for their wands, the other being the yew. In the *Rennes Dindsenchas* or *History of Places*, two of the five most sacred trees of Ireland were yews, one of them being extolled as 'a king's wheel, a prince's right' and as 'a straight firm tree, a straight firm god'. It was, of course, yew trees which Lucan mentions as falling down to rise again. In *The Frenzy of Suibne* the magician King Suibne of Dalriada possesses the shamanistic gift for levitation, and escapes pursuit by flying up into a tree. The tree he most favours is the yew, for he tells Loingsechán, the one steadfast friend through his madness, that he flies 'from hill to hill on the mountain above the valley of the yews'.

Often a tree's fruit will have magical properties. The berries of the rowan tree in which Diarmait and Grainme hid could abolish sickness and renew youth. Those who ate the nuts from the hazel which grew by the Well of Segais, near the source of the Boyne, acquired the gifts of poetry and prophecy. The salmon belonging to the Druid Fingas which Finn tastes while cooking gives knowledge because the salmon itself has been feeding on the hazelnuts of wisdom. In the *Adventure of Cormac*, the hero sees a spring in which are five salmon who eat the nuts from nine ancient trees. It is consistent that in later times the hazel symbolised knowledge of the arts and sciences. The rods on which the Welsh bards were said to carve their poems were of hazel. In France rods of the same wood were used for beating the bounds and were also sometimes carried by heralds as a sign of office.

Forked twigs from the hazel are, of course, the traditional instrument of the water diviner. Many of the superstitions with which water diviners have surrounded its gathering, such as approaching the tree on which it grows walking backward, cutting it in silence while reaching their hands between their legs, sound Druidic and bring to mind Pliny's description of taking the selago, 'in the manner of a thief'.

Hazel as divining rod evokes the Underworld and its treasures. In Cu Chulainn's nightmare the man driving the cow is doing so with a hazel switch. The whole scene, with its one-legged, burial chamber horse, reeks of death and brings to mind the Breton Ankou who, with his assistants, drives his ghostly horse-drawn corpse wagon foreshadowing the death of any who see them.

Apples have specially strong magical and Otherworld overtones. Avalon, for example, is the Land of Apples. One of the punishments inflicted by Lugh on the sons of Tuirenn is to gather three apples from the Garden of Hesperides. The garden and apples are borrowed from Greek myth and the incident, like several others in *The Fate of the Sons of Tuirenn*, may be a late storyteller's interpolation. However, a typically Celtic characteristic of these apples is that they did not diminish when eaten, one which they shared with the apple given to Connle by the Otherworld woman. Magic apples which satisfy the hungry also occur in *The Voyage of Mael Duin*. One of the key poems of the bard Myrddin, probably the original Merlin of the late Arthurian stories, is 'The Apple Tree' in which he describes the terrible battle as a result of whose carnage he, like Suibne, loses his senses.

Another possible significance of apples is mentioned in the *Tain*.

We are told that above King Conchobhar's throne at Emain Macha was a silver rod from which hung three golden apples 'for keeping order over the throng'. When these were shaken 'everyone fell into such a respectful silence you would hear a needle drop to the floor'.

Magic apples can serve as an Otherworld passport. The warrior who visits Cormac and acts as his guide bears a branch on which are three golden apples he gives the hero. When shaken they emit a delightful music which converts pain or sorrow into sleep. But they also seem to serve as exit visas, for in *Gereint* the horn, whose winding is to end the bizarre games and free the hero, hangs from an apple tree.

Important as Druidic tree lore must once have been, its actual content is, with so much else, forever lost. In a poem Suibne apostrophises the oak, elder, blackthorn, apple, briar, yew, holly, birch and aspen. And the treatment of trees as though they were living beings is to be found in the highly cryptic *The Battle of the Trees*, claimed as the work of the sixth-century Welsh bard Taliesin, and which Markale regards as shot through with Druidic secrets. In *The White Goddess* Robert Graves attempts an ingenious interpretation of the work using as his basis the tree alphabet, supposedly Druidic, which is given by the seventeenth-century writer Roderick O'Flaherty in his *Ogyia*. The alphabet is made up of thirteen consonants and five vowels, each letter taking its name from the first letter of a tree or shrub. Unfortunately for the theory, many scholars regard O'Flaherty's tree alphabet as a late invention or, at best, a construct from shaky evidence.

A tree zodiac in which the various signs are given tree rather than the more usual names derived from the zodiac's Mesopotamian origins is equally doubtful.

It has also been suggested that *The Battle of the Trees* recalls the custom of tree metaphors whereby a hero will often be compared with one. This may be reflected in the use of trees in proper names such as McColl, son of hazel. In *Kulhwych* the heroine's cruel giant of a father is Ysbaddaden or 'Hawthorn' and in *The Dream of Oengus* the swan maiden is Caer Ibormeith or 'Yew berry'. Ibor, Yew, is also the name of the charioteer in the *Boyhood Deeds of Cu Chulainn*.

The tree which burns without being consumed is not the only sight to bedazzle the eyes of the errant Peredur. The river at whose side it stands divides the valley into two meadows and what he sees there, in my view, catches the essence of Druidism more completely than anything else. In one meadow black sheep are grazing; in the other, white ones. Each time one of the black sheep bleats, a white one crosses into their meadow turning black as it does so. The reverse occurs when a white sheep bleats. In the Irish story *The Voyage of Mael Duin* the hero and his fellow travellers have a similar experience, in their case on one of the marvellous islands they find on their travels.

It requires no very subtle discernment to recognise that what is figured here is the notion of Cosmic Balance between the two worlds. Caesar mentions the employment of Druids to offer sacrifice for an individual who was seriously ill or about to face danger. It is instructive that in the Peredur version the sheep have to cross a river, frequently the boundary between two worlds. Cosmic Balance must be restored whenever it is disturbed, a process complicated by the fact that it is not static, but dynamic, as is shown by the way the black and white sheep constantly change places. From one point of view it could be seen as the flow between the *yin* and *yang* of Chinese Taoism which, in certain of its aspects, Druidism resembles. But it is, of course, implicit in all religions. Wherever disaster strikes, religious leaders are always quick to see in it divine retribution for some collective sin which has disturbed the Cosmic Balance.

As Jean Marx points out, there is another aspect of the black and white sheep: their total number remains unchanged. It is 'as if there was a sort of limited capital of souls and spirits which circulated between the two worlds', he says.

This principle of balance is exemplified in the shamanistic image of an Otherworld which is a mirror image of our own. The two are in symmetry.

One emblem of the relationship between gods and mortals was what is perhaps the best known of all Celtic artefacts, the torc, or neck ring, of which hundreds of examples have been found, many of exquisite workmanship. Its religious function is evident from the fact that it often encircles the necks of male gods, even in otherwise rudimentary representations.

We know many instances of similar customs. Hilda Ellis-Davidson mentions one among the Semnones, a Germanic tribes inhabiting the area which is now Swabia, who bound worshippers with a cord before they were admitted to their most venerated sacred grove for the annual human sacrifice. The use of a cord is instructive, since the design of many Celtic torcs indicates that they must have been based on a twisted cord or rope.

Tacitus, recording the Semnones' practice, says the binding served to 'acknowledge the power of the deity'. Eliade, who devotes a chapter of his *Images and Symbols* to the 'God who binds', regards binding as the prerogative of Dumézil's 'Terrible Sovereign', most powerful of his three categories of Indo-European deity. Binding to a god meant, says Eliade, granting him power over life and death, a power obviously possessed by the god to whom human victims were dedicated.

Though the torc has been found among grave goods in female inhumations, goddesses are not portrayed as wearing it. Nor is it always worn by gods. On the Gundestrup Cauldron, for instance, the neck of the god in the act of immersing a sacrificial victim in a vat is bare, though some trouble has been taken to represent a torc on those gods on other panels. On the Reims stela which shows Apollo and Mercury flanking the enthroned Cernunnos, only Cernunnos is wearing one. He is, indeed, the deity most consistently so adorned and, in view of his markedly shamanistic traits and what I believe to be his intimate association with Druidism, might well be said to be 'a god who binds'.

However, the torc is not linked exclusively with him as it occurs on representations of other gods, for example the 3rd–2nd century BC warrior god from Entremont, Provence, and the particularly striking bronze and iron figurine from Bouray, near Paris.

As Dumézil associates the concept of binding particularly with the Indo-Europeans it is hardly surprising to find it among the Celts who preserved so much going back to these roots. Tacitus's passage on the Semnones makes clear that binding took place only before the sacrifice and this raises the question of whether the Celts wore the torc permanently or only for ritual occasions. Or did they, in fact, wear it at all? Merrifield points out that some found in graves would have been too small for most human necks and suggests that they may have accompanied the body as payment for admission to the Otherworld. Against this we have the evidence of Dio Cassio that Boudicca went into battle wearing one, and torc-wearing Celtic warriors are portrayed on several classical representations such as a Roman sarcophagus in which they encircle the necks of the otherwise naked Celtic spear throwers.

The practice of sacrifice is obviously broad enough a subject to deserve treatment on its own, but an aspect of what might be regarded as sacrifice, namely the making of votive offerings to a god in the form of valued objects, can be discussed here. The hoards found in ritual shafts, but most especially in rivers, lakes and marshes show this to have been widely practised. The deposits of gold and silver bullion mentioned by Strabo as found in the Lake Toulouse area are an example, and the Gundestrup Cauldron came from a Danish bog. Treasure found in Llyn Cerrig Bach in Anglesey included slave chains, trumpets, harness fittings and even entire chariots and it was, of course, from the shallows of Lake Neuchâtel that the La Tène hoard was dredged in the last century.

The central role played by water sources is abundantly clear from the vernacular literature. Cu Chulainn fights his mortal struggle at a ford. Arthur receives his sword from 'The Lady of the Lake' and, when mortally wounded at the Battle of Camlann, is conveyed over water to Avalon. Similar Stygian overtones are to be found in the ancient Breton story of the boatman summoned by an unseen voice to convey a freight of souls to one of those off-shore islands which are so often abodes of the dead in Celtic belief. The sixth-century Procopius of Caesarea has an almost exactly similar story from Britain according to which those living along its Atlantic shore acted as ferrymen of souls. This further confirms the fact that to the Druids, as to the shamans, water was an Otherworld entrance. According to a belief commonly held in the Celtic countries until late times, those pursued by fairies could escape by crossing water. The tactic is employed by Robert Burns's Tam O'Shanter when he blunders into a witches' Sabbath, and Pliny was advised by Druids that, when pursued by enchanted serpents, one should flee on horseback across the nearest stream as they were unable to cross it.

Among weapons which have been found in lake and river are scores of spears and swords. The shafts of the former were often broken and the latter bent. Some archaeologists have suggested this was regarded as 'killing' them, though the point of this is difficult to see.

There are, of course, sword-breaking episodes in myth. In the *First* or *Wauchier Continuation* of Chrétien's *Perceval*, Gauvain (Gawain), visiting the castle of the Fisher-King, sees a bier on which lies a corpse covered by a splendid silk pall. Across it lies the broken sword. Gauvain, seeking an explanation for the mysteries he has

witnessed at the castle, is told his curiosity will be satisfied only if
he is able to reunite the two parts of the sword. He fails, falls asleep
and awakens lying in a field with his horse grazing nearby, the castle
having vanished.

In *Peredur* the hero, on the instructions of the Fisher-King's brother,
who is his uncle, takes up a sword and thrice uses it to strike an iron
column. Each time both sword and column break in two. Twice they
rejoin when Peredur puts the pieces together. However, at the third
attempt he fails. There may well be a link here with the breaking of
swords before throwing them into rivers, but there are, to my mind,
more down-to-earth explanations. Often those offered were of such
high quality, it is hard to see their owners exposing them to the
hazards of the battle or how they could have escaped so unscathed.
Some would have been parade weapons, but others were probably
forged specifically as offerings to the gods. Besides such divine
gratitude as might accrue to the donor, there was the material
advantage that his readiness to discard such costly items asserted
his wealth and status among his peers. This was particularly
important because of the Celtic concept of 'honour price', whereby
every individual's social status was assessed, usually in cattle.
Honour price was used in such matters as adjusting grievances or
in the system of suretyship mentioned in the Irish *Intoxication of the
Ulstermen*. Under it one man could offer himself as surety for the
fulfilment of another's obligations, but before taking on such a
burden had to demonstrate the adequacy of his honour price, which
could be diminished if his client defaulted.

The system had its advantages. For example, in the case of fines
or other exactions imposed on a clan the liability of each member
was assessed according to his honour price, with no one bearing
more than he could afford. On the other hand, since the higher the
honour price the greater the individual's status in the eyes of his
fellows, any reduction could lead to social ostracism. In addition and
as will be seen later, it could entail effects so catastrophic that it is
understandable that even the most drastic methods should be
resorted to in order to maintain it.

The status and honour price of an individual would obviously be
enhanced if, before tossing into the waters the weapon for which he
had paid a considerable sum of money, he first rendered it unusable.
Apart from anything else, it would absolve him of the possible
accusation that he had secret plans to retrieve it.

The extravagance involved brings to mind the potlatches given by chieftains among the North Pacific Coast Indians of America. Besides lavish feasting, also popular among the Celts, these could involve the public destruction of the chieftain's own property as a means of demonstrating wealth. Besides maintaining his status among his own court, it could also be a weapon against enemies. An unusually expensive potlatch might be given in a bid to outdo a rival and humiliate him or force him to dissipate his own wealth in trying to match or surpass it. Indeed, at times potlatching was a form of surrogate warfare.

The making of votive offerings to the waters can be traced to Neolithic times and was still being practised centuries later. Finds of swords, knives and daggers in rivers stretch from Viking times to the sixteenth century and imply a continuing belief in water beings who require propitiation or from whom favours might be obtained. Among places from which such articles have been recovered is the Thames at Billingsgate whose association with Belinus has been mentioned.

Besides coins found at the same spot, there were Medieval pilgrim badges, some of which must have cost their owners quite large sums of money. These, like the weapons, had been bent, which seems to indicate that, if recovered, they would be valueless. The sixth-century Gregory of Tours records a lakeside festival in the Cevennes at which votive offerings were thrown into the water and animal sacrifice made, a pagan survival which, in however modified form, continued on the site until 1868. Parcels have been seen floating in the waters of the hilltop pool of Dow Loch in Dumfriesshire as late as the present century.

There are, in addition, the countless folk tales involving submarine palaces and cities like the Breton Ker-Ys. For example, Owain Glyndwyr was said to have a magic palace which could sink beneath the waters of one of the Welsh lakes.

The counterpart to the dropping of valued articles into water was the practice of inscribing a malediction against an enemy on metal, usually lead, and treating it in the same way. The under-lying assumption that the spirits or gods of the waters would take the necessary action implies a Celtic origin for the practice, though it continued throughout Roman times – many of those found are inscribed in Latin – and curses dated to the seventeenth century have been dredged from rivers and wells.

Plainly also linked with water is the custom found in Ireland, Wales and the Isle of Man of visiting wells dedicated to saints, particularly at Whitsun or on May Day. The rites involved may include circling the well sunwise – sometimes, in Ireland, on hands and knees. Relics of the votive offerings are the pins, buttons or sometimes coins dropped into the water. From some perspectives a pin could represent a midget sword or spear and a button or coin a shield, so these could well derive from the models of spears and shields, in some cases dating to the Bronze Age, which have been found in wells like that at Woodeaton temple, Oxfordshire.

Irish, Welsh and Scottish wells are generally credited with healing powers and one cure for toothache in the Isle of Man was to insert a pin between the troublesome tooth and its neighbour, then drop it into the well.

Sabine Baring-Gould records how, during some of the *pardons*, cripples would bathe in the waters of a particular well, while others drank it or bathed their sores in it. Breton mothers would soak their children's clothing in the well and put them back on still dripping, a practice obviously linked with ensuring their infants' health. Not only do wells feature in the pardons themselves, but most Breton churches have wells, always regarded to a greater or lesser degree as miraculous, within their precincts or close by.

The fountain of Barenton, which occurs in *Owein*, is also mentioned by Gerald of Wales who gives substantially the same account of its properties. In a typically Celtic juxtaposition it stands near a tree, by which are a stone and a cup. If the cup, filled with water from the fountain, is emptied over the stone, no matter how high the barometer, a torrential rainstorm will ensue. In *Owein*, when the tree is bereft of its last leaf the storm abates and a bird in the tree's branches sings an enchanted song, the first of many wonders the hero is to experience. Belief in its rain-making efficacy continued down to the mid-nineteenth century when, during a long drought, local people formed a procession with their priests leading them to the spring.

Gerald also describes a well in Munster which, he says, would cause a deluge 'if one touches or even looks at it'. This persists 'until a priest, who is virgin in body and mind' – surely an excessive demand – celebrates Mass in the chapel erected for the purpose nearby, then sprinkles holy water and milk from a cow of one colour, a touch which the author describes as 'barbarous' and is certainly Druidic.

Near Penzance in Cornwall is the holy well of St Madron, ceremonially visited in May. The name may be a corruption either of Modron, Mother, or, and in my view more credibly, of Mabon ap Modron since May was the season especially associated with the youth of gods. However, besides curative qualities, for which purpose the sick were plunged into it or had rags from their clothing hung on branches by it, the well had another purpose: if consulted by a young girl it was supposed to indicate with bubbles the number of years before she married.

Nor can one overlook the well-dressing ceremonies found in places like Buxton, Derbyshire; those in question also having a reputation for being curative. In these, pictures are made up primarily from leaves and nowadays depict scenes from Scripture, but must have been drawn from mythology in the past. A ceremony similar to the Derbyshire one also used to take place in London where, once a year, the city clerks dressed a well, thereby giving it and the surrounding area the name of Clerkenwell.

# Chapter 6
# The Blood of Sacrifice

By derivation the word 'sacrifice' means 'to make sacred' and it has been argued that for this reason one cannot describe material objects, such as votive offerings, as sacrifices, except in the widest sense. Only a living thing can, in the process of being offered, change its nature.

The distinction is to some extent a fine one. The hoards of war booty dedicated to the gods, which the Celts left openly displayed and which, to the obvious surprise of Greek and Roman writers, remained untouched, might from some points of view be said to have acquired a type of sanctity. A devout Catholic would certainly argue that the Eucharistic wafer totally changes its nature, indeed becomes sacred, at the consecration. The legendary Grail is an everyday article which by dint of the use to which it was put – that of containing the wine at the Last Supper – changed its nature. It could even be said to have taken on a sort of life of its own, for, we are told, it passed round a table apparently without human agency, feeding every member of the assembly with the food of his choice.

Nonetheless, only a living creature could be said to become sacred in the sense of becoming a divinity, as was thought to be the case with some victims of sacrifice. From many societies we know that even an animal, and particularly one of the totem's species, could be regarded as being raised to the divine at the moment of offering. The Celts undoubtedly practised animal sacrifice. We have Pliny's account of the white bull offered during the mistletoe-cutting ceremony and a bull was sacrificed during the ritual in which a new king was chosen, while one of the Gundestrup Cauldron plates shows a figure taken to be a god plunging a knife into a bull's neck.

The bull was undoubtedly important to Druidism and must once have been a totem. Besides the adoption of tribal names containing a bull element, a Galatian god is called Deiotarus or Bull God. Bull artefacts have been recovered from many parts of the Celtic world, and there are place names like Tarbes in southern France from Tarvos or bull. Skulls of bulls have been found in storage pits. However, perhaps the clearest hint of the bull's original place is to be found in myth. The magic bull, Donn of Cualnge, in the *Tain*, must at some remote epoch have been of immense significance and power comparable perhaps with the Bull of Minos.

At the same time, since the Celts reckoned wealth by livestock, animal sacrifices could also have been seen as giving the gods a valued possession and hence closer to something like a votive offering than a true sacrifice. It is plain from finds on excavation sites that the bull was only one of several species involved and others include pigs, goats, sheep, dogs and horses.

It is only in the case of the last that we have information on the rite involved. Gerald of Wales, though plainly not present himself, describes the slaying of a white mare in Ireland as part of a ceremony in confirming kingship. White mares were, as we saw, one of the aspects of Celtic goddesses, but the practice described by Gerald is also consistent with Indo-European reverence for the horse. Commentators have drawn attention to the similarity between his account and the Indian rite of *asvameda* in which a white stallion, not a mare, was slaughtered, and horse sacrifice was also connected with Scandinavian royalty.

That in several cases the sacrificed creature was cooked, then eaten by the assembly, is further evidence of its totemic nature. The eating of a member of the totem's species at a sacred feast so that all can absorb its divinity is found in numerous cultures.

Since animal sacrifice was practised in Rome it was not this but human sacrifice which inspired such horror among writers like Lucan, Tacitus and Caesar. The description in *The Conquest of Gaul* of the mass holocausts in giant wickerwork human images have become yet another of the popular stereotypes of Druidism. Caesar's source was probably Posidonius rather than a direct witness, for Strabo and Diodorus of Sicily, who both draw on Posidonius, have broadly similar descriptions. The reference by the early third century BC poet Sopater to the Galatians' mass burnings of prisoners of war in gratitude to the gods for victory may also be related.

Archaeology provides us with evidence of another type of sacrifice: that in which the victim was immured in a pit. At Wandelbury, Cambridgeshire, where T.C. Lethbridge uncovered the hill figure of a goddess mounted on a horse, the legless body of a child had been wrapped in a cloth and thrown into one. Besides traces of human

remains found at Swanwick and Holzhausen in Bavaria, a specially
dug pit at Danebury contained three human legs, a lower jaw and
part of a trunk. But of the archaeological evidence for sacrifice the
most dramatic is the bog bodies. The Iron Age male remains found
at Tollund Fen and near the village of Grauballe, both in Denmark,
and at Lindow Moss in northern Britain all appear to have been
sacrificed. They were naked except for, in the case of the Tollund
man, a sheepskin cap, and of the Lindow man two strips of fur,
possibly armbands. Both had been clubbed and then strangled, the
first with a plaited skin rope, the second with a thong of sinew. In
addition, they had both had their throats cut. One cannot entirely
rule out, however, the possibility that the head injuries to the
Grauballe body, which suggested he had been clubbed, may actually
have occurred with the disturbance of the corpse when it was found.
The well-manicured fingernails and neatly-clipped moustache of the
Lindow Moss body show him to have been a member of the upper
classes.

Bogs and marshes plainly had a religious significance, perhaps as
the transition zone between earth and water, and the Berne
Scholiasts who annotated Lucan between the fourth and ninth
centuries describe how victims dedicated to Toutatis had their heads
held down in a vat of water until they drowned. The Gundestrup
Cauldron scene has been interpreted as showing this, though it is
debatable whether it shows sacrifice at all. Jan de Vries sees it as an
initiation ceremony for young warriors. Those shown arriving on foot
in the lower part of the panel become, by a species of baptism, the
knights shown leaving the scene on horses. By contrast, Markale
argues that the foot soldiers are the dead restored to life by
immersion in a Cauldron of Rebirth and so links it with those in the
myths. However, one must remember that human sacrifice was itself
frequently seen as equivalent to rebirth.

Victims dedicated to Esus, on the other hand, were hung from trees
and then stabbed so that their blood flowed into the earth beneath.

The associations of water in the one case and earth in the other
has led some to see a link with the three elements of earth, air and
fire, reinforced by the sacrificing of victims to Taranis by burning.
In any event, the use of fire was undoubtedly appropriate as Taranis
was associated with lightning. Before the discovery of ways of making
fire, lightning strikes, which can leave the trunk of a tree aglow for
hours afterwards, were a source. It would therefore be logical to

express gratitude to the provider of this much needed amenity by using fire to offer him victims and the Scholiasts declare that the victim was actually burnt in a tree trunk.

However, not all methods of sacrifice fit readily into the three-elements thesis. For example, there is impalement, which may account for the human remains found on the stakes in ritual shafts, and shooting with arrows. The second is curious, as despite their contacts with the Scythians who were expert archers, the Celts did not use the bow as a weapon.

On the other hand, the triad sacred to the Druids may explain the so-called three-fold death. This could take several forms. In one, the victim was supposed to have been put in a building which was then set ablaze. He was caught as he tried to escape and had his head held under water before being stabbed.

The burning building evokes the mythical *bruidne* or 'hostels', such as that in *The Intoxication of the Ulstermen*, wherein the death of a hero is to be encompassed, and there is a hint of this as well as the three-fold death in the post-Christian Irish story *The Death of Muirchertach mac Erca*. Muirchertach, High King of Ireland, falls in love with the beautiful Sin, oblivious to warnings that she is a witch. One night he awakens to find the house ablaze. He tries to protect himself in a vat of wine, but instead is drowned in it.

Tolstoy points out that the complicated instructions for the killing of Lleu – one of the Welsh forms of Lugh – given in *Math son of Mathonwy* may be a three-fold death. Certainly a ritual element is present in the description of the making of the lethal spear which must be forged over a year, work being carried out only during the time of Sunday Mass, a stipulation which, by causing the maker to miss his devotions, would make him guilty of an additional sin.

Tolstoy sees the three-fold motif in the deaths of Suibne of Dalriada and of another madman, Lailoken, who is mentioned in the twelfth-century *Life of St Kentigern*. Suibne, in his madness, was succoured by a swineherd's compassionate wife who would fill a dried cow pat in one of the fields with milk for him to drink. Her husband, suspecting Suibne had designs on her, one day took a spear and impaled him as he lapped. Some versions say that, besides the spear, the swineherd had half buried the pointed horn of a deer in such a position that it pierced the drinker's breast as he lay on the ground. It may well be that drinking from the cow pat actually represents drowning.

On three different occasions Lailoken, usually taken to be an alias
for Myrddin, bardic prototype of Merlin, forecast the manner of his
death to St Kentigern who had befriended him. On one occasion he
said he would be stoned and beaten to death with cudgels; on
another that he would be speared with a sharp stake and on the third
that he would be drowned.

The triad was, of course, sacred to other Indo-European peoples
and victims dedicated to Odin, for example, were burnt, strangled
and stabbed. Graves draws attention to the remarkable parallel
between the killing of Lleu and that of Agamemnon after his return
from Troy, both of which involve a bath and stabbing. Mallory,
applying Dumézil's tripartition, suggests that those devoted to a god
occupying a priestly or juridical function were hanged; stabbing with
a weapon was reserved for those devoted to a war god; and drowning
for those devoted to fertility gods. On such a hypothesis the infliction
of death on a single victim in three different ways suggests either that
three gods were being propitiated by one victim or else that the god
to whom he or she was devoted was of such importance as to require
more than simple, straightforward dispatch.

The Celtic custom of head hunting must be regarded as another form
of sacrifice since, apart from other uses to which they put decapitated
heads, they were certainly offered to the gods. They have been found
on temple sites and there are other examples of piled up heads
obviously devoted in the same way as other booty of war. The
Entremont figure portrays a god squatting in the traditional buddhic
posture with his right hand resting on a head. Beheading incidents
recur even in the Medieval stories where knights almost invariably
decapitate enemies they have vanquished.

The most likely purpose of the practice was to prove how many
enemies one had vanquished in battle, but there are other
possibilities. According to Onians, the belief that the head was the
seat of the soul was universal among ancient peoples, including the
Romans. Hence, possession of the head was a safeguard against the
anger of the spirit. In a Highland story recorded by MacKay, one of
the characters speaks of staying with the head he has just severed
'for two days and two nights', keeping it apart from the body 'until
the spinal marrow froze'. Obviously here the fear is that the two may
rejoin, but in a footnote the author mentions a superstition that
heads could fling themselves on the decapitator. Finally, it may have

been that it was thought necessary as the means of releasing the soul which is supported by the discovery of beheaded bodies, as in the Romano-British cemetery at Lankhills, Winchester. It is also significant that in some parts of the Christian world it was customary to exhume skeletons from graves after a certain lapse of time and remove the skull for preservation in a separate ossuary. There is an example at Hallstatt in Austria, a place which, on account of discoveries made there in the last century, has given its name to the first major phase of the European Iron Age.

However, belief in the head as housing for the brain, itself frequently regarded as the 'soul', must lie behind another Celtic practice, that of making slingshot balls by mixing the brain of decapitated enemies with clay and allowing them to harden. The Druidic doctors who attended King Conchobhar decided that one lodged in his forehead should be left where it was as it was reckoned too dangerous to remove it. (The story goes that, during a fit of rage against the enemies of Christ when he heard of the Crucifixion, it burst out and he died.)

Frequently a well had a skull associated with it. In later times this was said to be that of a saint and preserved as a relic in a nearby church. Some wells actually have the word 'head' in their names, as in Tobar na Ceann, Well of the Head, in the Outer Hebrides. This brings to mind other pagan wells such as that of Norse Mimir which was supposed to contain the giant's magical head.

There is, however, an even more familiar survival in the use of representations of heads in architectural decoration. A carved triplicate head is to be found in Llandaff Cathedral, South Wales, and carved stone heads decorate several Irish Romanesque churches. Among these is St Brendan's Cathedral at Clonfert, County Galway, where more than twenty heads embellish the west door with ten of them set in the triangular niches favoured by the Celts. What makes this intriguing is that St Brendan is frequently confounded with the god Bran who, of course, underwent voluntary decapitation.

Perhaps even more surprising is the Victorian and Edwardian penchant for mouldings of heads as decoration. That these are often placed over door lintels precisely matches the Celtic custom, while the lintels themselves are often triangular in shape.

Countless attempts have been made to classify sacrifice. It has been said, for example, that there are 'regular sacrifices', that is to say those carried out during the yearly festivals, and 'occasional sacrifices' carried out for a variety of purposes. Among the types of sacrifice are expiatory ones to assuage divine wrath manifest in some natural disaster, those of gratitude for some favour received, or supplicatory sacrifices in which a request is made.

All such attempts at classification fail to take account of the enormous diversity of motive. The youths or maidens devoted during spring rites were undoubtedly intended as mates for the young god, relics of which remain in customs like the choosing of the May Queen. There are also the examples of a human being dispatched as an emissary to the Otherworld on behalf of his fellows. This shows surprising durability. It is recorded that during the Greek War of Independence from the Turks (1821-29) the defenders of the island of Santorini, finding themselves hard pressed, killed one of their number so he might intervene on their behalf with St Michael.

Yet another form of sacrifice is that associated with the foundations of buildings and was presumably intended to placate whatever Underworld gods might be disturbed in the process. In many cases, the victims are children. Besides such important sites as Stonehenge and Avebury, child burials are associated with the shrines at Maiden Castle in Dorset and that at Frilford, while at South Cadbury a young man was found in a pit near the hillfort.

This was yet another custom that continued down to late times. Geoffrey of Monmouth mentions the search made by the fifth-century British ruler Vortigern for a suitable infant to bury in the foundations of a projected citadel. Baring-Gould, who came across relics of foundation sacrifice in Brittany in the early years of the century, offers an explanation for its purpose: 'No man could assure himself undisputed and inalienable landed property till he was dead', he writes. 'When once a body was placed in the earth it became the centre of the clan and of the tribal worship'. This would accord with the element of ancestor worship in shamanism.

The same writer goes on to quote two legends. According to one when St Patrick planned to found a monastery at Clocmacnois, a leper whom he had cared for volunteered for live burial to secure the place in perpetuity. The other involved St Columba's establishment of a community on Iona where a monk volunteered to be buried alive. In neither case are we told whether the offer was accepted.

What must have been a relic of the practice was found by workmen restoring Aître St Maclou, the Rouen charnel house. In this case the body of a kitten was buried in the original sixteenth-century foundations. Merrifield notes the discovery of pilgrim badges in house foundations in Buckinghamshire, Northampton and Oxford which may, he thinks, have been foundation offerings.

Probably related to foundation sacrifice is the custom of Beating the Bounds practised in many parts of Europe including Britain until recent times. In this, civic dignitaries, including mayor and local clergy, lead a group of youngsters, usually choirboys, round the bounds of the town. At certain points, often boundary stones, one of the boys is 'bumped' by being held at the feet and arms and repeatedly struck against the ground. Various explanations have been advanced, among them that it is intended to inculcate into the young the boundaries of their town. A more likely one is that the bumping is a relic of child sacrifice and this is underlined by the presence of clergy and the religious associations with the custom. I am indebted to Alan Cleaver of the Association for the Study of Anomalous Phenomena (ASSAP) for what, as far as I can discover, was the last instance of the custom being carried out. This was at High Wycombe in 1985, the town's 700th anniversary when the organisers were its Strange Folklore Society. Two previous occasions were in 1928 and 1911.

Sacrifice was also employed for divinatory purposes, the death throes of the victim being prophetically interpreted. This is mentioned by Strabo and, according to the Scholiasts, sacrifices to Esus were for this purpose, with omens being drawn from the way in which the blood from the stabbed victim flowed.

The principal times for sacrifice, human and animal, were the great festivals. Four of these are known, but insofar as folk custom is any guide, there were others. For example, there is the Festival of the Deermen at Abbots Bromley in Staffordshire every 4th September. Participants, wearing spans of antlers, dance through the streets as escort to 'Robin Hood' who, as a green-clothed, forest-dwelling hunter may well be an epiphany of Cernunnos and is certainly evoked by the dancers' antlers. At the end of the day these are returned to the church for safekeeping and the continuity of the custom is proved by the fact that when one of the spans was carbon dated it was found to predate the Norman invasion.

The festival takes place nine days before the Breton *pardon* of St Cornély – were it not for calendrical changes the two occasions would probably have coincided. St Cornély, who seems to be a local invention, is patron saint of horned animals and it can scarcely be a coincidence that his name contains the horn element *corn-*.

The four most widely attested festivals correspond with nodal points of the seasonal cycle. They are Imbolc, the lactation of the ewes, in early February; Beltaine corresponding to our May Day, traditionally connected with the sprouting of the spring shoots, though also the time when the cattle were driven into the open pastures; Lugnasad, the Christian Lammas when loaves made from the first ripe grain were taken to the church to be blessed; and Samain, corresponding to our own Hallowe'en, which marked the end of the Celtic year and was the time when the cattle were brought in.

Since Imbolc has been superseded in the Christian calendar by St Bridget's Day it is likely it was originally dedicated to the goddess Brigid. Her name is recalled in the rivers Brent in Middlesex and Braint in Anglesey, while in the form of Brigantia she was invoked by the Brigantes tribe whose huge territory covered what are now six counties in northern England. Brigid is represented in a number of artefacts, including one dated to the third century AD in which she is dressed as a Roman matron. She is also commemorated in 'St Bridget's Wells' or Bridewells, whose distribution up and down the country indicates the popularity of her cult.

She must be Caesar's Gaulish 'Minerva', Roman counterpart of the Greek Athena, many of whose characteristics she shares. In Ireland she is the daughter of the high god In Dagda just as Athena was the daughter of Zeus. She is patroness of poetry, arts and crafts, while her association with fire links her, like Athena, with the hearth and the maintenance of the communal fires. St Bridget, who has her own fire associations, was supposedly the midwife to the Virgin Mary, suggesting that her pagan prototype may have been invoked during childbirth.

Beltaine, which means literally 'the fires of Beli', seems to have been primarily a feast of fire renewal. In Wales fires were laid by nine men from nine different types of wood and were lit by rubbing together two sticks of oak, a method which also seems to have been used in Ireland. Here, according to William Evans, all fires were quenched until the Druids rekindled the sacred flame at Tara, whence runners with blazing torches ran the length and breadth of the island bearing the gift of the new fire. However, another aspect

of Beltaine was the lighting of huge bonfires between which cattle
were driven to exorcise the evil spirits which might have taken up
residence through the winter. The custom survived until recent times
in the Scottish Highlands and in Ireland. In the Isle of Man gorse
was set ablaze 'to burn out witches' and, as further protection,
crosses made from rowan were hidden in the tails of cattle, while
houses were decorated with brilliant yellow spring flowers.

The colour of the flowers betrays the character of the festival. Fire
festivals are invariably linked with the ultimate givers of fire, the sun
gods. This and the name Beltaine supports the belief that it was
dedicated to Belinus, whose own solar character is beyond doubt.
We know that in Ireland St Patrick was condemning sun worship in
the fifth century and vestiges were to be found until very recent times.
In the Shetlands it was customary on May Day to look skyward and
greet the sun with the words, 'Good morning and show your eye'.
Hebridean islanders climbed to highest points and saluted the sun
as it rose over the mountains to the east, christianising what is
patently a pagan custom by claiming that the rising sun symbolised
Christ's resurrection. As late as 1875 an aged inhabitant of another
Hebridean island, South Uist, could be spotted furtively ascending
a local mound at sunrise where he would kill a lamb.

The solar connection is endorsed by the practice of circling holy
wells, normally visited on this day, sunwise. However, in the
Hebrides, a graveyard rather than a well was circuited and a dance,
in which the death and resurrection of the year was symbolised by
a woman, took place. In the Isle of Man, where the day was called
Laa Boaldyn, an island form of Beltaine Day, sham battles were
fought up to the eighteenth century between the partisans of the May
Queen and those of the Queen of Winter, actually a man dressed in
furs and wool.

In Cornwall, apart from the May 'Furry Days' in some towns, there
is the Helston Furry festival on the eighth which includes dancing
in the streets by white clad girls and youths whose progress takes
them in and out of houses, such visitations being supposed to bring
good fortune to their occupants. The choice of venue is appropriate
enough since 'Helston' derives from Hele Stone or Stone of the Sun.

The human sacrifices which took place at this time are recalled in
a number of customs. In the Orkneys and Shetlands as well as in
the Scottish Highlands, youths would leap through the flames of the
fires. Fire leaping was also practised in Wales and here, as elsewhere,

was connected with the Beltaine cake, a barley or oatmeal scone divided into portions equal in number to the participants. The recipe varies from area to area, so that in the Scottish Highlands, for example, it had a pattern of raised knobs, each dedicated to some being thought to be the preserver or destroyer of domestic animals. Every person present broke off one of the knobs and threw it over their left shoulder with an invocation to spare or protect the animals. In other places, small round Beltaine cakes were rolled down a slope, supposedly in imitation of the sun's motion. If the cake broke during its journey it foretold its maker's death within the year.

In an ominous old English proverb 'dying within the year' was said to be the fate of the May Queen. It may have been a formulary used of a sacrificial victim who, having been chosen, could literally be said to 'die within the year'. (We know, of course, that in the pre-Colombian Americas, the chosen victim often was granted a year's lease of life before being led to the altar.)

The Beltaine cake is directly linked with sacrifice in another custom. At Beltany Ring in Donegal the cake, one part of which had deliberately been burnt, was placed on the top of a post around which dancers circled. At the climax of the dance they closed upon the post and divided the cake among themselves. Whoever got the burnt portion was subject to a special forfeit. In Perthshire, until the eighteenth century, a bannock with a burnt corner was divided among participants in a Beltaine festival. The unlucky recipient of the burnt portion was spoken of as 'devoted' and thereafter referred to as dead.

Near Callander in Scotland and in some parts of Wales boys would light a fire in a specially-dug trench. The Beltaine cake, again with one side burnt, was broken into pieces and put into a bonnet. The participants were then blindfolded and the bonnet passed round. Whoever got the burnt portion was supposed to be sacrificed and had to leap over the fire three times.

Testimony to the antiquity of the Beltaine cake is the discovery of traces of charred oatmeal in the stomach of Lindow Man.

If there is lingering doubt about the link between Beltaine and Belinus, there is none in the case of the early August festival of Lugnasad which was dedicated to Lugh and supposedly commemorated his marriage.

Legends of its origins differ from area to area, though most centre round a young god, making it in some ways comparable with the Eleussinian Mysteries which celebrated the youth of Dionysus. Given the references to apple trees, whose fruit would have been ripe in August, the games in *Gereint and Enide* must, as Tolstoy argues, have been those held at Lugnasad. This would also help to account for Chrétien's Mabonagrain, 'the Little King', and further confirms that Mabon and Lugh are one and the same. The young god and vegetation myth aspects were clear in the Isle of Man festivities which commemorated his victory over the oppressions of the malevolent Crom Dubh. There may be something similar behind celebrations held until the late nineteenth century at Morvah near Land's End, for among stories told was one of a magician who ascended a local hill to rid the area of an 'evil oppressor'.

In Ireland, the vegetation element is more oblique and the festival is marked by fairs. These certainly descend from the fairs of pagan times likened by de Vries to the great *kermesses* of the Middle Ages with large crowds descending on the place where it was held, staying at the local inns or under improvised cover. While jugglers and acrobats would have provided virtually non-stop entertainment, the main events are likely to have included competitions of craftsmen and of bards as in the *eisteddfodau* and undoubtedly the horse races to which the Celts were – and have remained – so addicted. It may well be that the race in which Macha was forced to compete took place at Lugnasad. As Lugh was patron of commerce, it is also likely that the fairs provided an opportunity for merchants to meet, discuss mutual interests and transact deals.

Appropriately, in view of the Druidic preoccupation with the sacred centre, the greatest of the Lugnasad fairs was at Telltown in County Meath. Telltown gets its name from the goddess Tailtiu, reputed foster-mother of Lugh, in whose honour the Tailtean Games or Aonach Tailteann were held until AD 1180. Among the events was a weight-throwing contest called the wheel feat in which a chariot wheel was thrown by its axle, an exercise in which Cu Chulainn is said to have excelled. There is evidence that the Aonach Tailteann may go back as far as the early second millennium BC, not only making them the oldest games on record but also both them and Tailtiu herself pre-Celtic.

The ways in which it continued to be marked show that the central vegetation myth theme of the marriage of the young god was never totally lost. According to the seventeenth-century author Geoffrey

Keating the Telltown Fair was the occasion for parents to draw up marriage contracts and, in pagan times, weddings were solemnised nearby. Until recently young men and women would pledge themselves to trial marriages here and, should it prove a failure, returned the following year to dissolve them. As a result irregular unions came to be called 'Telltown marriages'.

Somewhat in the nature of 'a trial marriage' was the Lammas Fair custom at Kirkwall in the Orkneys in which young men and girls chose 'Lammas' brothers and sisters for themselves and shared the night on an improvised bed of sheaves.

The generally festive and celebratory character of Lugnasad should not blind us to the fact that it was probably an occasion when the Druids announced their legal decisions and sentences. In any case, the 'marriage' of Lugh probably meant his ritual union with the mortal partner dedicated to him.

However, both its importance and its popularity were immense. When Caesar Augustus made Lugdunum (the present Lyons) the Gaulish capital he decreed that the First of August should be a general feast day merging the cult of the deified emperor, who has given his name to the month, with that of the Celtic god.

The festival of Lugnasad certainly survived. As Tolstoy says, the pagan celebration in Cornwall which the seventh-century St Samson successfully put a stop to sounds very much like it.

The fourth of the great festivals of which we have knowledge is Samain marking the end of the Celtic year. Save that its appearance in the Coligny Calendar shows it to have been marked in Gaul as well as the British Isles, we have no direct knowledge regarding who it was principally dedicated to. However, in *The Intoxication of the Ulstermen* there is a reference to an 'iron house' in which Cu Chulainn and two other Ulstermen are trapped at Samain by their Connaught enemies with the intention that they should be roasted alive. They escape only through the superhuman strength of Cu Chulainn.

In a Scottish story, the hot-tempered Conan corrals a group of women who have enraged him into a cabin which he then attempts to burn down. Both stories are very similar to the myths surrounding the smith's craft which are found in many cultures and are further discussed in the next chapter.

We can certainly conjecture that Samain was the festival of the dead when the dwellers in the *sidhs* mingled with the living and tried to lure them to the Otherworld. It was at Samain that Connle's temptress appeared and he made the fatal mistake of tasting the magic apple she offered him and so was unable to return to the Mortal World. (The taboo on eating Underworld food also, of course, occurs in the Greek legend of Persephone. That the idea is not exclusively Indo-European is proved by the fact that it is found, not only in the Finnish *Kalevala*, but as far away as Melanesia, as well as among several of the North American Indian tribes.)

It was not only from the *sidhs* that dangers threatened at Samain. Cities like the Breton *Ker-Ys* rise from the sea and stories of submerged cities are to be found round the coasts of all the Celtic lands. A Breton story tells how the lovely Soutbinnen gave rowdy parties at her house by the sea from which her guests never returned and of how, long after, a tunnel leading from it to the depths beneath the waters was found.

As to how Samain was marked, analogy from folk custom may give us at least an inkling. Most obvious is 5th November with its bonfires, fireworks and Guy. It is difficult to see the Guy other than as a sacrifice relic and this is supported by a Jersey custom. As with the Northern European Yule Logs, towards the end of the year island families would go into the local woods, cut down and trim the branches from a suitable tree, and drag it home. Then, on the last night of the year, it would be dressed in old clothes and burnt, under the name of *le vieux bout de l'an*, the end of the old year. With the introduction of Guy Fawkes celebrations to the island, the term *boudelau*, a corruption of *bout de l'an* was applied by country people to the Guy. This might seem like little more than coincidence until it is realised that the island has had its own Parliament, the Jersey States, from earliest times and thus cannot be expected to feel a deep emotional involvement at the threat to the Westminster one.

Further confirmation is the fact that in the Orkneys Hallowe'en and 5th November customs have been fused, with bonfires and fireworks on the former. In Scotland Hallowe'en is often celebrated on 11th November which would have corresponded with Samain in the old calendar. Again it was marked by enormous bonfires, the most favoured sites being the tops of the burial mounds, in other words the *sidhs*. Bonfires were also lit in Ireland and in one custom, very like that at Beltaine, peat fires were extinguished to be rekindled next morning.

The question of dedication is more difficult, though there are several hints in the vernacular literature connecting In Dagda with it. Caer Ibormeith, with whom his son Oengus mac Oc is enamoured, changes from human to swan form at Samain and she offers her favours on condition that he too becomes a swan. When he agrees their congress also takes place at Samain. As In Dagda himself mates with the Morrigan at this season, de Vries suggests it was the regular festival of divine couplings.

A poem in the metrical *Dindsenchas* describes an idol called Cromm Cruaich at Mag Slecht in County Cavan to which, until the practice was stopped by St Patrick, children were sacrificed each Samain. That the idol may have represented In Dagda is suggested by a sentence in the *Book of Leinster* which speaks of his destroying the milk and corn of the Milesians. The *Dindsenchas* poem says that the purpose of the bloody sacrifice to Crom Cruaich was to ensure a supply of milk and corn.

While we have no conclusive evidence, it is hard to believe that the winter solstice, important to all agricultural communities, was not marked by the Druids. *The Life of St Samson* mentions New Year celebrations in Guernsey which the saint tried to suppress, while two other Breton saints, St Brieuc and St Ninnoc, denounced the orgies which took place on this day.

Until recent times a wren hunt was held in Ireland, the Isle of Man and the Channel Islands on St Stephen's Day, 26 December. In Man and Jersey, this tiny bird was regarded both as a transformed witch and presager of disaster, but one cannot help wondering if, in origin, it derives from an incident in *Math son of Mathonwy*. According to this Arianrhod is tricked against her will into naming the son she has disowned. She sees the boy, whom she does not recognise, shoot at a wren with his slingshot. He hits it in the leg 'between the sinew and the bone', causing her to comment that he has a very skilful hand, so becoming Lleu or Lugh of the Skilful Hand. Since Arianrhod is one of the many witch-like goddesses of Celtic mythology it may well be she who had taken on the form of wren and who is thus wounded by her son. An injury inflicted on one who has undergone transformation invariably causes a reversion to their normal state.

It is now the best part of three decades since the last of the latterday Druidic bodies abandoned its summer solstice rites at Stonehenge.

In any event, the belief that it had been erected by the Druids had been demolished a good three decades before that. Nonetheless, even if the Stonehenge antics had no sanction, the summer solstice was another occasion marked by almost every agricultural society and it seems inconceivable that the Druids could have ignored it. The fact that the Church apportioned the day to one of its most illustrious saints, John the Baptist, cousin of the Saviour himself, suggests it was attempting to provide a substitute for a festival too deeply imbedded to be abolished by simple decree. Almost everywhere in Europe it was marked by the lighting of public bonfires and by a licence totally at odds with the austere nature of its patron. Thus in the Isle of Man the eve was marked by crowds carrying green meadow grass to the top of Barule in payment of rent to Manannan mac Lir, the Celtic sea god from whom the island gets its name and who was regarded as its protector. After this relatively innocuous start, the day ended in revels 'too shocking to be told', while similar revels took place in Jersey.

In Ireland and Scotland it was a time for fires and one custom was to circumambulate the cattle and sheep pens with blazing brands. Ashes from the fires were frequently mixed with the seeds later to be used for planting, showing that the fires were thought to have special properties. In Brittany where the Plougastel *pardon* took place on Midsummer's Day children were passed over or through the fires and, in a custom which may be linked with the mixing of ashes with the seeds, the assembly would kneel round the fire rubbing their eyes with its dead ash while saying the Lord's Prayer and the Hail Mary. Purification by ash is found in many places including India where the Brahmins rub their bodies with it, and Ireland, the Isle of Man and Lancashire where it is used for divinatory purposes.

Midsummer may well have been the time when the holocausts in man-shaped wickerwork cages recorded by Strabo and Caesar actually took place. Frazer mentions a custom in the Pyrenean town of Luch, a name probably derived from Lugh, in which a wicker column, decorated with flowers and foliage, was filled with flammable material and set ablaze as the climax of a procession by townsfolk and clergy. While the column was burning, snakes collected from the countryside were thrown into it, wriggling their way to the top in a vain effort to escape the flames. At Metz cats were burned in wicker cages.

From Arrian, of course, we learn of a custom by which Celtic hunters offered an annual sacrifice to Artemis on her birthday. As these were bought with fines paid into her treasury, the plain implication is that the creatures taken were regarded as belonging to her. Artemis's 'birthday' and that of her Roman alter ego, Diana, was Midsummer Day and both are mistresses of the hunt. However, Caesar, while listing Apollo among his Gaulish gods, omits his sister. Traces of a cult of Diana have been found in Britain and, in some cases, accompanying material suggests that it was a native one. In two stories, a pool in the Forest of Brocéliande is called Lake Diana, but these tales are late and regionalised and cannot be taken as supporting what Arrian plainly regards as a general practice.

However, folk custom provides several tantalising clues. In many places Midsummer's Eve was the time when a phantom hunt was seen, bringing to mind Artemis/Diana's role as divine huntress. For centuries members of the Isle of Man's parliament, the House of Keys, marked the day by wearing sprigs of St John's Wort in honour of the saint. Then, in the nineteenth century, they took to wearing mug wort, the excuse being that it was one of the local flora. But under its botanical name it is *Artemisia vulgaris* and in Rome and Greece was used to decorate shrines and temples of Artemis/Diana on her feast day.

The fact that the mistletoe-gathering customs earlier referred to all took place at this time may point to Midsummer as the day on which the Druids held the ceremony mentioned by Pliny. Furthermore, it was widely believed that the Herbs of St John, which included St John's Wort itself, as well as vervain and mistletoe – the last two with Druidic connections – were an infallible protection against lightning strikes if gathered at midnight on Midsummer's Eve or at the stroke of noon on the day itself.

Nonetheless, we are still left with the problem of identifying the mysterious Celtic Diana. Phonetically there is one goddess she brings to mind: Dana, founder of Tuatha de Danann. What is almost certainly an alternative form of her name, Ana, is commemorated in a pair of hills in Killarney, Da Chích Annan or the Breasts of Ana, but neither form appears in the epigraphy and she plays no active part in the vernacular literatures. In Irish myth she is known solely through her divine clan and her British counterpart only because three gods – Gilvaethy, Gwyddion and Amathaon – are surnamed 'ap Don', son of Don, and a goddess – Arianrhod – is described as her daughter. However, the fact she is in both the Goidelic and

Brythonic literatures shows her to have been a deity known to the
Celts before they divided into two linguistic groups. At some time
she must also have occupied an important position. As late as the
ninth century the glossarist Cormac is calling her 'mother god of the
Irish'. Two British rivers, one in Scotland and the other in Yorkshire,
are called the Don. The River Marne, whose name comes from
Matrona, the Mother, a goddess invoked from northern Italy to the
mouth of the Rhine, may be connected with her. So, in all likelihood
is the Danube, associated with the Celts by Herodotus. Another
Don, in Russia, runs through what was once Scythian territory and
within its boundaries are the Dniepr and the Dniestr, all of which
suggest a possible connection.

It is possible that a mutated form of Ana is preserved in the name
of the Munster *sidh* woman, Aine, claimed to have taken a mortal
lover to whom she bore Gerald, the fourth earl of Drummond, and
to have been violated by a Munster king whom she killed with her
magic. There is a slightly less doubtful link with the Leicestershire
'Black Annis' said to have demanded human victims. In addition,
there is the recurrence of Anne's Wells and 'Saint' Anne's Wells
throughout the British Isles. It must have been more than hazard that
led the Bretons to choose St Anne for patron and to make her the
focus of two important *pardons*, those of St Anne d'Auray and St
Anne de la Palude. In Breton legend Anne is an early local duchess
who, turned out of doors by her wicked husband, is carried in an
angel-guided boat to Jerusalem. Here she gave birth to the Virgin
Mary whom she brought up in ways of piety before returning to her
duchy.

As we have seen, Diana's Roman counterpart had a deep antiquity.
In point of fact the suffix *Di-* is an Indo-European one attached to
god names and meaning, roughly, 'the bright, shining one'.
Sometimes it was elided into a J, so 'Diuppiter' becomes 'Jupiter'
and 'Dianus', 'Janus'. Sometimes it was dropped altogether, in which
case 'Diana' would become 'Ana', Cormac's 'mother god of the Irish'.
At others, the I was dropped, making it 'Dana'.

# Chapter 7
# Druidism and Royalty

Besides the known annual festivals there were certainly occasional ones. Of these the ones on which we are best informed are those connected with kingship.

In Ireland, we know of three ranks of kings. At the bottom the tribal one, then the provincial one or *rí cóicid* ruler of several tribes and, at the apex, the *ard rí* or High King, who ruled all Ireland from his palace at Tara. Jean Markale suggests that a similar situation may have occurred in central Gaul with the Bituriges' tribe, whose name means 'Kings of the World', providing the High Kings. In Britain we have little evidence for anything remotely like a High King until the time of Arthur who, according to Geoffrey of Monmouth, when he held plenary court at Caerleon-on-Usk, was attended by the kings of Scotland, Moray, North and South Wales, Cornwall and Brittany.

What one can also make out in Arthur are traces of the unique position the Celtic king occupied in society. Geoffrey's Arthur is a vigorous potentate who keeps the Saxons at bay and between times successfully campaigns in Scotland, Ireland, Iceland, Norway and in Gaul, finally taking on the Romans in a great continental campaign, but rashly leaving his nephew Mordred as regent of Britain. This can hardly be said to tally with the picture of him we get from other accounts. In these he seems marked by inertia, holding courts and organising tournaments and hunts, but taking little part in more hazardous enterprises. He fails to react even when an intruder knight deliberately empties the queen's cup over her in full view of the court and it is left to others to avenge the insult.

Much the same kind of infirmity seems to seize other legendary kings. The reputation of Cormac, the Irish High King in the Fenian Cycle, rests on his skill as legislator. King Conchobhar of Ulster participates in the great war with the men of Connaught only in its final stages and the incident in which a slingshot ball penetrates his skull occurs during a drunken carouse. His enemy, King Ailill, plays no part whatever in the struggle.

In point of fact it is expressly stated of Cormac and Conchobhar that they were kept away from every kind of danger. The person of the king was sacrosanct in the eyes of his subjects and he sustained his dignity in other ways, in particular that with which Geoffrey repeatedly credits Arthur: liberality. Chief among these in pagan times was liberality towards the gods. This would certainly include a readiness to consign expensive, possibly specially-made weapons or other votive offerings to the waters and an equal readiness, especially in times of crisis, to maintain the supply of victims for the sacrificial altar. In addition, kings, perhaps more than anyone else, had to guard against any diminution in honour price, not least because it might give rivals an advantage in trade deals or alliances.

Of Arthur we are told that his 'generosity was known throughout all the world and this made all men love him'. One form it took was in his rewarding of knights. The same goes for Conchobhar of whom it is said that at any given moment 'thirty noble heroes' could be found enjoying the hospitality of his copious vat. Typically a Celtic king would offer to those who brought him or were about to bring him some benefit 'any gift they asked', leaving it to the recipient to name it, a custom recalling the ostentatious present-giving of the potlatch discussed in Chapter 5.

Bran, liberal in his life, continues to be so when all that remains of him is his head. By contrast, such is the meanness of Bress when he is made king of the Tuatha De Danann that he becomes the target of what is claimed to be the first *glam dicin* sung against him by the bard, Cairpré. As a consequence red blotches break out all over the king's face.

The failure of royal liberality for whatever reason is always catastrophic. When Cormac, hitherto renowned for open-handedness, doubles taxes on his people, his forces are defeated. In *Perlesvaus*, one of many Medieval romances based on the Perceval story, the Court of Arthur declines when the hero fails to ask the essential questions about the Grail and spear in the palace of the Fisher-King. One symptom of this decline is that the king 'began to lose his talent for largesse'.

Reduction could lead to the desertion of champions in favour of one who was enjoying better fortune. Such defections were not solely because a king had become less open-handed, but also because the decline implied that he was losing the favour of the gods, which might contaminate those around him.

According to the *Perlesvaus*, something of the sort was happening to Arthur, for in one passage the author laments the gradual decline of his court and the declining number of his followers. It may even account for the desertion of his queen to his nephew Mordred, for it is plain that this is exactly what happened. She not only lives with him – in Geoffrey of Monmouth's view 'adulterously' – but, as Jean Marx emphasises, she has actually been crowned with him.

There were others constantly watching for any sign of divine displeasure. The relationship between king and Druid is complex and ambiguous. Celtic kingship was hereditary only in the sense that occupants of the throne were drawn from 'royal' clans, an example being the Scottish Stuarts. When a choice had to be made, all the freemen of the realm, commoners as well as nobles, assembled for the purpose, an apparent example of early Celtic democracy in action.

Nonetheless other data shows that, like the court Brahmins of India, the Druids wielded immense power. It was said of King Conchobhar, himself son of a Druid, that no Ulsterman spoke before he had and that he did not speak before his Druids had done so. The rule was maintained with unbending rigidity. When Cu Chulainn's father, Sualdam Setanta, bursts into the royal presence, the Druid Cathbad says he should be executed for his impertinence, though the old man has acted solely out of his desperation to bring succour to his son who is holding off the Connaught army single-handed.

Even the decision of the electors of the new king required Druidic ratification, given after they had held a *Tarbfeis*, or bull dream, to discover the will of the Otherworld in the matter. A bull was sacrificed and a broth made from its flesh. While the rest chanted over him, one of the Druids would sleep on its hide and was supposed to see the new king in a vision. A description of the *Tarbfeis* is found in the Irish *Destruction of Da Derga's Hostel*, and a reference to it may well be concealed in the Welsh *The Dream of Rhonabwy* in which the eponymous hero, while sleeping on a yellow bullhide, has a dream in which kings figure.

Given that the Druids had this ultimate and decisive role in king-making, Caesar could be accused of erring on the conservative side in bracketing them with the knights. They had powers no Celtic knight possessed and one wonders whether Dio Chrysostom is exaggerating when he calls the king 'a mere minister of the Druids'.

In fact, there were good reasons for their mediation.

The Irish myth usually known as the *Baile in Scáil* or 'The Frenzy of the Phantom' tells of the origins of the Stone of Destiny. Conn, following his custom of rising early and climbing to the peak of the Hill of Tara to make sure no threat to Ireland from the Otherworld has manifested itself during the night, chances to tread on a stone which gives a cry heard in all the surrounding countryside. When he asks his Druids to interpret they tell him it is the sacred stone of Fál, the number of whose cries indicated the number of kings of his line who would reign. At that instant mist descends and from it Conn and his companions hear the sound of hooves. A few moments later three spears land. When the Druids warn the spear thrower whom he is endangering he stops and orders Conn to follow him. He is taken to a magnificent dwelling where, with a vat and a silver goblet before her, sits a maiden whose royalty is proclaimed by the crown she wears. The horseman identifies himself as Lugh, explains that the maiden is the personification of the sovereignty and that Conn has been brought thither to hear the roll of his successors. The maiden repeatedly serves red ale from the vat and asks the god to whom it is to be given. Each time he names a future king. The prophecies complete, palace, Lugh and maiden vanish and Conn finds himself back at Tara but in possession of the silver cup, itself the symbol of sovereignty.

The symbolism of the story becomes clearer in the light of a British one. Jean Markale draws attention to the little known fifteenth-century *The Marriage of Sir Gawain*. That he believes the central character not to be Gawain at all, but Arthur, lends it profound significance. Wandering in a forest Gawain/Arthur is challenged by a man with a club who has a grievance against him. The hero's life will be spared only if, within a year, he can answer the riddle: what is it that women love most of all? For twelve months Gawain/Arthur ponders, then, having arrived at no satisfactory conclusion, returns to the forest. He is waylaid by an ugly woman who offers to help him if he promises to marry her. To save his life he agrees and she tells him the answer is 'Sovereignty'. It then emerges that she is the club wielder's sister. When he meets the giant, Gawain/Arthur gives his answer. It is the right one and, to his enemy's chagrin, he has to be spared.

In due course the account, in the form of the ugly woman, arrives for payment. The marriage takes place and the reluctant groom retires to the bridal chamber. However, given a kiss, his bride undergoes the usual transformation into a beauty.

The Celtic forest is a spirit-haunted place and there can be no doubt that those Gawain/Arthur meets are gods. The club, in fact, would seem to identify the male one as a proto-god, the Lord of the Forest, encountered by Kynon.

A cup is one of the many everyday utensils which has acquired a heavy charge of symbolism and one does not have to be a convinced Freudian to recognise that, as a container, this includes the feminine principle. It is proved by scores of examples. The cup Conn is given by the hand of the maiden unites him with the principle of sovereignty which is itself feminine. There is little room for doubt that the maiden here was Eriu who, with her two alter egos, Fotla and Banba, personified Ireland. One can now understand why the coronation of the early Irish High Kings was called the *fled baindsi* or wedding feast, mythologically exemplified in the union of In Dagda and the Morrigan which takes place over a river. The cry from the stone is, as de Vries says, the cry of his goddess-bride. It is the involuntary cry of a woman in sexual ecstasy.

Details of the ritual by which mortal king and territorial sovereignty were united are not known, though Gerald of Wales's description of the white mare sacrifice at Kenelcunill in Ulster is probably not far off the mark. As he goes on to record, with appropriate ecclesiastical horror, custom demanded that the king indulge in public intercourse with the animal which, when it had been killed and butchered, was made into a broth which he drank while at the same time bathing in it. (Intercourse with a horse was also part of the Indian *asvameda* rite mentioned earlier, although in this case the principal actors were a stallion and a queen.) It is, in other words, a relic of the sacred feast of the totemic animal.

We have many examples of these unions between mortal king and goddess. King Ailill of Connaught has for wife Queen Mebd. She is proclaimed a goddess, not only by the formidable sexual prowess of which she boasts, but also by the fact that she has her sacred tree, the *Bile Meibde*. In addition, as de Vries points out, Ailill is only the latest of her husbands. His predecessors include Conchobhar and collectively they represent all the provinces of Ireland. (Mebd may well be the fairy-midwife, Queen Mab, in Shakespeare's *Romeo and Juliet*, and who is mentioned by Ben Jonson, Herrick and Drayton.)

There is another, perhaps more surprising, example: namely Arthur and his consort, Guinevere. It is unnecessary to repeat all the arguments for regarding Guinevere as divine rather than mortal which were fully deployed in my book *Celtic Mythology*, except perhaps to recall that Guinevere has her Irish counterpart in Finnabair, whose divinity is inarguable. The same conclusion is reached by de Vries, who points out that in a Breton version of one of the Arthurian stories, an ugly sorceress arrives at the court only to change into a beautiful maiden bearing a cup, the Grail. Guinevere, too, has a cup, the one which the uncouth Red Knight empties over her before leaving with it, challenging the knights to recover it. As Marx says, he could well be challenging the possession of sovereignty.

By his marriage, the king has surrendered sovereignty to his divine spouse, but this is, at the same time, the condition on which he alone is entitled to rule and whereby he becomes the channel through which her divine goodwill flows, displaying itself in the health of people and livestock and the very fertility of the soil. In Medieval Denmark mothers brought their children into the royal presence and farmers their seed that they might receive the benefaction of contact with the *mana* of which he is the conduit. A relic of this must have been the Royal Touch said to cure scrofula which William III brought to an end by telling the only person he was ever importuned into touching, 'God give you better health and more sense'.

One could say that there existed between the king and his divine spouse a contract from which came two major consequences. One was that he who ignored custom and seized the throne – the usurper – courted the wrath of the gods. In Wales down to late times, it was believed that usurpation of a throne would result in bad harvests. In Scotland, no usurper could be interred in the royal burial place of Iona.

The other sprang from the nature of Celtic law.

That deep concern for truth and justice on the part of their would-be converts which the early Christian missionaries found so admirable was more than an abstract ethical principle. King Cormac was told that the Otherworld was a place where only truth reigned and where no jealousy, hatred or arrogance existed. Interpreting the will of the Otherworld was, as Caesar confirms, the function of the Druids as supreme lawmakers and judges. At every Welsh coronation the bards recited verses reminding the new king of the necessity of reigning justly to prevent famine or plague falling on his people.

The Celtic king, unlike those of other societies, was not the maker of the law, he was its upholder and, under the guidance of his Druids, its administrator. We are told that King Conchobhar 'never gave a judgment until it was ripe for fear it might be wrong and the crops worsen'. St Patrick, in listing the blessings of a just king as 'fine weather, calm seas, abundant crops and trees laden with fruit' was merely reiterating ancient belief.

Unfortunately, experience showed that, no matter how conscientious the king might be in keeping his side of the bargain, divine favour could still be withheld or removed. This would manifest itself in some disaster: the harvests would fail, the cattle abort, there would be drought and famine.

It could happen if he acquired a physical blemish. Nuada, king of the Tuatha De Danann, was forced to abdicate even though the hand he had lost was replaced by one of silver. In the *Chanson de Roland* which, like most of the *Chansons de Geste*, is full of Celtic allusions, the Saracen King Marsile also gives up his throne after losing a hand in battle. In *The Wooing of Etain* King Mider, having had an eye knocked out, laments that he can 'neither see the land he has come to nor return to one he left'. The disqualification of a king on account of some bodily imperfection is not uniquely Celtic. In the Hindu epic, *The Mahabharata*, in which many themes known in Celtic mythology are to be found, King Dhritarashtra is forced to give up his throne because of his blindness.

Since the insatiable Celtic goddesses could hardly be expected to take kindly to the loss of sexual capacity by their mortal partners, the most calamitous of all wounds were those in the genital region. It is after sustaining such an injury that Bran orders his companions to behead him. The disaster which could befall a people in these circumstances is illustrated by the Fisher-King whose realm is rendered a wasteland when he receives a wound which Wolfram von Eschenbach, the German author of *Parzival*, tells us explicitly was in the scrotum. Traces of the belief that royal impotence affected the prosperity of the kingdom were still to be found in twelfth-century France. In Brittany the cattle were said to have strayed and the harvests to have failed after the castration of King Alain.

It would follow that, of all his attributes, it was his virility which Celtic kings strove hardest to maintain and this could well solve another mystery. There is little doubt that the legal system developed by the tenth-century Welsh king Hywel Dda is largely a codification of the Druidic oral one. Among the officials of his court is listed a *troediawc*, literally a footstool, whose task it was to cradle the royal feet from the time the king sat down at table until he went to bed. A girl who plays such a role is mentioned in *Math son of Mathonwy* where the most important qualification for the job was that she should be a virgin.

What we have here must be the practice of shunamitism which is the belief that a younger person can transfer vital energies to an older one. The word comes from a passage in the Bible. King David, who, on account of advancing years, 'gat no heat', is told that he needs a young damsel to 'lie in his bosom'. The one duly appointed, Abishag the Shunamite, thereafter shares David's bed, though without intercourse taking place. This form of sex therapy was also used in Greece, while in Rome one seventy-year-old who took it up was said to have lived to 115. The German Emperor Barbarossa held young boys against his stomach and genitals and Pope Innocent VIII employed healthy children to stroke him and so transfer their energy to him.

In eighteenth-century London and Paris shunamite parlours offered a highly expensive service and demanded from their clients a substantial deposit lest, temptation growing too strong, any of the forty young ladies of the establishment lost her virginity and her value to her employers.

Math and the other Welsh kings with their feet in their virgin *troediawc*'s lap would, of course, have been close to the source of rejuvenation, her genitals. The fact that the story in question turns on the discovery that the footholder has lost her virginity seems to clinch the case. Another hint of shunamitism is to be found in a Breton folk story. In search of a cure for the sick king, a youth named Luduenn finds himself in a strange castle. In one of its apartments he comes upon a sleeping princess lying on a purple bed and it transpires that the only way the sick king can be cured is by sharing his bed with her though, the text implies, intercourse must not take place.

However, there was one infirmity from which nothing could, in the long run, protect the king – that of old age. As the king aged, his consort aged in sympathy, ultimately turning into one of those ugly hags which populate the vernacular literature. Egyptian kings marked the thirtieth anniversary of their accession with the Festival of Hebsed, which some commentators believe had once included ritual regicide of those whose powers were thought to be diminishing. Spartan seers scanned the skies every eight years and if they saw a shooting star or meteor would seek the arbitration of the Delphic Oracle as to whether the king should continue to rule. After nine years' occupancy of the throne, a Scandinavian king was liable to have life and reign simultaneously terminated if the omens, which included the fertility of the soil, were inauspicious. Almost from the moment it happened in 1100, stories were circulating that William Rufus's death while hunting in the New Forest was ritual regicide, in which he was the compliant victim. The theory that he was the devotee of a witchcraft cult was explored in Margaret Murray's now discredited *The God of the Witches*, published in 1933, and much was made of the fact that the king's death took place at Lammas, coinciding with the Celtic Lugnasad.

Whatever the case here, as Powell comments, there is little doubt that Celtic kings tended to meet a violent, but ritual, end at the hands of the Druids and de Vries points out that in a list of Irish kings from the beginning of our era only four died in bed. Of the rest, some met their deaths in battle, others at the hands of their nearest relatives. Others died *during* epidemics, which is not to say they died *from* the illness, as such an outbreak would probably have been viewed as a token of divine disfavour. Often, too, death was said to have been the result of accidents with a profoundly suspicious ring about them, such as falling from a horse, being struck by lightning or even mortally wounding themselves with their own swords.

A story from Brittany tells how an aging king sends the young Efflam as envoy to the palace of the radiant Sun Princess whom he wants to marry. She sets him three tasks: to spend one night in a lion's den, a second with an ogre and a third sorting out a pile of grains of wheat. When he succeeds in all of them the princess still refuses to marry him on the grounds that he is too old and suggests that she kill him, then use her own magic to restore him to life as a young man. He rashly agrees, but once dead she decides not to revive him but to marry Efflam instead.

The story of Efflam contains a number of elements with echoes in the vernacular literature. One is the motif of the Young Rival. Best known among these is that of *Kulhwych and Olwen* in which the giant Ysbaddaden will die if anyone succeeds in taking his daughter in marriage. Hence, like the Sun Princess, he sets her suitor a series of seemingly impossible tasks. We also have the rivalries between Conchobhar and Noisiu for the love of Deirdriu, Finn and Diarmait for Grainme's, and King Mark and Tristan for Isoult's. Often the rival appears to be the youngest of a group of potential suitors. Stress is laid on the youth of both Tristan and Diarmait and in the Eochaid and Ossianic stories it is the youngest of the group of males who accedes to a hag's demands for a kiss and, by the gesture, restores her youth.

The best known rivalry must be that between Arthur and Lancelot and we may well have here an example of another of the perils by which the Celtic, in common with all Indo-European kings, were hedged: the abduction of his divine consort by the ruler of the Underworld. It is the seizure of Rama's wife, Sita, by Ravana which sets in train the epic war of the Hindu *Ramayana*, as Paris's theft of Helen starts the Trojan War.

In a Welsh story King Arthur is asked to decide how Isoult is to be shared between Mark and Tristan. He rules that one of them shall have her when the leaves are on the trees, that is summer; the other when the trees are bare or in winter. Mark, accorded the right to choose, decides in favour of winter because the nights are longer. Isoult finds a way of circumventing the judgment by applying its letter rather than its spirit. Not all trees shed their leaves. Some, such as the holly, the ivy and yew, keep them summer and winter. Thus she need never be parted from her true love, Tristan. But one cannot fail to notice that Mark's choice of winter links him with the Underworld. Isoult has been in danger of falling into the hands of an Underworld king.

Arthur makes a similar judgment in another case. *Kulhwych and Olwen* contains a passing reference to 'Creiddylad, daughter of Llud Silver Hand'. She is one of the 'gentle, gold-torqued women of this island' and 'the most majestic girl ever in Britain or the three offshore islands' and for her favours Gwythyr son of Greidyawl and Gwynn ap Nudd fight 'every May Day until Judgment'. Later in the story the reason is explained. Gwythyr and Creiddylad's plans to marry have been thwarted when Gwynn ap Nudd abducts her. In this instance the Underworld link is clear enough, for we have already encountered Gwynn as the master of an Underworld hunt. The rescue force Gwythyr musters is defeated and a number of nobles captured. When this comes to the ears of Arthur, he intervenes, frees the prisoners and makes peace between Gwynn and Gwythyr. The terms are that whichever of the two wins the next annual duel will have Creiddylad for that year.

The similarity between this and another abduction story, that of

Persephone by Hades, is inescapable and shows that all are vegetation myths. But there is another similarity with the Celtic stories. Gwynn and Gwythyr fight for Creiddylad every May Day or Beltaine. Persephone must also have been abducted during the same season for she was snatched by Hades while plucking spring flowers. But neither case is unique. Thus Malory: 'So it befell in the month of May, Queen Guinevere called unto her the knights of the Round Table; and she gave them warning that early upon the morrow she would ride on Maying into the woods and fields beside Westminster'. Go she does and it is while she is thus amaying that she is abducted by Meleagant. That he belongs to the Otherworld is shown by the ordeals that Lancelot is forced to undergo to rescue her from the Gorre, the Isle of Glass; ordeals which include making the crossing of the Sword Bridge, the typical Narrow Bridge of shamanism.

# Chapter 8
# The Wisdom of the Druids

The Druids have aroused strong emotions from earliest times. On the one hand we have Lucan and Tacitus turning them into savage juju-men indulging in primitive and bloodthirsty rites. On the other are those in the tradition of Posidonius who praise their wisdom and knowledge or who, like Diogenes Laertius, regard them as one of the four founders of philosophy, the others being the Persian Magi, the Mesopotamian priesthoods and the Indian Brahmins. Diogenes is quoting two lost books, the *Magicus* of Aristotle and *The Succession of the Philosophers*, by Sotion of Alexandria.

This view gets some indirect backing from Hecateus of Abdera among whose more startling claims is that the Greek philosopher Pythagoras had been instructed by a Druid named Abaris, a claim he would have made only if he took Druidic knowledge seriously.

Like so much else about them the dispute has survived. Kendrick, writing in 1927, can find little positive to say, though he ascribes this to lack of available information. For Piggott, whose short study was first published in 1968, the Druids were probably no more than 'conditionally' literate.

Next to such contemporary opinions as these must be set those of their admirers from the eighteenth century down to the Druidic movements of our own times.

Judgments of this kind are always subjective. Lucan and Tacitus were writing as dyed-in-the-wool patriots. Caesar aimed to portray himself as the liberator from a barbaric past. All could therefore be expected to emphasise the darker aspects of Druidism. Posidonius and Strabo were Stoic philosophers who, having convinced themselves that the troubles of their age stemmed from the enfeebling ease of civilised urban life, were eager to prove that true merit was to be found among the Noble Savages of other societies. All the same, to believe that either was so blinded by his preconceptions that he was unable to make a disinterested judgment is to malign them. Both were highly intelligent men and seasoned, observant travellers.

Before joining either party in the debate we ought at least to examine the evidence and there is one witness who should give us pause. Among those who, in 60 BC, listened rapt as the Aeduan chieftain Diviciacus addressed the Roman Senate was Marcus Tullius Cicero. He later attributed to him 'that knowledge of nature which the Greeks call "Physiologia"'. One might take this as another case of uncritical adulation of Noble Savagery and J.J. Tierney comments on the difficulty of reconciling customs like sacrifice or nailing human heads above doors with 'the rarefied levels of Greek philosophy'. To this it could well be answered that such cases are less uncommon than he appears to think. Spanish Inquisitors, once they had left the shriek and stench of the torture chamber, were perfectly capable of engaging in recondite discussions on Aquinian philosophy which, as they knew full well, owed a considerable debt to the logic of the pagan Aristotle.

The image of the tall, rugged figure of Diviciacus leaning on his shield before the assembled Roman senators is one so romantic that it is bound to rouse scepticism in many breasts. Piggott even questions whether he could speak adequate Latin. However, Cicero is entitled to serious consideration. He can hardly have been entirely ignorant of the Celts for he had studied at the Platonic Academy in Athens at the time when its dominant philosophy was Stoic and when Posidonius was actually at its head. Master and pupil remained in contact for the rest of their lives and Cicero had visited him in retirement at his native Rhodes not long before Diviciacus's visit to Rome. In any case, besides statesman and orator, Cicero was a distinguished lawyer who had proved himself more than a match for the best advocates of his day. In these circumstances it is hard to believe he could easily have been deceived into taking mumbo-jumbo for Greek natural science.

To his audience Diviciacus may well have exemplified one area in which Celtic preeminence was recognised: that of eloquence. After their occupation of Gaul, upper class Romans sought out its orators as tutors for their sons. Even in the fourth century the great Roman orator Quintus Aurelius Symmachus boasted of his Gaulish training and among those who entered Roman employment was the Bordeaux-born rhetor Decimus Magnus Ausonius who, before becoming tutor to the son of the Emperor Valentinian, taught at the university of his native city. According to a series of poems he wrote, its school of rhetoric had been founded by Druids from Armorica or Brittany.

But there are, to my mind, other reasons why the thesis of Druidic knowledge is not easily to be dismissed. There were the Culdee establishments, such as that at Scone, with their reputation as Christian heirs of the Druids. In *Celtic Mythology* I suggested that the high international reputation of Irish scholarship was a kind of indirect legacy from the Druids. Because of their considerable knowledge, at the time of the conversion, it had been found necessary to send to the country missionaries of the highest intellectual calibre.

St Patrick's monastery at Clocmacnois, as well as others founded on what were believed to be Druidic sacred sites, became famous as a seat of learning throughout Europe. The phenomenon of Irish scholarship is one which Arnold Toynbee discusses in *The Study of History*. By the mid-sixth century, less than a hundred years after St Patrick's mission (AD 432–61), 'the Irish Church had not only developed its distinctive features but had in many respects shot ahead of Continental Catholicism', he writes. Irish missionaries and scholars were warmly welcomed in Britain and on the Continent, with students vying for places in their schools.

Taken overall the evidence seems to provide at least a *prima facie* case for believing in a tradition of scholarship among the Druids which would accord with Caesar's statement that the Druids were 'held in great honour by the people'.

But what did they actually know? Like the shamans, they were regarded as magicians. So, too, were the Mesopotamian and Egyptian priesthoods. However, in societies in which only a minority have a basic education, even things like writing and simple arithmetic can be regarded as esoteric knowledge. Goldsmith's village parson was held in awe by his parishioners because he could 'read and cipher too'. Of the Mesopotamians and Egyptians we also know they were astronomers, mathematicians, physicians, possibly chemists, though we might also call them astrologers, numerologists, herb doctors and alchemists. We are similarly well informed on the Brahmins but, though we know of their many similarities with the Druids, as to the actual content of the latter's knowledge we are once again frustrated by their pathological secrecy.

There is another difficulty. Historically, knowledge has tended to move from east to west. That is to say the knowledge of the Mesopotamians, Persians and Egyptians was transmitted westward, first to the Greeks (Herodotus believed that Greek religion originated in Egypt). Then, about the mid-second century BC, as Greece was falling under Roman domination, it was disseminated throughout the Empire. East-west transmission may have been because it was only in the east that anything deemed worthy of transmission was to be found. On the other hand, it may have come about by sheer historical and geographical chance. For the Romans, and even more the Greeks, Egypt or Persia were simply closer than the remote island off the coast of Gaul and if anything of significance was happening there it was likely to go unrecorded.

But significant things may have been happening. The cyclic theory of time, that whereby it moves in a sort of huge circle ultimately returning to the same point, is to be found in Plato's *Timaeus* and Virgil's *Fourth Eclogue*. Toynbee may well be right in declaring that Plato got it from the Mesopotamians. Yet the Druids and, there is little doubt, their Neolithic predecessors in Britain, the builders of the megaliths, also had a cyclic theory of time. It could have been that Plato got it from this source, though possibly secondhand. There may even have existed some third, unknown source from whom all got it.

One feasible medium for its transmission to Britain is by way of the Mycenaean Bronze Age civilisations of the Aegean. From about the sixteenth century BC signs of their influence are demonstrated, among other things, by a scatter of artefacts along the east coast of Ireland and across Britain. The track stretches as far north as the Orkneys, but the greatest concentration is in the south west, seat of the Wessex Culture. This compares with an almost total absence of such material over much of continental Europe except for some on the Breton peninsula and in the Channel Islands.

More significant than objects is the technique used in building the last stage of what was the Wessex Culture's most dazzling achievement, Stonehenge. Here the tops of the uprights have been very precisely cut away to leave stone studs into which equally accurately bored holes in the lintels fit, a technique used in Mycenae. It could have been that the builder of Stonehenge was wealthy enough to import Aegean stone dressers and masons. The pattern cut into one of the stones, tentatively interpreted as representing a Mycenaean dagger, has been taken as support.

But there is support of another kind – in the labyrinth patterns incised, among other places, on some of the stones of New Grange in County Meath. These are similar to the most famous one of all, that from another Aegean civilisation, the early Bronze Age Minoan labyrinth of Crete. Its image was used on Minoan coinage and represented that in which the dangerous Minotaur was constrained. In Wales, where similar mazes were sometimes cut into the turf or outlined in pebbles, they were called 'Caerau Droia', Cities of Troy. Homer's Troy was linked with the Aegean culture-province as the city invaded by a Greek (actually Mycenaean) army under Agamemnon which was seeking to rescue the abducted Helen and punish the Trojans. (This obviously raises the question of whether there can actually have been a connection between the British and Trojans, as Geoffrey of Monmouth claims.)

The astronomical function of cursuses and henges such as Stonehenge, which are a wholly British phenomenon, is today finding increased acceptance. Indeed the possibility was first mooted in connection with the Breton monuments by Jacques Cambry in *Monumens celtiques*, published in 1805. If this is the case then they harmonised solar and lunar years by means of the nineteen-year cycle also used in Mesopotamia and taken over by the Greeks (it is still used for calculating movable religious feasts like Easter). That the Druids employed a similar system is confirmed by the Coligny Calendar.

Whether or not the calendar can in itself be taken as proof of a high degree of astronomical and accompanying mathematical knowledge is disputed. Piggott points out that, accurate calendography being essential in determining the main events of the farming year, such skills are to be found among even the least developed societies.

As far as the astronomy which underlies calendography is concerned, besides a highly dubious tree zodiac, we know that terms derived from mythology were used to describe much that could be seen in the night sky. The Milky Way was 'Caer Gwyddion'. The constellation Corona Borealis was called 'Caer Arianrhod' after Lugh's stony-hearted mother, while Cassiopeia is 'Llys Don', the Palace of Don, who is the Irish Dana. Sir Walter Scott who, in *The Lay of the Last Minstrel*, refers to the Great Bear as 'Arthur's Wain' is obviously using an expression current in his time, though possibly restricted to Scotland. But it is probable that Arthur's name was a late substitute for that of a pagan god, in much the same way as 'Gwynn's Hunt' became 'Arthur's Hunt' in many places. However, evidence now emerging may cast a new light on Druidic astronomy.

The last of the great stone circles was built from about 1800 BC which is much earlier than the date traditionally accepted for the Celts' arrival in Britain. We have no direct testimony of their using it. On the other hand, there are indications of a Celtic connection at the site at Godmanchester near Cambridge, for it was here that a dedication to a local god, Abandinus, was found. Nearby, archaeologists have unearthed the remains of a large Neolithic temple both older and, as an astronomical calculator, more sophisticated than Stonehenge. Its main alignment is towards the sunrise on May Day and the First of August, corresponding with the festivals of Beltaine and Lugnasad respectively. Nonetheless, before taking this as conclusive, one must remember that if the Druids had learnt their principal doctrines from a late Neolithic and Bronze Age priesthood in Britain, their instructors would have marked these two dates as key points in the agricultural year.

We are on firmer ground in considering the Druids as healers. References to them in this role occur in the Irish story of the death of King Conchobhar and in an episode in the Cu Chulainn cycle. When the hero lies ill, his wife Emer upbraids his Ulster companions for failing to find a competent physician. Had any of them been sick, Cu Chulainn would not have rested until a Druid had made his examination or 'a doctor found to heal him', she laments.

There can be little doubt that Druidic medicine was based largely on herbs. Mistletoe is well documented, of course, verbena slightly less so, and they may have extracted drugs from the poppy and certain fungi, though it is uncertain whether these were employed medicinally or solely for ritual purposes, as the Brahmins used the ritual drug Soma. The name 'all heal', which Pliny tells us they applied to mistletoe, was retained in folk medicine. In Wales it was so prized, not only medicinally, but also for magical purposes, that the Laws of Wales set the high value of three score pence on it. The herbalist Culpeper corroborates Pliny when he tells us that mistletoe from an oak tree was particular valued as it 'partakes of the nature of Jupiter'. From Pliny's time down to the present it was thought to be a cure for epilepsy and hysteria and, in fact, its pharmacologically-active ingredient, *guipsine*, is actually employed by modern medicine in the treatment of hypertension and nervous disorders. This gives some backing to the belief that the Druids practised psychiatry and even had clinics devoted to it. One, the hospital of 'Foolish Thought', was supposed to have been located in the Forest of Brocéliande.

The white robes worn by the Druids for the mistletoe-culling were also, according to Pliny, worn for gathering the *selago* which, though used medicinally, has remained unidentified.

Outside strictly herbal treatment was a so-called magic egg which Pliny calls an *anguinem*, extracted, he was told, from the secretions of angry snakes. A number of explanations have been advanced for it, ranging from the shells of sea urchins to the egg cases of the whelk, but we should not dismiss the possibility that it may actually have been some kind of extract of snake venom which is, of course, used medicinally.

Especially impressive is the evidence for Druidic surgery. A second century BC grave at Obernebzingen in Bavaria yielded, besides weapons, three surgical instruments: a retractor for holding back skin or layers of muscle liable to impede the surgeon during operations, a probe for exploring wounds and a trephining saw for cutting through bone. All three differ only slightly from those found in modern operating theatres. That a trephining saw is used in brain surgery to remove areas of the skull suggests that the Druids may have had some knowledge in this highly specialised area. They must also have practised eye surgery, for instruments for the removal of cataracts were found at Mont Auxois near Alise Sainte-Reine in Burgundy.

It is difficult to imagine how delicate operations on the brain or eyes could have been carried out without anaesthesia. One possibility is that they employed hypnosis. This was certainly known by the priests of Egypt and Greece and the vernacular literature contains references to a 'magic sleep'. Among the secrets Merlin rashly imparts to Viviane is that of inducing sleep, enabling her to gain power over him. As an anaesthetic, hypnosis has been shown to be extremely successful and in the mid-nineteenth century the surgeons John Elliotson in London and James Esdaile in Calcutta used it for major surgery.

Somewhat analogous to hypnosis which, besides its use in anaesthesia also had direct therapeutic applications, was incubation or curative sleep. Pausanias mentions an area in the Aesklepion or clinic at Epidaurus in the Peloponnese 'where the suppliants sleep', and evidence of the use of extended periods of sleep for healing purposes comes from elsewhere. An inscription in a temple associated with a curative shrine at Grand in the Vosges implies that it was practised there, while Sir Mortimer Wheeler suggested that the long building forming part of the Lydney Park complex served a similar function.

Borvo, god of bubbling springs, seems to have been patron of health spas. His most important cult sites Aix-les-Bains, Bourbonne-les-Bains, Bourbon-Lancy and Bourbon-l'Archambault are spa towns, and his association with them suggests they were used in early Celtic times.

As the Celts were a metal-working people, first in bronze, then in iron, we have to consider another possible aspect of Druidic knowledge. Eliade points out that the smith is close to the shaman and undergoes a very similar initiation. Indeed, one of the legends of the North Asian Yakut smiths which he quotes is reminiscent of the mythological 'iron houses' which are used for imprisoning heroes and then heated to red heat in an attempt to destroy them. According to Eliade, Yakut smiths learned their craft from K'daai Maqsin, chief smith of the underworld, who lives in an iron house, surrounded by slag iron. (The underworld connection so commonly found probably comes from the fact that metallic ores occur underground.) Smith gods who impart their skill to humans are universal and the accounts of its direct transmission from the gods repeatedly leads back to shamanistic origins.

For the Celts the smith god was Goibniu, the Welsh Govannon, one of the Tuatha De Danann. In Irish mythology, as in that of other societies, the smith god is particularly celebrated as the maker of invincible weapons. This is itself instructive, for the forging of swords with purported magical properties is a recurring folk-tale motif. Often the weapons come from mysterious foundries in the depths of forests. Such places may well have existed for, besides the secrecy the location would offer, it would have provided the timber to yield the charcoal to produce the high temperatures needed to soften metal.

One step in the manufacturing process particularly lends itself to magic: the tempering which gives the blade the surface hardness allowing it to take a sharp, durable cutting edge. This is carried out by heating the blade to red heat then quenching it in a liquid, depending on the type of surface required. Normally oil or water is used, but in the past some smiths preferred blood, the phosphorus

from which, according to contemporary swordsmiths, combined
with the metal to convert it to phosphor-steel. The practice was
maintained by the Toledo swordmakers, who learnt their craft from
the Arab occupiers of Spain. It is likely that their teachers had been
the Celts, whose reputation was such that foreign rulers often tried
to persuade them to set up workshops in their countries and
sometimes succeeded. The word 'Galata', given to an area of the
former Turkish capital of Istanbul, has the same root as Gaul and
Galatia and derives from the fact it was at one time the area where
Celtic swordsmiths worked.

The tempering blood was obtained by plunging the hot blade into
a live animal – a method suggestive of ritual. However, it is likely
that, at an earlier time, human blood was preferred, so it was actually
a form of sacrifice. This is certainly the implication of one of the
Scottish versions of the Fenian stories. In it Fionn (the Irish Finn)
is accosted by a fairy smith who leads him to his forge in a remote
highland glen. There he makes Fionn's sword. As the process is
nearing its climax the smith's daughter whispers in Fionn's ear that,
at the moment the sword appears to be finished, her father will ask
him. 'What else is left to do?' Fionn was then to take the red-hot
weapon and plunge it through the smith's body to temper it – which
he did.

Caesar writes of the Druids being given to long discussions on the
'heavenly bodies and their movements, the size of the universe and
of the earth, and the physical constitution of the world'. Frustratingly
he tells us no more, either because, as a man of action, he was
uninterested in such speculation, or because showing the Druids as
learned metaphysicians would have injured his main thesis. Hence
we are thrown back into the morass of uncertainty. This is a great
pity as the 'physical constitution of the world', which is to say the
nature of the universal substance, was a problem exercising the
minds of early Greek philosophers, among them Pythagoras, whom
Hecateus specifically links with the Druids. It may be that it was their
now lost contributions to the debate which led to their being credited
by Cicero with a knowledge of *physiologia*.

The only hint we have comes from the so-called *Barddas
Manuscripts*. For all its inflated claim to be 'a collection of original
documents, illustrative of the theology, wisdom and usage of Bardo-
Druidic system of the Isle of Britain', it has to be treated with

scepticism. First, the earliest record of the manuscript goes back only to the sixteenth century when a two-volume compilation was made by Llewelyn Sion of Glamorgan. Secondly, in the eighteenth century it caught the eye of Edward Williams, alias Iolo Morganwg ('Iolo of Glamorgan'), one of a group of London Welshmen who immersed themselves in the burgeoning fashion for things Celtic and, in his efforts to prove a continuity of tradition, was not past forging documents or embellishing those he chanced upon. Thirdly, there is a flavour about it of the Neoplatonism then also in vogue.

Nonetheless, some elements in the *Barddas* manuscripts do have a genuine ring and can, to a degree, be said to echo what is known from elsewhere. For example, its doctrine of reincarnation and the three circles of existence, *Ceugant*, *Abred* and *Gwynvyd*, which it posits, are in accord with known Druidic teaching.

Overall, what it presents is a system in which the destructive and ultimately nihilistic forces of 'the not-world', Annwvyn, are in ceaseless conflict with God, representing life. The potentiality for life came into being when God created Manred, the primal substance of the universe, comparable perhaps with the ether of the sixth century BC Greek philosopher Anaximenes.

The concentric circles of Ceugant, Abred and Gwynvyd stand respectively for: infinity where animate and inanimate as we recognise them do not exist; the place of rebirth where the spirits awaiting reincarnation sojourn; and perfection (or 'whiteness'), where life reasserts itself and the individual develops through the impact of experience. Thus, in Evans Wentz's exposition of the *Barddas* doctrine, each soul begins its journey as a mere water-animalcule ascending at death to the next rung of the ladder of creation, a process which continues, until it becomes fully human. Humanity once achieved, a new period of spiritual growth begins as a progress leading ultimately to divinity.

The inherent dualism of God versus Annwvyn is to be found in many of the world's religions, including Hinduism with its other parallels with Druidism. At various times it has even made its appearance in such Christian heresies as Gnosticism and Catharism. There are, to be sure, elements in the myths which give intimations of just such cosmic contests as, for example, in the great battles between Otherworld peoples, such as the Tuatha De Danann and the Fomors. On the other hand, there is nothing in Druidism which suggests any kind of spiritual progression and certainly not one leading ultimately to divinity. In point of fact, for all the ease with which mortal and immortal worlds coexist in Druidism, there is every indication that each remained separate.

In any event, if there ever was a Druidic belief in a progression to divinity it would be interesting to learn what steps were necessary in order to achieve it. In other words, to know something of Druidic ethics.

Generosity has already emerged as a prized virtue. In the *Accallam na Senórech* or Colloquy of the Elders, the aged Cailte, last of the Fenians, finds himself in the monastery of Drogheda where he engages in a somewhat testy debate with St Patrick, making unfavourable references to the saint's God whom he regards as vengeful, petty-minded and parsimonious. He tells him that if the leaves of the autumn trees were true gold or 'the white wave silver', Finn would have given it all away.

No less important a virtue was a robust self-reliance and integrity. Asked by St Patrick what maintained them through life, Cailte answers, 'The truth that was in our hearts, the strength in our arms and the fulfilment in our tongues'. The tripartite form of this indicates it may have a genuinely Druidic origin and a somewhat similar tripartite list is given by Diogenes Laertius who tells us the Druids taught that 'the gods must be worshipped, no evil done and manly behaviour maintained'. We are also told that the Otherworld was a place where truth reigned.

Manly behaviour was obviously important. Alexander the Great, who asked a Celt what he most feared, was told, nothing 'so long as the sky does not fall or the sea burst its bounds'. The phrase is peculiarly insistent. Sualdam Setanta, trying to rally the Ulstermen to the support of his son, Cu Chulainn, shouts, 'Are the heavens rent? Is the sea bursting its bounds? Is the end of the world upon us?' Later in the same epic, the warriors of Conchobhar assure him they will continue to fight until overcome by these cataclysms.

In 1282, when news reached his fellow countrymen that Llewelyn, the last Prince of Wales, had been killed by the English, the bard Gruffydd ab yr Ynad Coch, lamented:

> Oh, God, why does not the sea cover the land?
> Why are we left to linger?

# PART 2
# THE DRUIDS IN ECLIPSE

# Chapter 9
# Rome Triumphant

The Roman occupation of the Celtic lands took place, not in a single sweep, but by the exploitation of opportunities as they arose. Men like Caesar, eager to extend the bounds of empire, who even felt a mission to do so, had to contend with those at home who were suspicious of their ambitions. To gain the resources he needed Caesar had to justify his every move and each time limits were placed upon its scope by the senate.

Nonetheless, by the middle of the second century southern Gaul, the modern Provence, including the cities of Marseilles, Nice and Narbonne, was in his hands. The next step was his intervention to forestall an advance by the Helvetii from what is now Switzerland, through the territory of the Sequani in central Gaul. Ostensibly this was done in the name of an alliance with the Aedui and its leader Diviciacus whose land the Helvetii were threatening to overrun. The true reason was that Caesar could see a potential threat to the Roman territories in southern Gaul and the loss of access to their Spanish colonies. As it proved, by the stationing of forces in the area he had also put himself in a position to control the main arteries of Gaul, the routes between the Rhône, Saône and Loire rivers.

Too late the Gauls awoke to the danger: the Romans could strike wherever they chose and against whomsoever they chose. They were strategically placed to make themselves masters of the country. In 56 BC the Gauls attempted to reverse the situation by making use of the element in which the Romans were regarded as being at their weakest – the sea. The Armorican peninsula was dominated by the powerful Veneti. Confident in their control over the harbours and inlets with which the coast abounded and in the invincibility of their fleet, they summoned their client tribes as well as volunteers from across the Channel to support them and issued a challenge.

Forced to respond, the local Roman commander was at a double disadvantage. He was numerically inferior and his vessels lighter, weaker and propelled by oarsmen, whereas the Venetians had sails. On the day of the engagement the Gaulish ships bore down with a following wind, threatening to drive the Romans from the sea. Then, with an abruptness typical of the area, the wind dropped. The attackers were becalmed and paralysed amid an enemy who, with his oars, now had the advantage of mobility. Grapnels hurled into the rigging of the Venetian ships were used to haul down masts and sails before boarding parties overcame their crews.

The next and last serious revolt came from central Gaul where Vercingetorix, the young king of the Arverni, the present Auvergne, attempted to unite the tribes under his leadership for an all-out land offensive. Failing to bring this about, he was still able to take the field with forces superior in numbers to the Romans. At first successful, the superior discipline and mobility of their enemy in the end compelled his retreat on Alésia. Besieged here, he held out in the belief a relief column was on its way, but had to surrender when it failed to appear.

Though sporadic revolts were to continue, Gaul was now largely under Caesar's control and he began looking beyond. The Romans were known to have covetous eyes on Britain with its thriving economy. However, partly because he lacked the men and supplies for what was likely to prove a major operation, and partly because he was concerned about events at home, he contented himself with two sorties and the island was spared occupation until AD 43, when it was invaded by Claudius. In a short time, the territories of the principal Celtic king Cunobelinus (Shakespeare's Cymbeline) submitted and his capital Camulodunum (Colchester) made that of a Roman province. The Celts could be said to have been nullified as a military threat and, in AD 59, the legionaries stood on the Menai shore contemplating the island of Môn, or Anglesey, with its great Druidic centre.

The British Isles were never, of course, completely occupied. Ireland was not entered and in Britain the zone of occupation ended in the north at Hadrian's Wall.

Môn was taken, however, and it is clear from Tacitus's description that its capture was the result of a major and carefully planned operation. To transport the infantry over the shifting shallows of the strait, flat-bottomed boats were built, a large cavalry force was concentrated and the whole was put under the direct command of a brilliant soldier, the recently arrived imperial governor, Gaius Suetonius Paulinus.

The island's population had been swollen by large numbers of Druidic fugitives from Gaul, fiercely antagonistic to Rome, yet, since even their presence can hardly have made it a military threat, one is forced to question why it should have been thought necessary to invest so much effort into taking it. The answer lies in the determination of the Romans, on the whole tolerant towards the religions of their subject peoples, to destroy that of the Celts insofar as it was represented by the Druids.

Among the justifications advanced is that they were involved in the magical practices prohibited to Roman citizens, and in their propaganda much is made of human sacrifice. But the horror at this rings hollow when one places it beside the barbaric 'entertainments' in the Circus Maximus which Caesar himself had rebuilt. In any event, it is doubtful whether these sentiments were universal. Though human sacrifice had been abolished in Rome not long before Caesar's birth, there is evidence of its continuation in secret. We even have indications of the troops in Britain practising it. A body, with votive deposits above and below it, in a ritual pit at Newstead in the Scottish frontier zone, was almost certainly a Roman sacrificial victim. The bodies of babies found at a barrack block, at Reculver fort and at Springhead, Kent, date to the second century and must have been foundation sacrifices.

As such things could hardly have been done without the authorities turning a blind eye, it is hard to accept that human sacrifice raised the kind of abhorrence in the Roman breast that Tacitus or Lucan would have us believe. The hostility to Druidism must therefore have had other causes. To be sure, more than anything else, it was the ideology of a national culture and Piggott is probably right in comparing the Roman occupiers of the Celtic lands with the sixteenth-century English in Ireland. Here too the key to suppressing national aspiration was seen as wiping out those who embodied its culture.

There was probably a second, more important reason why Druidism was seen as a danger. Important and far reaching political developments were taking place in the Celtic world in the years immediately preceding the Roman conquest. The tribal kings with their wide autonomous powers were undergoing a process of demotion in favour of annually elected magistrates or *vergobretos*.

The abolition of a tier of the political structure bespeaks a movement towards centralised authority. In other words, the old loose and querulous confederacy was in the process of conversion into a nation.

The moving spirits behind it can only have been the Druids. As a supratribal body they could intervene and enforce peace during conflicts, were called upon to settle disputes between tribes and could ban from participation in sacrifice those refusing to accept their arbitration. This lends strength to Anne Ross's thesis of two categories of gods, the local ones and a pantheon of 'national' or Druidic gods. The second are those who, like Lugh, not only appear in the mythology but whose wide distribution is known from epigraphy. Encouraging their cults would, of course, have been a way of fostering a national consciousness.

Further support to this view is given by another event. In AD 68 a rebellion against Roman rule took place in Gaul. Its leader was Civilis, the commander of the cohort guarding the Rhine frontier who was also chieftain of the Batavi tribe. The degree to which his family had become romanised is shown by the fact that he had been given the same first names as Caesar himself, Gaius Julius. At that time Rome was torn by a civil struggle between the rival imperial claims of Aulus Vitellius and Vespasian. Civilis threw his weight in with Vespasian and used his troops to block the movement of reinforcements to the Rhineland army, which supported Vitellius. However, when Vespasian became emperor, Civilis kept up the struggle, with Rome itself as the enemy. Joined by other tribes, he declared a Gallic Empire and Vespasian found himself forced into drastic action against his erstwhile ally. He gave command of a large army to a relative, Petilius Cerealis, who won a victory which dissuaded those tribes still wavering from joining the revolt, and Civilis himself was compelled to surrender. Unlike Vercingetorix, who was paraded in irons at Caesar's Roman triumph and then secretly strangled, he seems to have been treated honourably, while every trace of his 'Gallic Empire' was expunged.

There is no reason to doubt the Roman charge that Civilis was supported and urged on in his imperial ambitions by his Druids. They can therefore be seen as the *éminences grises*, not only behind a revolt against their principal persecutor, Rome, but in a move towards Celtic unification. One is left to wonder about their role in other rebellions such as that of Cunobelinus's son, Caratacus, which, but for the treachery of the Brigantian queen, Cartimandua, might even have been more successful than that of Civilis.

Rebellion and resistance were to continue. Suetonius had hardly completed the suppression of Môn before he had to dash southwards to East Anglia to meet the threat from Bouddica. And, even with Môn subjugated, the mountainous region in the west, one day to be known as Wales, continued to resist. On the admission of Tacitus, by AD 78, the Ordovices, whose wide swathe of territory included Môn itself, were virtually exterminated in an attempt at pacification. Even then much of Wales remained a military zone throughout the Roman occupation. Besides a line of forts from Caernarvon in the north to Cardiff in the south, there was one military headquarters at Caerleon-on-Usk (the name means 'City of the Legions') and another across the border at Chester. When the Romans, in the period just before withdrawal from Britain, had reduced their garrison to four legions, they still had two tied down in Wales. Despite these forces they ventured into the more isolated regions of the interior as seldom as possible, leaving the remoter communities to live much as they had always lived.

The general feeling one gains is that here, at least, the occupiers were living an existence among the occupied rather like that portrayed in the Goscinny and Uderzo's *Astérix le Gaulois*.

Where the two were thrown into contact and wherever the Romans were able to enforce their writ, attitudes varied widely. Relations between occupier and occupied are far less black and white than the images presented in Resistance drama would suggest. Some among the native population were beguiled by the propaganda which presented the Romans as the wave of the future, much as the Nazis presented themselves to the occupied of Europe in the 1940s. There was also, of course, the admiration of a warrior people for Roman military skill and prowess. This could manifest itself, for example, in giving children names derived from Roman history as in the case of Civilis or the British client-king Cogidubnus, whose first names were Tiberius and Claudius.

Others simply saw the personal advantage that could flow from collaboration – as the Romans intended they should. These were considerable. In its final stage, Cogidubnus's palace, whose ruins are to be seen at Fishbourne, Sussex, could vie with the Palatine mansions of the wealthy Roman nobility.

In continental Europe, one fundamental change brought about by romanisation was in language. The low Latin of the troops became the basis of a linguistic group which, besides Italian, includes French, Spanish, Portuguese and Romanian. In Britain, typically some might say, this alien tongue was never adopted by the population at large, though there is some evidence that it was fairly widely understood. A handful of Latin loan words, such as port, colony and legion, entered and have remained part of the English language. Among words which must have been current throughout Britain and have survived in Welsh are *pont* (bridge), *fenestr* (window) and *mur* (wall).

Loan words generally enter a language for two reasons. First, when some previously unknown commodity or new technology is introduced. The computer spawned a whole vocabulary of English words worldwide. Many of our herbs still have the Arabic-derived names that record the fact that they were brought back by the Crusaders. 'Chocolate' comes from the Aztec *xocoatyl*, while 'tea' is an anglicisation of the Chinese word *te*.

Secondly, they occur when a language is regarded as representing a higher or more successful civilisation. This is the same sort of backhanded compliment that the French and the British pay one another from time to time. Thus, we have our egregious menu French, stemming from the belief that French cooking was superior to our own. Or there are such strange neologisms in French as *le camping* (campsite), *le parking*, *le shampooing* (shampoo), *le weekend* and, more recently, *le shopping*, *le look* (especially *le look anglais* in fashion) and even *le car*.

As far as the Romans' attitudes to their subjects went, as we have already seen, they often employed Celts as tutors for their sons, but otherwise any fraternisation seems to have been exclusively with the romanised native aristocracy.

The ban on Druidism did not, of course, extend to Celtic religion and the worship of the gods continued during the occupation. Indeed, the temple to Nodens at Lydney Park was built in Roman times, its design imitating Mediterranean models.

It was under Roman occupation that the Celts began the wholesale portrayal of their gods in human terms, adopting classical ideas even as to dress and hairstyle with such enthusiasm that some have seen the hand of Roman sculptors behind them. However, we know that in many instances, as at Bath and Cirencester, native sculptors were responsible, and, on the whole, these representations retain their essential Celtic characteristics. On the Reims stela, while Apollo holds the lyre and Mercury wears his winged helmet and bears the caduceus, Cernunnos is adorned with horns and torc.

The Romans actually adopted some of the Celtic gods. The cult of the horse goddess Epona was introduced into cavalry units, possibly because they contained a large native element and she became, in fact, the only Celtic deity to enter the official pantheon. Epona, like her British and Irish counterparts, Rhiannon and Macha, possesses the characteristics of a mother goddess and there are several instances of the Romans invoking Celtic mother goddesses. In most cases the shrines, which show a seated figure with the cornucopia on her lap, seem to have been dedicated by men of low rank, though at Castlesteads on Hadrian's Wall one was rebuilt by a centurion, and Romans of substance seem to have been responsible in a number of other places.

Nor was it only goddesses who were invoked, for Cocidius, often equated with Mars, also occurs particularly in the northern dedications.

How thoroughly the various edicts against Druidism were actually enforced during the occupation is unclear, but evading surveillance was probably not unduly difficult as the main religious activities took place in remote and unfrequented places. We have a parallel in the witches' Sabbaths of the Middle Ages which continued despite the vigilance and the appalling sanctions applied by the Church. It can hardly have been difficult, therefore, for Druidism to survive in isolated areas like rural Wales where, in any case, the legions feared to tread.

In addition there were a number of subterfuges the Druids could have adopted. During the Elizabethan period of Catholic persecution, groups of Welsh recusants acquired inns near some of the more popular shrines which, under this facade, served as pilgrim hostels. Whether this was done by Druids or their followers we cannot be sure, though the Gaulish 'Druidess' said to have foretold Diocletian's ascent to the purple was his landlady at the inn at which he was staying.

There was another disguise available to the Druids. No hard and fast division can ever have existed between the three groups the classical observers call 'learned and holy men', the Druids, the Vates and the bards. Bards could at the same time be Druids and the distinction between one and the other was probably dependent, as much as anything, on inclination or talent. Nonetheless the bards possessed an advantage in that their activities were never proscribed. Hence, by taking up the harp the Druids, within obvious limits, would have been free to continue their activities. In *Math son of Mathonwy* Gwyddion and his companions dress themselves as bards and are welcomed at the court of Pryderi. Gwyddion is an interesting case since his name contains the root *Gwydd* or knowledge. A related word, *gwyddon*, means both scientist and magician, and it is Gwyddion's magical skill which enables him to defraud Pryderi of a herd of pigs. Thus, he must originally have been one of the Otherworld Druids frequently encountered in the literature. The prestige and rewards of the bard were considerable and in many ways comparable to those of a Druid. In the *Laws of Hywel Dda* a royal bard was granted a freeholding of land, while he received his harp, often extremely valuable, as well as a horse from the king and a gold ring from the queen. He normally sat next to the king's heir with the right to a seat next to the king himself. Taliesin is said to have received a hundred racehorses, a hundred purple cloaks, a hundred bracelets, fifty brooches and a fine sword from his royal patron.

The original distinction between Druid and bard must have been between those primarily concerned, on the one hand, with the religious, scientific and juridical aspects of his society and, on the other, those concerned with its history and mythology. However, through the period of occupation the two would have become thoroughly intermingled, especially once the Druids began passing themselves off as bards, and the two would probably have gradually merged. It could well have been that it was in this process that the Druidic doctrine with which they were later credited got into the hands of the bards.

In any case, the bards had always retained some quasimagical functions, as in the singing of the *glam dicin*. From now on these seem to have increased and bard and Druid become ever more similar. Bardic colleges provided twelve-year training courses where, as in the Druidic *bangor*, teaching was oral and students were required to learn stories by heart. Once graduated, the bard adopted the title 'Ollave' roughly equivalent to our own 'doctor' which, the evidence suggests, had been used by the Druids.

Taliesin describes himself as having 'at length become a gwydd', a word whose magical connotation has just been discussed. Myrddin, later the Merlin of the Arthurian stories, was probably a northern bard. In *The Triads of the Islands of Britain* Welsh bards are even described as astronomers and, according to Gerald of Wales, kept the genealogies of princes which they would recite from memory.

Even the poetic muse has a quasimagical quality and was spoken of as *awen* or ecstasy. Gerald mentions *awenyddion*, a word meaning 'poets', but here used to describe individuals able to induce trances in which they lost control of their senses 'as if they are possessed by devils' and uttered gibberish taken to be 'prophecies'. One is reminded of the Delphic Pythia and it is difficult not to believe that such practices came from the Druids.

Though the degree of romanisation might have varied from country to country and even among the sectors of population, four centuries of occupation produced vast changes in lifestyle. In some measure these reached even the most isolated hamlet and it is undeniable that they brought great benefits.

There was Roman technological superiority. Cities had been built and communications between them improved. They had introduced a monetary and, to some extent, an industrialised economy. Administrative bodies had been set up at all levels. Trained secular judges, appointed to administer a comprehensive, codified legal system, had largely eradicated such things as the resolution of interfamily quarrels through feuds.

The latter years of occupation brought what was the greatest change of all: the adoption of Christianity. Accounts of Constantine's conversion and his choice of state religion vary widely. In later life he was given to sermons in which he ascribed his own successes to the favour of the Christian God. In fact there are intimations that the conversion was almost arbitrary. It is said that while in Gaul he had had a vision of a huge *chi-rho*, the Greek monogram formed from the first two letters of the name of Christ which had become a Christian symbol and which he thereafter adopted as his standard. However the fact that, in some versions, the vision came to him in a Gallic temple has led French scholars to suggest that, rather than the *chi-rho*, it was actually the symbol of the god Taranis he saw and that he might even at one point have considered making Druidism, whose ideas he could have encountered while in Britain, the Roman religion.

Some Christian conversion had, of course, gone on before Constantine's proclamation of the Edict of Milan in AD 312 established religious toleration throughout the empire. Nennius's account of the British King Lucius accepting baptism in 167 is likely to be legend, as were the stories of Joseph of Arimathea's visit to Britain with his nephew, the boy Christ, during the 'hidden years' – the inspiration for William Blake's 'Jerusalem' – as well as of Joseph's return to found a monastery at Glastonbury. The last is not, however, without its distinctly Celtic resonances exemplified by the marvellous objects he was supposed to have brought with him: his staff which, planted in the earth, took root as the Glastonbury Thorn, flowering on the day of Christ's nativity; the phial containing drops of the precious blood; and the chalice from which the apostles had drunk at the Last Supper.

Nevertheless, that there was an active Christian community in Britain is shown by the fact that several Britons, including the proto-martyr, St Alban, were executed during the third- and early fourth-century persecutions, and that the bishops of York, London and Lincoln were among those who attended the Council of Arles only a year after the Edict of Milan. For the British church already to have been organised into dioceses in this way must mean that it was firmly established. From around the same period, too, come hoards of Roman silverware engraved with the *chi-rho* and the fish, another Christian symbol, while a mosaic floor in the remains of a villa at Hinton St Mary, Somerset, has what is taken to be a representation of Christ. Small churches dating to the fourth century, such as those at Silchester (*c.* 360) and Caerwent have been found, but the evidence from Hinton St Mary as well as from another villa at Lullingstone suggests that most worship went on in private houses.

This supports the view that the Christianity of the time was something of a cult movement among both the Romans and native population; one of the many cults, some of them bizarre and esoteric, which had spread through the empire in its declining years. It was, indeed, during the fourth century that the invocation by Romans of the Celtic gods began in earnest.

As far as the great mass of the British population was concerned there seems to have been little attempt to wean them from paganism. In Gaul, though there was a whole succession of saints – Trophimus,

Saturninus, Martial, Denis, Austremoine, Gratian – their activities were largely restricted to the towns and it was not until the election of St Martin as bishop of Tours in 372 that an attempt was made to proselytise the countryside. David Edwards suggests that the fault lay with the native landowners' failure to convert their slaves and tenants. But the truth is that among many of those landowners, conversion had been less than skin-deep and only accepted, as it continued to be accepted, as a matter of political expediency.

For the greater majority, at all social levels, it is likely that Christianity remained what it had been from the time of Constantine's edict – yet another imposition by the occupiers, ignored where possible and, where this was not possible, resented and resisted. As Toynbee says, conquered peoples have frequently maintained their cultural identity by the intense cultivation of their religion, as the Jews did after the Diaspora. Never, since the Roman occupation, have the Celtic peoples known a time when their culture was not threatened in one way or another, yet that they maintained a cultural identity can scarcely be doubted and we know that Druidism continued even if in a radically diluted and corrupted form. Indeed, if we accept that Civilis's rebellion was encouraged by his Druids, they were active in Gaul over a century after it came into Roman hands and even in a household so romanised that one of its members held high rank in their army.

In point of fact, from the fourth century, Druids are again being spoken of as openly as if they had never left the scene. The claim by Decimus Magnus Ausonius that the rhetorical school at Bordeaux was founded by Armorican Druids is only one of his poetical allusions to them. Describing his fellow teachers, he mentions one Phoebicius, who himself came of Armorican Druidic stock and had been 'keeper of the temple of Belenos' until, finding this employment somewhat ill-rewarded, he used family connections to gain himself a chair at the university.

The sixth-century St Gildas wrote a series of denunciatory letters to the British native princes who were supposed to have converted. One of his charges is that their obedience to Christian precept is little more than lip service. In one mordant sentence he assails them for their self-congratulation 'because they do not publicly sacrifice to the gods'. His use of the word 'publicly' in this context may be significant, implying as it does that something might be going on out of public view. Indeed, despite the supposed conversion, there is evidence from Britain and the continent of a revival of Celtic paganism following the Romans' departure. The shrine of the Aeduan territorial deity Bibracte at what is now Mount Beuvray near Autun continued to be a place of pilgrimage (and remained one until the sixteenth century). *The Acts of St Vincent* contain a reference to a custom in Aquitaine in which a flaming wheel was rolled downhill into a river to extinguish itself in the water, whereafter it was reassembled 'in the temple of the god'. The flaming wheel can only be a sun symbol and reminds one of the wheels associated with Taranis.

Curative shrines such as Lydney Park, Farley Heath or Pagan's Hill remained open and those who managed and administered them may well have been pagans and, in that sense, successors of the old Druidic physicians.

*Peredur son of Evrawg* tells, in briefer form, the same story as Chrétien's unfinished *Perceval* and contains many of the same incidents. While it is true that *Perceval* was written in the twelfth century and the earliest extant version of *Peredur* was two centuries later, internal evidence suggests an earlier, possibly tenth-century date for the latter.

In one incident, Peredur, rejected by Angharad, vows he 'will speak to no Christian' until he has forced her to confess her love for him, and in a subsequent adventure he gives vanquished opponents the choice between death or baptism. If we agree to the tenth-century date for its committal to writing, the conclusion has to be that there were heathens to be found at that time.

While we have no indisputable evidence that such practices as human sacrifice were taking place, a third-century burial at Lankhills near Winchester contained a coffin, empty save for coins and the remains of two dogs. One had had its backbone bent backwards and its head bound to its tail to form a sort of rough circle. Nearby was a second grave containing the body of a young man with his severed head placed between his knees and a coin in his mouth. In the same context, we should perhaps remember that there is still some controversy about the age of the Lindow Moss body, with some experts claiming it dates from the third century of our own era.

# Chapter 10
# The Missionaries Arrive

The reversion to paganism was not limited to the Celtic areas of the former Roman empire. In the old Germanic provinces Odin and Thor were once more being invoked. Some have suggested that the apostasy of the fourth-century emperor Julian, who tried to reinstate the old Roman pantheon, created an encouraging climate, but his reign was surely too short for its effects to have been so far reaching.

In any case, as late as the sixth century, Gregory of Tours was lamenting the excesses of the Frankish King Chilperic and his brother Theudebert. Their crimes were said to have included the burning and sacking of churches, the theft of church vessels and violence to the religious and the clergy. What Gregory deplored was, in fact, merely symptomatic of the turmoil of the times and, according to ecclesiastical history, that the faith did not atrophy completely was due to the tenacious courage and fervour with which a minority held on to it.

At least as far as Britain was concerned its survival may actually have had rather more to do with the depth to which a large segment of the upper classes and intelligentsia had been romanised. Almost as a reflex, they had come to regard anything bearing the Roman imprimatur as immeasurably superior to the native product. The attitude of mind which produced images of the Celtic gods largely indistinguishable from Graeco-Roman ones had no difficulty in later convincing itself of the merits of Christianity and embracing it as part of Rome's civilising legacy. Among the most instructive of the loan words taken from Latin is that for 'church'. It comes from the Celtic *ciric* and is to be found in many place names; for example, Falkirk in Scotland, Kirkham in Lancashire and Dunkirk in France. The word adopted by the British and still in use in Wales was *eglwys*, plainly derived from the Latin *ecclesia*.

Further evidence of romanisation comes in the letters of St Gildas. Among those picked out for his vituperation was Maelgwyn, Christian King of Gwynedd, North Wales. The list of charges against him included maintaining what are obviously household bards. That their tales of full-blooded violence should be preferred to edifyingly insipid ones from Scripture or the lives of the saints was obviously reprehensible enough, but by employing them Maelgwyn was seen as abandoning civilised Roman in favour of primitive native usage. To make matters worse, it can hardly have escaped men like Gildas that the bards were continuing to regard themselves as successors to the Druids and, in some cases, were accepted as such and were, therefore, contributing to the perpetuation of heathenism. Many commentators see the ghosts of the Druids haunting even Christianity itself. During the fifth century the British-born monk and theologian Pelagius challenged the doctrine, promulgated by St Augustine of Hippo, that humans were so incorrigibly sunk in iniquity as to be incapable of winning redemption save by divine grace. Pelagius argued that such dependency merely absolved humans from all responsibility for their actions, since whether these were good or evil depended entirely on the granting or withholding of a grace over which they had no control. In such circumstances conduct was immaterial – the reason, he believed, for the lax morality found even in the Church. Though he would hardly have admitted to Druidic mediation, there is something close to their teachings in the idea of humans taking responsibility for their actions. It recalls Cailte's answer to St Patrick's question as to what had sustained them in the past: 'The truth that was in our hearts, the strength in our arms and the fulfilment in our tongues.'

In any event, Pelagius's critique of orthodox doctrine points both to an intellectual ferment in British Christianity and to a desire to make its teachings more reflective of the national temperament. One twentieth-century French Catholic commentator, Dom Louis Gougaud, has gone so far as to describe Pelagianism as 'the national heresy of the Britons'. This may have been one reason why Pelagius acquired such a tremendous following in his native land.

His views represented an acceptable compromise between old and new creeds and it could be said that one lesson to be learnt from the success of Pelagius was that the Church's teachings would find no acceptance as long as they continued to appear as survivals of Roman domination. Its greatest successes had been in Scotland and Ireland where, as early as the mid-second century, Tertullian of Carthage was writing that 'parts of Britain inaccessible to the Romans were indeed conquered for Christ'. Here the missionaries were coming into a society in which Druids were still active. Though we do not know exactly what changes had taken place in Druidism at that time or what powers its functionaries retained, there is every sign of considerable respect for them on the part of the missionaries.

Through these pages we have come across a number of instances where, even though the missionaries christianised them, they adopted practices from the Druids. They were probably imitated in matters of dress; possibly, too, in their way of praying, for whereas the orthodox mode was on the knees with clasped hands, members of the Gallican, or French Celtic Church, prayed standing with upraised arms, a gesture which Tacitus describes as that adopted by the Druids at Môn. That this was used in Britain is indicated by the remains of a fourth-century Roman villa at Lullingstone, Kent, four rooms of which had been converted into a 'house church'. A mural in one portrays a group praying standing up with upstretched arms and this method is still, in fact, used by the more fundamentalist Protestant sects of Northern Ireland. The missionaries may even have imitated the Druidic tonsure. In the sixth century it was one of the bones of contention between the Roman and Gallican churches of France. The monks of the former had taken to wearing the so-called 'tonsure of St Peter' in imitation of the saint's bald crown. The Gallicans, on the other hand, shaved a swathe of hair from ear to ear, with the hairline starting at the crown and the hair growing freely therefrom. According to an early Irish manuscript the Druids treated their hair similarly, leaving just one lock over the brow. It is illuminating that the Catholic Church condemned it as 'the tonsure of Simon Magus'. Simon Magus, strictly speaking Simon the Magus, was the magician denounced in *The Acts of the Apostles* for trying to bribe the apostles Peter and John into parting with the secret of transmitting the Holy Spirit by the laying-on of hands. Almost any practice with a magical or, as we might say, shamanistic tinge – one which could justifiably have been applied to Druidism – was linked by the church with Simon Magus.

Missionary emulation of the usages of the people they have come to proselytise are far from unusual. The seventeenth-century Jesuits who went to China adopted local dress and an argument as to whether ceremonies honouring Kung-Tzu – it was the Jesuits who latinised his name to 'Confucius' – were permissible as part of the liturgy was not finally resolved until Vatican II. Invariably, however, imitations occur where, as in China, the Church has to advance its claims against those of high intellectual calibre and can hope to win converts only if its missionaries can prove themselves their equals.

In Scotland and Ireland imitation seems to have extended even to church organisation. Unlike Britain, where authority resided with the bishop, here administration was in the hands of monks whose functions included the ordination of priests. Heading them was an abbot, said to be a 'nobly born' member of whatever tribe inhabited the area where the monastery was located. The sixth-century St Columkill, for example, born in Donegal, was a member of the royal clan of O'Neill. One recalls Caesar's assertion, borne out by the vernacular literature, that the Druids were drawn from the tribal aristocracies. Markale is probably right in regarding the monk-missionaries as 'Christian Druids' and their establishments as 'following directly in the tradition of the Druidic *bangor*'.

As to the actual buildings, they were in most cases little more than huts and primitive chapels built from whatever materials lay to hand. Here the monks lived, sang the offices and ventured forth to serve the community, teaching a theology so strictly biblical that, according to David Edwards, even the food regulations in the Old Testament were observed.

All the same, it was not quite all austere Christian primitivism, for it was from their rudimentary *scriptoria* that there issued those masterpieces, unmistakably in the great Celtic mould – the magnificently illuminated Bibles which represent some of the finest artistic achievements of the epoch.

It may or may not have been a direct result of imitation, but we know it was among the Druids and the *filid*, or bards, that the earliest converts were made. A *fili* named Dubtach became adviser to St Patrick and another, Fiacc, the first Irish-born bishop.

David Edwards sees other factors at work in bringing about such conversions. Some aspects of scripture must have seemed familiar to the Celts. For example, just as their own society was a tribal one given cohesion by a strong common culture based on their shared faith, so too was that of Ancient Israel.

This factor may have been contributory, but I believe there were two others. One was Christ's forty days and temptations in the wilderness, so like the shamanic crisis, which would have made him recognisable to the Druids as one like themselves. The second was the rebirth principle explicit in the Gospel and, specifically, its association with water as enunciated in St John's Gospel: 'Except a man be born of water and of the Spirit, he cannot enter into the kingdom of God'. We know the importance of water to Druidism and baptism recalls the vat drownings of victims dedicated to Toutatis. Even if one accepts Markale's hypothesis that the Gundestrup panel represents a Cauldron of Resurrection or de Vries's of an initiation ceremony, we surely have something analogous to baptism. At the same time, it is easy to paint an over-idealised picture of the situation in Scotland and Ireland. Tertullian was writing from afar and may well have heard inflated accounts of their own successes from the missionaries. Far from supposing that either country was peopled by hymn-singing converts of whom none were more ardent than the Druids, the evidence suggests that, side by side with the undoubted zeal among some, there was opposition and even violent hostility among others. The Battle of Cuil Dremne was fought in 561 between a group of Christian kings and the pagan Diarmait mac Cerbaill, and it is reported that Diarmait's Druids raised a fog which impeded the Christians until St Columba dispelled it. Later, while visiting the Pictish king at Inverness, the saint was threatened by a Druid with an 'adverse wind' and 'a mist of darkness'. There are also instances which prove the monasteries were not past adopting some of the excesses of the pagan society they had come to change, with the monks raiding one another's monasteries, sometimes for cattle or goods, sometimes for religious relics.

For all the following he attracted in his native country, Pelagius's questioning of accepted dogma rendered him heretical and, to counter his appeal, the eminently orthodox Bishop Germanus of Auxerre, accompanied by Bishop Lupus of Troyes, was sent to Britain in about 429. In characteristic phraseology we are told how the visitors, after first being exposed to the hostility of the assembled Pelagians, won them over with the superiority of their arguments.

During his visit, Germanus had an opportunity to witness at first hand how the turmoil of the times was affecting Britain. Even before the Romans' departure, coastal and riverside settlements had suffered from the sudden descents of seaborne raiders who raped the women, slaughtered the men and carried off anything portable, including such humans as might find a ready sale in the slave markets. This had necessitated a drastic reorganisation of the Roman command structure and a redeployment of forces which helped to bring about some reduction in the raids. Now largely unopposed, the raiders became ever more audacious with Picts from the north, Irish from the west and even the bishop's own countrymen, the Gauls, joining in from the south.

On the occasion of his visit the threat came from the fourth quarter, the east, where Saxon bands had landed. Before ordination Germanus had been a soldier and was invited to join an expedition against them. It is plain that the British forces were by no means entirely Christian for, we are told, as it was Lent the bishop used the opportunity to instruct them in the faith, baptising them on Easter Day. Still soaking from their immersion they advanced on the enemy, unarmed, but shouting 'Alleluia'. The Saxons, possibly concluding they were faced, not by an army, but a horde of madmen for which nothing in training or past experience had fitted them, quailed and fled. Victories against the German invaders were not always so easily won, or, in the end, won at all. Edwards suggests that one reason why the British were in no position to fend off the attackers was because of the devastation wrought among the battleworthy by an outbreak of bubonic plague in 549. It was certainly followed by fresh invasions from about 570.

As to how it was to defend itself there seems to have been basic agreement on one point. The original Roman conquest of the Celtic lands had been facilitated by the lack of a central, coordinating authority, making it possible to pick off the tribes one after another. Often, too, the Romans had been able to exploit intertribal jealousies. If the new invaders were not to be allowed similar advantages, it was vital to have unity.

Typically, there was fresh ground for disagreement as to how it was to be achieved. For one party it was a question of continuing along the lines the Romans had laid down – namely centralism. The other, represented by those who had waited 400 years for the restoration of the old kingdoms and who, in many cases, had re-established them, found themselves unable to stomach fresh sacrifices of power and freedom of action.

One can have some sympathy with both, but also understand why men like Gildas would see the turning away from Roman models and harking back to a more distant past as regression to the primitive as well as to a time when the weaknesses of division had been so costly. While unity remained elusive the raids increased in frequency and scope. When troubles overwhelm, like the man who tries to solve his immediate cash problem by recourse to the moneylender, the most immediate crisis may be solved by means which will bring other and more serious ones in its train. This is perhaps the justification for the behaviour of Vortigern. Ruler of the Cantii, the people of what is now Kent, he seems to have taken over responsibility for the defence of the whole of eastern Britain. Finding himself hard pressed by the Picts, he invited Saxon auxiliaries to augment his own depleted forces, offering them territories for settlement as an inducement. The decision, taken with the approval of the local *ordo* or council, a body set up by the Romans, nevertheless led to his later execration and his being accused, without evidence, of a number of other crimes. In the *Triads*, not only is he branded as one of the 'three arrant traitors of the Island of Britain', he is said to have murdered Constantine the Blessed and seized the crown.

In any event he had opened a door it was going to prove impossible to squeeze closed. In 442 his Saxon mercenaries rebelled and began seizing land for themselves. Settlements were established in Kent, Sussex and southern Hampshire, spread into Essex, East Anglia, Lindsey and the East Riding of Yorkshire, as well as inland along the upper Thames including what were to become the cities of Oxford and Cambridge.

Something, it is plain, had to be done. The first to take up arms against them was Ambrosianus Aurelius, usually regarded as a Roman who had remained in the country after most of his compatriots had left. Acclaimed king, he succeeded in binding the various factions in the country in some kind of military alliance and took the field, possessing a marked military advantage in that he had cavalry whereas the Saxon forces were made up entirely of infantry. A series of victories gained, he drew to his banner those who had wavered and the federation was still in being when he withdrew from active soldiering in about AD 500.

It is now that Arthur enters the scene, linked, according to the little we know of him, with a decisive victory at Mount Badon, a site never identified. He too seems to have led a confederacy of forces, for Nennius speaks of his fighting 'alongside the kings of the Britons'. This would fit with Celtic practice. Kings were prohibited from the battlefield, not only because their persons were sacrosanct, but also because in any pan-tribal military enterprise they would inevitably be identified with their own people. Hence, as discussed in the case of 'Brennus' and the march on Delphi, a war leader was chosen by an assembly of all the tribes involved which would explain the title of *dux bellorum*, leader of war, which Nennius gives Arthur.

Whether it was from the need to preserve a coalition, some of whose members were still pagan, or whether it was simply that such practices were attributed to the legendary Arthur by storytellers, he seems to have kept up ancient tradition. Besides his ritual marriage to the territorial goddess, Guinevere, the major court events are said to take place at Pentecost, coinciding with Beltaine.

His Mount Badon victory ushered in a period of peace lasting, we are told, for fifty years. At the same time, the British kingdom established a line in the west from Cornwall to Strathclyde which was probably the nearest the Celts of Britain ever came to nationhood. However, internecine dissent could not be silenced for long, enfeebling resistance and, after its short independent life, the British nation was extinguished largely as a result of what seems to have been a dynastic quarrel.

Nonetheless, in a number of ways, Saxon colonisation remained less than complete. Cumbria kept its independence as two kingdoms, Deira and Bernicia. Even Vortigern's former realm continued to be called the Land of the Cantii. In other areas the struggle against the invaders was continued by means of guerilla warfare, in some cases successfully enough to keep the Saxons out entirely, as in Wales. Even in England the area north of the Humber was not colonised for some years and that around Glastonbury not until 710–20.

Disputes among the conquerors themselves helped. Penda, the powerful Saxon king of Mercia, seized the territory of the West Saxon Hwicce people, and with Cadwallon, the British king of Gwynedd, as his ally, invaded Northumbria.

In the meantime, seaborne migrations from Britain were taking place. One colony was established in northern Spain where language and culture were preserved for several centuries until the migrants were finally absorbed into the existing population. Another migration had a closer destination, the west Gaulish peninsula, the old Armorica, which was to acquire the name of Brittany or Petit Bretagne from the newcomers. At the time it was largely depopulated, partly from the plague, partly because of exactions by the Romans in their last years and partly because constant raiders had forced most of its inhabitants to live within the more easily fortified cities.

Gildas paints a harrowing picture of the British fugitives bidding farewell to their native heath as they shuffled into exile to escape a cruel and rapacious occupier. Cruelty and atrocities there had undoubtedly been. So bitter were British feelings towards the people now called the English, they could not bring themselves to carry the Christian faith to them. The Welsh clergy, according to St Adhelm, would have no truck with any Englishman unless he came to take refuge with them. Even then he had first to do forty days penance for the sin of being English.

Besides the acts of wanton cruelty, there was a trade in slaves and the English are known so to have used many of the British who fell into their hands. But none of these crimes was one sided. Inquiring about the blond, fair-skinned slaves he saw being offered for sale in the Rome slave market, Bishop (later Pope) Gregory was told they were Angles, inspiring him to his quip that they looked more like angels. After seeing them he wrote to an agent asking him to buy any young Englishmen he came across for training in the monasteries.

In fact, the movement across the channel lamented by Gildas had begun much earlier as more and more inhabitants, particularly of Cornwall, sought to escape, not the Saxons, but the sea raiders, some of whom were their fellow Celts.

The much bigger later movement was, as Nora Chadwick says, carefully planned and organised to ensure it was orderly and that the rights of the earlier colonists were not infringed. An advance group was sent to make reception arrangements and only when these had been completed did the main body, Welsh and Cornish, embark. It appears to have been led by native chieftains, thereby recapitulating the migrations which centuries previously had taken the Celts through so much of Europe and beyond.

Large as the migration might have been, like all such movements it would have represented only a tiny proportion of the total population. The majority remained, doing what it had always done – tilling the soil from which it drew sustenance. The English newcomers were, of course, doing the same, and what would have begun as hostility must have settled first into a *de facto* truce, then into peace. Throughout history there have been times when the exigencies of the agricultural year have taken precedence. During the summer of 1940, when Hitler's armies were sweeping over the plains of France, here and there a German soldier, himself a son of the soil, would drop his Mauser, throw off his field-grey tunic and help the toilers in the fields.

There was even intermarriage, and not always among the humbler strata of society. The Northumbrian king Oswy married a British princess of the kingdom of Rheged.

The received picture of the life of the time is of heathen English and Christian Britons. We have seen that this was far from being the case. There were, however, numerous similarities between many of the Norse and Celtic beliefs about the supernatural, no doubt derived from their common Indo-European ancestry. *Tir na nOg*, the Land of Youth, may be compared with the *Odainsakr*, the Norse Land of Immortality. Those fortunate enough to go there either 'do not die, but live from generation to generation'. The thunder god Thor, especially in the alternative form of his name, Tanar, resembles Taranis. Jan de Vries compares In Dagda and Thor, the one with his club, the other with his hammer, *Mjöllnir*. Tyr, like Nuada, has lost a hand. The habit of Celtic gods of closing one eye brings to mind the fact that Odin exchanged one of his to gain the secret of magic from Mimir's well of wisdom. He also bears several striking similarities to Lugh. Both are connected with poetry, are guardians of the highway and patrons of travellers and commerce (Roman writers like Tacitus actually called Odin Mercury). Odin's Valkyries, rather than the serene figures of later literature, were actually blood-thirsty demons of battle and slaughter, resembling the Babd.

There are also many common elements in the myths of Lugh and Woden. (It has also been pointed out by a number of writers that Odin is blind in one eye, as is Cu Chulainn, son of Lugh.) The German god hangs from the World Tree, is wounded by a spear and, after winning the precious mead of poetic inspiration, turns into an eagle. Lugh, as the Welsh Lleu, is struck by a spear, hangs on a tree and flies off as an eagle. The spear serves, too, as their favourite weapon and both make often unscrupulous use of magic. Woden, like Gwynn ap Nudd, is associated with a wild hunt.

The list of correspondences could be extended almost infinitely and it is therefore to be expected that there would have been some syncretisation between the autochthonous population and incomers. Besides English place names commemorating Germanic gods, such as Woden in the name Wednesbury, there is another group, fewer in number, where a Celtic godname is incorporated into an Anglo-Saxon matrix. Examples are Billingshurst in Sussex and Billingsgate in London which contain a mutated form of the name Belinus.

From some points of view it could be said that, where left alone, the signs are that the two populations found a perfectly acceptable *modus vivendi*.

# Chapter 11

# Conversion Completed

The regression to paganism had not gone unnoticed by the Church which, as soon as it could summon resources, embarked on a campaign of reconversion. In 597 its legates reached England in the person of St Augustine, whose mission is traditionally supposed to have been prompted by Pope Gregory's sighting of the fair English slaves. What Augustine was to find was an extremely complex situation. As far as one can unravel the threads, there was a basically Celtic population, a large part of which was either still holding or had lapsed into its old beliefs, while another had embraced Christianity in varying degrees of ardour. Some of these had become Christians during the Roman occupation. At the time of his conversion Constantine's capital was not Rome, but Byzantium, the present Istanbul, and his Christianity was of the Eastern Orthodox kind. Its introduction in Britain may account for the traces of Eastern practice and liturgy to be found in the christianised versions of Arthurian legend. This was, and has remained, very different from the Roman Catholicism which Augustine and his monks had come to preach.

Living more or less cheek by jowl with the British were the English settlers. In spite of the reluctance of the British Christians to mount any evangelising effort among them, the English had not been allowed totally to wallow in heathenism. Missionaries had come from the churches of Ireland and Scotland who, having had no direct experience of them as cruel, pitiless enemies, felt no bitterness towards them. Their converts were therefore absorbed into a distinctive Celtic church, though this too had absorbed some of the eastern liturgical practices via the Romans.

Though the Anglo-Saxons had moved into Britain as militant pagans, at the time of St Augustine's arrival this attitude was undergoing modification – for good reason. In the early fifth century the Franks had made themselves masters of Gaul, thereby becoming the most formidable power in Europe. Pagan like the English, in 498 their king, Clovis, had accepted baptism and he and his successors had thrown their enthusiastic support behind the Church's reconversion drive. Hence, any action against it risked incurring the Franks' wrath.

The ripples crossed the Channel when King Ethelbert of Kent married Bertha, Christian daughter of Charibert, the Frankish king of Paris. She brought to her new home at Canterbury Bishop Liudard who set up his oratory in a small Roman-built church just outside the city walls. It was, therefore, on to a congenial shore that Augustine and his forty monks stepped when they arrived from Rome. Nonetheless, it was not thought to be an entirely safe one, for, according to the twelfth-century Henry of Huntingdon's *Historia Anglorum*, the first meeting between Augustine and the king took place in the open air as both parties feared Druidic enchantments if it were held within four walls.

Pope Gregory's slave-market peregrinations and the reconversion campaign had been only two in a number of interdependent factors leading to Augustine's dispatch. David Edwards mentions the belief current in Rome that the entire British church had become indolent and had sunk so low in esteem that even its most extreme sanction of excommunication, in certain circumstances equivalent to the damnation of the anathematised, failed to arouse awe. But, to the papacy, what made the church in Britain particularly suspect was its sturdy, confident and frequently exhibited sense of independence which made it difficult to keep under control. It was a situation Rome wanted rectified as soon as possible, on the declared ground that unless the British churchmen were prepared to accept the guidance of a greater and wiser church, they lived in the ever-present danger of a lapse into a heresy like that of Pelagius.

This independent spirit had, to a considerable extent, fed on the isolation in which its native church had for so long existed and was content to exist. Its leaders could argue that, having solved their own problems, whether of faith, morals or administration, in their own way, they had found their solutions perfectly acceptable and saw no reason to abandon them. In addition there must also have been that Celtic conviction, the conviction which had provoked the laughter at Delphi, that they retained a purity of belief others had lost. It was to survive through the history of Celtic Christianity in all its shades, whether in Scotland, Wales, Brittany or in Ireland, North or South. One cannot helping agreeing with Toynbee that, rather than taking an alien religion as they found it and allowing it to break up their native tradition, the Celts had a special gift for reshaping it to fit their own heritage. As Ernest Renan, put it, 'No race showed such originality in its way of taking Christianity'.

But isolation and independence had its reverse side, too: lack of dialogue with the Church at large had stunted intellectual growth. Nonetheless, with the normal human unwillingness to admit to failings, the Welsh clergy whom Augustine tried to win over to his own brand of Christianity bluntly rejected his arguments. At the same time, possibly because of the lingering embers of the old hatred for the Saxons, they were equally uncompromising in their refusal to join forces with him in his mission to the English.

Undeterred, Augustine, his monks and the various reinforcements dispatched from Rome launched their crusade. Yet, for all this evangelising effort, the majority of the population still proved obstinately recalcitrant. Not only Augustine and his fellow labourers, but several generations of their successors had come and gone before it could be claimed that even the English kings and the nobility had been won. And almost every court reverted to paganism at some point and had to be reconverted. As David Edwards points out, as far as the countryside was concerned, it was 'a question of centuries'. The vacillation of royalty and the nobility can largely be explained by those political motives which had prompted many of them to accept conversion in the first place – Frankish power. When the situation demanded conciliation, an appearance of devout Christianity was given. The crisis past or the Frankish gaze averted, the old gods were invoked once more.

A good example is to be found in Ethelbert's Kentish kingdom. Having embraced the new creed himself, he showed all the zeal of the converted. He passed laws by which theft of the bishop's property was to be made good elevenfold, whereas the theft of royal property required only ninefold restitution. He also did his best to persuade his brother kings to convert. One of them was Redwald, King of the East Angles, who accepted baptism while on a state visit to Canterbury. Back in his own realm, Redwald's queen not only refused baptism, but persuaded her husband to limit his own religious activity to the installation of a Christian altar beside the pagan one in his private chapel. Many believe the Sutton Hoo ship burial near Woodbridge, Suffolk, one of the richest Germanic graves in Europe, to be Redwald's, whose funeral rites show him to have died a pagan or, at any rate, show that his family were anxious to make it appear he had.

When Ethelbert himself died, his son and successor Eadbald renounced Christianity as did the sons of Sebert, the king of the East Saxons (what is now Essex). Among the British, Urien, King of Rheged, patron of Taliesin, was probably a pagan as were many of his British contemporaries.

Nonetheless, Augustine's failure to enlist the native church behind his banner and the fact that the English had been allowed to remain largely unconverted before his arrival actually had one positive advantage: it meant that his new converts were definitively won for Rome.

In fact, relations between his own and Celtic churches had on the whole been amicable, though there were differences. These tended to increase as each went its own way more and more and, as was inevitable, ultimately came to a head. The cause was an outwardly minor issue: the dating of Easter. To settle this and other matters a Synod, with delegates from both communions, was held at Whitby to decide whether Roman Catholic or Celtic usage should prevail. The decision went in the Catholics' favour largely because Oswy, the Christian king of Northumbria, gave his support to their side. Since his realm had been converted by Celtic missionaries led by St Aidan, this can only have come as a shock, even a defection, clearing the way, as it did, to a Catholic ascendancy. It was made absolute when Theodore of Tarsus was sent to Canterbury to reorganise the church on the Roman system with metropolitan sees both in his own city and at York. Only the Scots, while accepting the new dating of Easter from the eighth century, continued as an independent church until the eleventh.

Among other questions which came under scrutiny at Whitby were several which seem to illustrate the continuing influence of Byzantine Orthodoxy. They included, for example, the administration of the communion in both kinds, that is to say bread and wine, whereas only the bread, in the form of the unleavened wafer, was administered in the Catholic church. There were others, specifically Celtic, which demonstrate its uniqueness. Particularly damnable in Catholic eyes was the use of *conhospitiae*: women who, in some places, actually dispensed the communion. Supposedly abandoned after the Synod of Whitby, its continuation is proved by extant sixth-century letters denouncing it, written by the bishops of the province of Tours to Breton clergy.

Given the tenacity of paganism and the fact that, even in those areas supposedly won for the Church, relics were doggedly surviving, a change in the dating of Easter, if known of at all by the majority of the population or even the rural parish priest, can only have seemed uniquely abstruse and irrelevant. As subsequent history shows, it had little effect on traditional custom and belief. Just how intractable these were has been shown by some of the examples in these pages.

To begin with every attempt was made to stamp out every last trace of paganism. As early as the Council of Arles in 314 an edict condemning the veneration of trees, fountains and stones was passed and was reiterated by the Council of Tours in 567 and again by the Council of Nantes in 658. Those who flouted warnings were liable to excommunication. The secular powers joined the ecclesiastical by adding laws and sanctions of their own. In Gaul, Charlemagne and, in England, Canute conducted campaigns against all survivals of pagan worship. Since neither was a Celt we may suspect that their motives, as with the decrees against the Welsh bardism passed by Henry IV during the rebellion of the Owain Glyndwyr, were also aimed at suppressing Celtic nationalist aspirations.

In any event, spiritual and temporal prohibition failing to produce results, other methods were adopted. The author of *The Life of St Samson* tells us it was the sixth-century holy man's custom to pay an annual pastoral visit to the island of Guernsey, then part of his diocese of Dol. On one such occasion he made a point of arriving on New Year's Day, which the islanders insisted on celebrating 'according to the vile custom of their fathers'. The writer goes on to tell us that out of affection for their bishop the Guernesiais agreed to abandon it.

Another time, travelling through rural Cornwall, he came across a group enacting a play in honour of what the writer calls an 'idol', but which appears to have been a standing stone. Admonished, they pleaded that 'it was not wrong to celebrate the mysteries of their progenitors in play', but were won over when St Samson miraculously restored to health a boy injured in a fall from a horse. However, to make assurance doubly certain, before departing he carved a cross on the stone.

In Brittany, where standing stones are abundant, the practice of christianising by disfiguring became common. A rough cross was carved on one at Trégastel and on its face were carved representations of the instruments of the Passion which for centuries afterwards were picked out in lurid colours. At Pouancé, a hole was cut through the stone and an image of the Virgin Mary inset. The ineffectiveness of all such devices is shown by the fact that down the centuries infertile Breton couples continued to turn to the menhirs for a cure, and young women rubbed their naked bodies against them in the hope of a husband.

Baring-Gould records the strange history of the 'Venus' of Quinipili, a two metre high stone statue of a naked woman which was the centre of a cult in the Lannion area of Brittany. Among its properties was that of easing labour pains, so that pregnant women from all over the duchy had recourse to it. Attempts to abolish these practices were still continuing in the seventeenth century when the Count of Lannion transferred it from the mound on which it had always stood to the courtyard of his château.

As it continued to attract veneration on its new site, the Bishop of Vannes ordered its destruction and, in 1660, the count had it mutilated and thrown into a local river. A drought and the failure of the corn crop the next year was blamed on this mistreatment and in 1664 peasants dragged it on to the bank and, in spite of its damaged state, revived its cult. In 1670 yet another attempt was made to destroy it and it was rolled into the river. In 1696, a new Count of Lannion had it brought to the surface again, intending to use it as a piece of garden statuary. The locals, unwilling that it should be placed out of their reach in this way, sued and, having lost, continued to venerate it by the expedient of breaking into the castle grounds.

It has been contended that the Church had, in some measure, brought such problems on itself by choosing to regard the old gods, not as fictions which would vanish before the light of Gospel truth, but as spiritual realities, albeit evil ones. Having convinced themselves that the gods were the denizens of Satan's kingdom, it is as if, influenced by the images presented by writers like Lucan, they had then persuaded themselves they must have been worshipped out of superstitious terror of their powers. They had not. They were actually loved. A Breton woman encountered by Evans Wentz invoked a blessing on the name of Viviane. She was 'as good as she was beautiful', his informant told him, and went on to describe how she had saved the life of her husband, a woodcutter by day who made family ends meet with a little nocturnal poaching. Spotted by armed gamekeepers, they had fired at him as he tried to flee, hitting him in the thigh. He fell, and while he lay waiting for seizure and possibly death, a thick mist interposed itself between himself and his pursuers. A gentle voice urged him to save himself, promising concealment till he had crawled home.

Baring-Gould, himself an Anglican divine, discusses the dilemma faced by the country clergy. Experience had shown that compulsion invariably failed and that the priest who endorsed it simply brought the odium of his flock down on his head. As a consequence he was forced to use his own discretion. In addition there was the ignorance factor. Throughout the Middle Ages, the clergy was drawn mainly from the peasantry. Coming from families whose means were insufficient to pay for university study, the novice-priest picked up the rudiments of theology and a modicum of church Latin from his village priest. Ordained, he brought to his calling prejudices and superstitions little different from those of his congregation.

In the end the Church was forced to adopt a policy of 'if you can't beat 'em, join 'em'. Oak groves, with their markedly Druidic overtones, were rededicated to the Virgin Mary, who also received a number of distinctly strange titles: not only Our Lady of the Briars, Our Lady of the Pines and even Our Lady of the Nettles, but also Our Lady of the Waters and, most Druidic of all, Our Lady of the Mounds and Our Lady of the Menhirs. The great festivals were allowed to continue, but now under the patronage of a suitable saint.

At the same time many of the gods were canonised. Brigid became 'Saint' Bridget, and Ana, as 'Saint Anne', became patron saint of Brittany. (It should be pointed out that many believe there was an actual St Bridget. Her story, according to which she was sold as slave to a Druid whom she converted and later refused to marry the King of Ulster, has elements of legend, but this does not detract from her historicity. Such legends have gathered around the heads of many historically-attested saints.) The smith god Govannon ap Don became St Govan in Scotland, St Gobain in France. Mabon ap Modron, the Young Son, reached the *Book of Saints* as the legendary builder of the church at Llanfabon (or Llan-mabon) in the parish of that name on the eastern border of Glamorganshire. Bran becomes 'Bran Bendigeit' or Bran the Blessed, though this may have been due to a confusion between the obsolete word *benedight*, blessed, and the Celtic word for head, *ben*. The historical existence of a Brendan, born in Tralee, County Kerry about AD 484 is not in doubt. Nor is there any doubt that he, like many later Celts, was a great traveller and explorer (among his destinations were the Canary Islands). On the other hand, many of the marvellous places which the tenth-century *Navigatio Brendani* claims he visited owe more to *imramma* like that of Bran than to history. Nor can one help wondering if the various forms of his name under which he is commemorated, for example as 'St Brelade' in Jersey and 'St Broladre' in Brittany, do not recall the god rather than the saint.

No translation to the company of the saints was made by Cernunnos who, as the horned, Underworld 'hunter of souls' seemed naturally cast for the role of Satan though, as a matter of fact, his outline is plainly detectable as the Breton St Cornély, patron saint of horned animals.

In many ways, the Church's attitudes to paganism were highly ambivalent. Pigs, recurrent in Celtic as in many other Indo-European mythologies, were used to indicate places where churches should be built. When looking for a site for his church in Wye, St Dubricius used a pig. One must suppose that the animal was thought to be particularly sensitive to those places where the supernatural forces were at their most potent. It is the pursuit of a white boar that brings Pryderi and then his mother, Rhiannon, to the Castle of the Golden Bowl.

Ambivalence extended particularly to pagan knowledge. The princes of the Church, no less than the wealthier laity, eagerly resorted to Arab and Jewish doctors and there is evidence that British Christians had no qualms at all about consulting those who drew their knowledge from the Druidic font.

This is illustrated in the life of St Samson. Anna, wife of Amon, a nobleman of Gwynedd, North Wales, has failed to produce a child. The couple hear of a 'wise man' in the remote north and resolve to consult him. While he is not described as a pagan, neither is he accorded the tribute to his piety usual in such contexts. In any case, as we have seen, much of the north was pagan at that time. The text calls him a *librarius*, probably a latinisation of the Welsh *llyfrawr* which meant a prophet-magician. He tells Anna that she will have a child, that he is to be called Samson and would be 'an holy and a high priest before Almighty God'. The couple stay overnight at his dwelling in what Tolstoy suggests was probably an 'incubation chamber' like those at Lydney Park and elsewhere.

Next day, the master repeats his assertion, adding that 'at the proper time' he is to be handed over 'to be taught knowledge'. In due course a son is born. At the age of five he expresses a desire 'to go to the school of Christ'. Despite hesitation on the father's part he is handed over to the care of 'the famous master of the Britons, Illtyd by name'. Besides being a priest, Illtyd is versed in geometry, rhetoric, grammar and arithmetic and all theories of philosophy. As we have seen, rhetoric was particularly associated with Druids and, even more significantly, he is said to be 'a most wise magician, having knowledge of the future'. In any event, the community founded by St Illtyd became one of the great international centres of Celtic Christianity.

Suspicion of Druidic mediation is supported by incidents in St Samson's own life. The sixth-century Breton monk-bard Huarvé is said to have aided him in his struggle against the usurper Duke Conmore. Having assembled the 'six saints of Brittany', the group, led by Huarvé, ascended a hill on which a thorn tree grew and, with their backs to it, uttered a curse. From the description, which comes from a biography of Huarvé, it is plain that this was the *glam dicin*.

There were actually seven saints of Brittany: Samson, Malo, Tugdual, Brioc, Paul de Léon, Corentin and Padarn. However, on this occasion St Samson probably took no part. Since he does not appear to have been among the six saints one might say that St Samson was permitting rather than participating in pagan practice. There are other instances where this defence fails. When attempting to cure a monk who had been bitten by a poisonous snake, he was accused by his superior of using magical means. What was involved is not explained, though we are told that the saint persisted in his unorthodox cure and that it was successful.

Even more reminiscent of magic is the means by which he destroyed a serpent. He first drew a circle round it from which, as is the nature of magic circles, the reptile was unable to escape. At the end of the day St Samson ordered it to die, invoking the name of Jesus Christ. The writer tells us: 'At once the serpent stood on its tail, and raising its head aloft, and absurdly making a bow of itself, cast forth all its venom and was dead.'

These legends of serpent mastery, the most famous of which is attached to St Patrick, have pagan echoes. In the Irish *Cattle Raid of Fraech*, one impediment to recovering the stolen animals is the serpent guardian of the courtyard where they are stabled. However, at the bidding of Fraech's principal companion, Conall Cernach, it leaps into his belt, enabling them to perform the rescue. Thereafter Conall releases the serpent and, as the writer says, 'neither did harm to the other'. Ross equates Conall Cernach with Cernunnos, who is shown on the Gundestrup Cauldron grasping a ram-headed serpent in his left hand.

As we know, every attempt to suppress the traces of the past or control them by superficial christianising had limited success. They survived, not just side by side, but in conjunction with Christian belief. This is by no means unusual. Tribes of North American Indians who were won over to Christianity practised their new religion with a devotion and zeal far greater than that to be found among the people from whom the missionaries had come, while keeping up most of their old practices.

And there are parallels nearer home. In the 1970s Dr Anne Ross came across communities, not in the fastnesses of Wales, Scotland or Ireland, but in Derbyshire and Cheshire, maintaining and passing from generation to generation the ancient Celtic traditions. She has evidence of similar groups in the Scottish Highlands and believes that others are to be found outside Britain. Though the names of gods are known among them and traditions such as the cult of the severed head remembered, these are not seen as in any way conflicting with Christian beliefs and practices.

In Britain, successively conquered by Romans, Anglo-Saxons, Danes and Normans, the Celtic tradition also provided a rallying point for nationalism and continued to do so throughout subsequent history.

With so much of the past, the stories survived, but now with names from scripture or Christian myth replacing the pagan ones.

Yet in its war against the survival of paganism there was one device which had not so far been adopted. It was one which men like Clement of Alexandria had used as early as the second century, and consisted in transforming pagan mythological tales into Christian allegories. In Homer's *Odyssey*, Odysseus, to prevent his crew from being lured on to the rocks by the Sirens' song, orders them to fill their ears with wax while he himself is tied to the mast. The incident was used by Clement to demonstrate how the Christian can sail past the temptations of the world as long as he ties himself securely to the cross of Christ, the 'mast' of the Church which is itself often likened to a ship.

It was one device which the Church in the west was much slower to adopt.

# Chapter 12
# The Genesis of Arthurian Myth

But adopted it was – in the form of the stories of the legendary King Arthur, the knightly prince *sans peur et sans reproche*. They were to seize such a hold on the imagination of countless generations that many came to believe in the reality not only of the characters, but even of the incidents and objects in them. Perfectly serious expeditions were mounted to find the Holy Grail, for example.

One of the more recent was launched under the sponsorship of the Nazi SS at the height of the war. The story known to every German of the Teutonic Knights who conquered the pagans occupying the area that became Prussia was one so well contrived to serve the ideology of National Socialism that even Hitler's unheroic lineaments were portrayed in the armour of a Teutonic knight. It was no doubt the pseudo-mystical ideas derived from such sources that had played their part in his urge to acquire the Spear of Destiny.

One of the people most imbued with these fantasies was Himmler, the Reichsführer-SS, who, in an effort to make legend reality, inaugurated his *Ahnenerbe*, or Ancestry Institute, recruiting to its ranks such German archaeologists as were prepared to risk attaching their names to its fatuities.

In 1933, the year of Hitler's accession to power, Otto Rahn had published his *Kreuzzug gegen Gral* or Crusade Against the Grail. Using Wolfram's *Parzival* as his basis, Rahn advanced the thesis that the Grail was part of a fabled treasure said to have belonged to the heretical thirteenth-century Cathars, or Albigensians, of southern France and, furthermore, that their last stronghold at Mont Ségur was the original Grail Castle. Ever since the time of their annihilation by Catholic forces in 1244 stories of an undiscovered Cathar treasure buried on the mountain had persisted and, in the version taken over by Rahn, this included the Grail itself.

One of his principal pieces of evidence was that at the time of its subjugation the warden of Mont Ségur was a Raymond de Pereilhe and that, when rendered into Latin, this became Perilla, coinciding with the name Wolfram von Eschenbach gives to his custodian of the Grail castle.

It was on this flimsy basis that several futile and expensive months were spent in excavations by an *Ahnenerbe* party. According to René Nelli, the leading scholar of Catharism, during a conclave of German archaeologists at the castle in 1944, a Luftwaffe aircraft flew over and traced the outline of a Greek cross in smoke in the sky!

The same accretion of gossip and legend expanded from mere shadows of history obviously surrounds the principal character of the stories, Arthur himself. The theories are many and various. It has been suggested that he and Ambrosianus Aurelius were one and the same person, a Roman professional soldier. In the period leading up to their withdrawal, the occupiers, concerned at the increasing temerity of seaborne raiders, had reorganised their four military provinces into three. Ambrosianus/Arthur may have held command of one of these and, when the army was withdrawn, stayed on, hiring out the services of his mercenary band to any British king ready to employ them. Such successes as they enjoyed came about partly because of their Roman military training, but also because, as indicated previously, they fought as a cavalry unit, whereas the Saxons fought on foot.

According to another theory, Ambrosianus and Arthur were separate individuals, the latter being Ambrosianus's successor. Others take the fact that even the majority of Latin authors use the British form 'Arthur' as evidence that he was a native.

The seventh century Welsh poem *Y Gododdin*, ascribed to the bard Aneirin, which contains the first reference to Arthur, tells of a defeat inflicted on the Britons by the Angles at Catterick, Yorkshire, and may have a historical basis. (Among the casualties of the battle, according to the poem, was Peredur.)

In such supposedly contemporary accounts as we have, Arthur is by no means always presented in a noble light. The early twelfth-century *Life of St Cadoc* tells how he and his troop invaded the abbey of Llancarfan to demand the handing over of a man who had taken sanctuary after killing three of Arthur's men. The monks refused, but offered compensation. Arthur asked for a herd of cows, specifying that they must be half red and half white, a stipulation which makes them sound very much like Otherworld animals. The monks agreed and the handover took place at a ford – another location with Otherworld associations. However, as the animals were crossing they miraculously turned into clumps of fern. Arthur, though angry at being thwarted, realises that the powers from on high are teaching him a lesson and agrees to allow the fugitive to remain at the abbey, according to custom, for 'seven years, seven months and seven days'. Such physical changes as these are, of course, to be found in the myths. In the Welsh *Math ap Mathonwy*, Gwyddion persuades Pryderi to exchange his pigs for the stallions he has magicked into existence but which preserve their equine forms for only twenty-four hours.

In another twelfth-century story Arthur steals the miraculous altar of St Carrannog which has the magical quality of also serving as a boat. Arthur returns the altar in exchange for the saint's prayers to help destroy an enormous serpent which is laying the region waste.

In the more or less contemporary *Life of St Padarn* Arthur steals a tunic, a precious relic, which the saint has been sent by the Patriarch of Jerusalem. As he tries to escape with it the earth opens and he is swallowed up to the chin. St Padarn offers rescue only if Arthur solemnly begs the pardon of heaven. Though the miraculous interventions occurring in these stories plainly indicate that they are apocryphal, most resistance leaders down to our own times have found themselves forced to live at the margins of legality and not infrequently to cross it. Thus Arthur's acceptance of the monastic cattle and his thefts – assuming they ever occurred – is in the tradition of partisan leaders throughout history.

Lastly, there is the belief that he was an actual king, probably Cornish with a court at Kelliwic, while Camlann, the site of his final battle and defeat, has been located in the principality. In *The Discovery of Arthur* Geoffrey Ashe has gone much further and equates Arthur with Riothamus, the 'Great King' from 'over the water' who allied himself with the Burgundian king, Gundioc, against the invading Goths. The corollary to this is that the stories of Arthur's continental campaigns mentioned by Geoffrey of Monmouth and by subsequent authors have a basis in fact. Ashe suggests that some time after his defeat at the hands of the Goths in about 470, Riothamus (or Arthur) died and was buried, not at the Avalon usually identified with Glastonbury in Somerset, but at Avallon near Vézelay in Burgundy.

This is not the place for an exhaustive discussion of Arthur's existence, though perhaps on balance it is difficult not to agree with Jean Markale who, in *Le roi Arthur*, writes: 'Despite the brevity of our information, despite that aura of legend which masks him from our

eyes, we are tempted to declare as a certainty his real existence . . .
There is, to be sure, no indisputable proof, but there are too many
facts, too many coincidences, too many memories for one to believe
he is simply the mythical creation of the human mind.'

One thing is indisputable: whether or not a real Arthur ever existed
and even if he was Geoffrey Ashe's Great King Riothamus, the reality
bears little relation to the legend and it is the latter who has had the
most enduring influence. The question is: where did he and his
stories come from?

With the Arthurian, as with other Celtic matter, we do not have
a single source, even if now lost, from which the rest derived. We have
a plethora of sources. These must have been the property of
unknown bards who retained them principally in oral form, passing
them from mouth to mouth. Finally they were committed to writing
and were passed to authors like Chrétien and Wolfram who are
known to us by name and works, but who were, nonetheless,
separated geographically and by language. Accordingly, there is wide
disparity. For example, where others are unanimous in describing
the Grail as a vessel of some description, in Wolfram's *Parzival* it is
a precious stone, the sparkling and radiant *lapsit exillis* borne by a
young queen, daughter of a line of royal custodians chosen by the
Grail itself. As this does not occur elsewhere it suggests that Wolfram
used a different source.

Sir Galahad does not turn up until the thirteenth century when he
figures in the Vulgate cycle of Arthurian stories. Because of his late
appearance and his Hebrew-sounding name, Markale suggests that
he may have been borrowed from one of the numerous apocryphal
scriptures. In fact, the name plainly derives from the comparatively
rare Gaelic word for 'beauty', *ghalad* pronounced gal-a-ad. He is as
definitively Celtic as his adventure and must come from an
authentic, now lost version.

Also from the thirteenth century is the earliest reference to the
incident of the sword in the stone, which is first found in Robert de
Boron. Yet, rather than a late interpolation or piece of imagination,
he seems to be recording what may well have been an Indo-European
rite in the choosing of kings. Theseus, King of Athens, discovers the
symbols of royalty, sandals and a sword, under a stone near his
birthplace, Troezen. A sword plunged into a rock is shown on a relief
portraying a sacred marriage found at the Hittite capital, Hattusa,
now Bogazköy in modern Turkey.

It is generally thought that the Jerseyman Wace used Geoffrey of Monmouth as his base text and that the Round Table, not mentioned by Geoffrey, was his own invention. However, there is reason to believe that he was referring to established Celtic practice. Though tables, as part of ordinary daily life, were a comparatively late innovation, at the great feasts such as are described in Irish myths like *Bricriu's Feast*, specially honoured guests seem to have been accommodated at individual tables arranged round a central, raised one reserved for the king. As Marx points out, in *Bricriu's Feast* there are twelve such tables. Wace's reference to an actual custom, but one not found in earlier authors, suggests that he too had access to yet another, so far unknown source. This may have been one of several earlier metrical versions of the stories now existing only as fragments of manuscripts.

However great the diversity, the first thing that strikes one when setting the Arthurian matter within the corpus of Celtic mythology as a whole are the innumerable correspondences with, for example, the Irish epics. Excalibur is Fergus's Caladbolg. Guinevere has her Irish counterpart in Finnabair, the daughter of Aillil of Connaught and his Otherworld queen, Mebd. Incidents like the reciprocal beheading theme in the story of Gawain and the Green Knight recur in the incident of Cu Chulainn and Uath mac Imoman.

Even more striking is the resemblance between the Knights of the Round Table and members of the Irish and Scottish *fianna* such as that of Finn mac Cumhail in the Fenian cycle. The *fianna* were bands of young men, drawn primarily from the warrior nobility, who lived away from the main population centres, subsisted by hunting and, to some extent, seemed to have fulfilled a kind of unofficial policing function.

The correspondences between *fianna* and the Round Table of knights are due to more than the fact that both were engaged in much the same sort of activities and came from the same cultural milieu, Celtic heroic society. (There is, of course, another such body: Robin Hood and his band of outlaws who are strongly reminiscent especially of the Fenians.) They are so numerous as to show either that one was copied from the other or that they derived from a single, common source. Thus, for example, both Arthur and Finn have dogs with a supernatural acuity and an important incident in both Irish and British cycles is the hunting of a magic boar.

As the Irish stories are older, one might suspect copying. For example, in the case of *Kulhwych and Olwen*, the first prose tale in which Arthur appears, his entourage contains a number of identifiable Irish heroes and gods. All the same, the weight of evidence has to be in favour of a common source. There are, to begin with, a number of instances where an Irish and a Welsh story, superficially dissimilar, prove on closer scrutiny to coincide on so many points that they must once have been a single one. The Irish Lugh is the son of Ethliu, the daughter of the Fomorian giant, Balor. His grandson kills him with a sling-stone in the eye during the great battle between the Fomorians and Tuatha de Danann. On the surface the only point of coincidence between this and the Welsh *Kulhwych* is that giants are involved, Balor in the one, Ysbaddaden in the other. The hero of *Kulhwych* is not a grandson, but a suitor of the giant's daughter. It could also be argued that there is no battle in *Kulhwych*. However, there is the terrible hunt of the boar Twrc Trwyth which takes on the aspect of a running battle. The death of both is encompassed by a young hero. If any man takes Ysbaddaden's daughter from him – as Kulhwych does – he is doomed to die, as Balor dies at the hand of Lugh. Furthermore, during a series of angry exchanges between prospective son- and father-in-law, a stone spear Ysbaddaden hurls is thrown back at him and hits him in the eye.

The stone of which Ysbaddaden's spear is made provides another similarity. The battle with the Fomorians is regarded as a mythologised account of the victory of an iron-using people over one still using weapons of stone. When the similarities are compared one can see that Balor and Ysbaddaden, both giants, both with characteristics recalling the Neolithic past, are both linked with a hero, both ultimately die through his intervention and both are struck in the eye with a stone missile.

Even better as evidence for a common source are the innumerable motifs common to the Indo-European mythologies which have turned up through these pages and whose recurrence in the Arthurian stories is evidence of their high antiquity. That they also contain relics of old Druidic hierophanies is shown by the way in which gods and incidents turn up and are recognisable even in Medieval retellings, despite differences in context or the corruption of names.

Thus, for example, R.S. Loomis has ingeniously and conclusively shown the Lancelot of the Lake of the Medieval romances to be the god Lugh. His mother, 'The Lady of the Lake', later becomes

'Viviane', but may well be the Welsh goddess Rhiannon, giving circumstantial support to Tolstoy's identification of Mabon ap Modron as the youthful Lugh and to Triad 124 in which Rhiannon rather than Arianrhod is said to be his mother. It may even have been a scribal error that made Rhiannon into Viviane. In Malory the horsewoman who bursts into Arthur's court is called 'The Lady of the Lake', but in the Huth Merlin she is 'Rhiannon'.

Her Irish counterpart, the Morrigan, has already been identified as Morgan le Fée, demonstrating by the role she plays the ambivalent and capricious nature which characterises her in the Irish matter.

The Fisher-King who appears under a diversity of names ranging from Anfortas in Wolfram von Eschenbach to Pelinor and King Bron in other versions, is certainly a god. Anfortas has been defined as a corrupt form of a word meaning 'infirm' which describes the Fisher-King's condition.

Pelinor, as well as other versions of his name such as Pelles, Pellehan and even Wolfram's Perilla bring to mind Pwyll in *Pwyll Lord of Dyved*. Pwyll is a god of the Underworld and, this being the source of wealth, may account for the riches attributed to the Fisher-King. But he has also been identified as Nodens. The Irish form of his name, Nuada, has been traced to a root *nuta*, meaning fisher, and his links with the sea are supported by a mosaic at Lydney Park showing tritons surrounded by marine monsters and fish.

King Bron plainly derives from Bran who is also King Ban of Benoic or Benwick, both corruptions of Bran Bendigeit. It is on account of a wound which renders him sexually impotent that Bran asks his comrades-in-arms to decapitate him, his head providing them with eighty-seven years of companionship and hospitality. Thus, it may well be his head which Peredur is shown at the Fisher-King's castle. It is certainly the wound which leads authors like Robert de Boron in his *Didot-Perceval* to equate Bran with the Fisher-King of the Grail Castle. Besides his appearances as Fisher-King he makes a number of others, for example as Bran de Lis and Brangore of Estragore. He has even been found as underlying Uther Pendragon, father of Arthur.

Just as characters and incidents in the Arthurian stories can be matched against those in earlier material, so too can its marvellous objects. One might go as far as to say that the presence of magical or miracle-working objects in themselves mark the stories as Celtic.

The spear or lance which appears with the Grail at the castle of the Fisher-King matches the spears of other contexts. Most famous is the spear of Lugh, irresistible in battle and 'so fiery that its blade must always be held under water, lest it destroy the city where it is kept'. A spear with the same characteristics is possessed by Oengus mac Oc, Irish counterpart to Mabon ap Modron, identified as the young Lugh. It reappears in the *Fate of the Sons of Tuirenn* and in *The Destruction of Da Derga's Hostel* as the spear from which great sparks fall when brandished. If it is not constantly dipped in a cauldron 'large enough for a bullock', filled with a black and horrible liquid, the whole spear would burst into flame. The cauldron recurs in *The Intoxication of the Ulstermen* and here it is established that the black and poisonous liquid is blood which spreads up the haft just as streams of blood are said to flow along the haft of the spear in the Grail procession.

However, another characteristic is associated with Lugh's spear. In *Mac Datho's Pig* Celtchar claims the champion's portion of pork, promptly to be challenged by Cet, son of Maga, who recalls that he threw a lance wounding Celtchar in the thighs and the top of the testicles, since when he had been unable to father children. Not only is this the situation of the Fisher-King, but, as we have seen, such wounds, by destroying the sexual capacity, would deprive the sufferer of the favour of the tutelary goddess who would be liable to demonstrate her displeasure by turning his land into a waste.

For all its many parallels with Chrétien's unfinished *Perceval, Peredur* diverges in so many details that each version must come from a different text. One such divergence lies in the second object Peredur sees: the salver with its freight of a bleeding head, most probably that of Bran, but undoubtedly the severed head of pagan times. Despite the christianising elsewhere in *Peredur*, there is no attempt at doing so in this passage and when the hero is finally given an explanation of what he has seen it is one so nonsensical it can only be the botched interpolation of some storyteller ignorant of the true origins.

But how is a salver with its gory content transmuted into the Grail? There was plainly a sequence of intermediary stages. In Chrétien's *Perceval* the dish is called a 'Graal' or 'Grail', from *gradalis*, a long flat platter normally used for serving fish, though Chrétien stresses it is being used not for this purpose, but to carry the single communion wafer, the Sacred Host, which is the Fisher-King's only source of nourishment[1]. But even here, as Marx points out, the witnesses display a singular lack of reverence considering the central object is one of such sanctity. No priest is mentioned as being present and no one genuflects as the devout do when entering a Church in which the Sacred Host is exhibited.

In fact, even when the scene becomes firmly Christian, incongruous elements remain. Marx draws attention to the similarity between the Grail procession and the liturgy of the Byzantine mass. At their entry the clergy are preceded by acolytes bearing lighted candelabra such as are described here. They are followed by a priest with the chalice and finally by the celebrant who carries a knife. This is not only shaped like a spear, but is actually called the Lance, expressly commemorating that with which Christ's side was pierced. It is used to cut the communion bread. In the last chapter we saw that elements of Byzantine ritual had found their way into the liturgy of the Celtic Church via the early Roman Christians.

But Chrétien's *gradalis* is still a long way from the Grail as marvellous object. There is the long Celtic tradition of vessels with such properties and these include drinking vessels. Titus Livy mentions the Celtic practice of converting the cerebral vault of the skull into a cup. The use of skulls in this way is implicitly linked with Bran and his head through the ancient Highland and Hebridean belief that a child, being weaned, will acquire supernatural powers if given his or her first taste of food from a raven's skull. Bran is, of course, the raven god – hence Lord of the Ravens – so that we plainly have here traces of an old belief. The wider significance of the skull as drinking vessel is, therefore, that it possesses magical qualities.

In addition there are the cauldrons. We know these to have figured prominently in Celtic daily life. Strabo writes of 'sacred cauldrons', and there is the archaeological evidence from Gundestrup. Mythological cauldrons include the Golden Bowl, symbol of the sun, which Pryderi and Rhiannon come upon in *Manawydan* and the cauldron which Taliesin, in his earlier incarnation as Gwyon Bach, is set to watch as it brews the potion that will compensate Cerridwen's son for his ugliness by making him an intellectual genius. Closer in character to the Grail, however, are the cauldrons of plenty and resuscitation. One of the objects Kulhwych and companions have to deliver to Olwen's father Ysbaddaden is the Cauldron of Diwrnach. It reappears as the Cauldron of Tyrnoc in *The Thirteen Treasures of the Island of Britain* and in Taliesin's *The Spoils of Annwyn*. Both have to be seized from their Irish owners, the dangers of the enterprise being justified by their marvellous character, for while they will instantly boil the meat for the brave they refuse to cook for cowards. As the Cauldron of the Dagda is similarly selective the conclusion is they are one and the same.

In the Welsh *Branwen*, Bran is also the owner of a cauldron whose particular property is that it restores the dead to life. It must, in fact, be the tub Peredur sees at the court of the sons of the King of Sufferings into which corpses are thrown to emerge alive.

However, cauldrons came in a variety of shapes and sizes and were not used exclusively for cooking. Posidonius mentions cups shaped like cooking pots made from clay or silver in which drinks were served.

The stories in which the Grail appears have one constant element: all the Grail-bearers are maidens, reminding Markale of the *conhospitiae*, the women servers of communion who caused such scandal to Catholicism. But there is another maiden who dispenses drink: the crowned one who serves Conn in *The Ecstasy of the Phantom*. Marx suggests that the Cup of Sovereignty motif lies behind the incident of the cup the Red Knight empties over Guinevere. And one should remember that sovereignty was essentially a feminine principle.

It is easy to see how the skull drinking vessels, the cups of sovereignty and the inexhaustible, revivifying cauldrons with their overlapping properties could combine as the Grail which unites all these properties.

For Marx, the true christianising begins with twelfth–thirteenth century Robert de Boron, a poet from Montbéliard in the Franche-Comté. His association with the Arthurian matter was probably inspired by another patron whose motives, crucial to the dissemination and popularisation of the stories among the Medieval French courts, will be addressed in the next chapter.

Naturally, popularisation was not due to any single factor. To begin with, one must not overlook the fact that they are quite simply splendid stories made up of an intriguing mixture of ingredients: romance, high life, adventure spiced with mystery and the unceasing struggle between the forces of light and darkness. Nor should one forget the skill of authors like Chrétien in France or Malory in Britain, who so brilliantly translated and adapted Arthur for their fellow countrymen. (I am aware that Thomas Malory is himself a source of mystery. There are at least three of the same name, including a Welshman. The most likely contender is an ex-soldier from Warwickshire who served a term of imprisonment for the crimes including assault and rape, the latter particularly at odds with the chivalry extolled in the book. But even if the author was, as some believe, the Welsh Thomas Malory, *The Morte d'Arthur* was written in English and intended for an English readership.)

Another and potent factor was the situation in which the British found themselves after the Anglo-Saxon Conquest. Those who had cherished the dream of a Celtic nationhood throughout the Roman occupation had seen it thwarted on the brink of fulfilment. The landowning aristocracy had found themselves dispossessed and, in many cases, reduced to penury. This alone would explain the burgeoning of a mythology celebrating a glorious and utopian past. It is totally consistent with our knowledge of how other societies have reacted to similar circumstances.

Those forced to cross the Channel as fugitives must have had an even stronger sense of deprivation. Whether or not Arthur had taken part in any continental adventures, it is likely that the settlers persuaded themselves that the land to which they were banished had once been part of his empire. New elements introduced into the stories came to carry such conviction that the city of Nantes, vying with Rennes to become the capital of Brittany, advanced its claims by presenting itself as the location of several key incidents.

The Arthurian Lyonesse, usually taken to be a mythical lost land connecting the Scilly Isles with Cornwall, was relocated in the ancient kingdom of Léon which lay in the region round Morlaix and Brest in Brittany. The Forest of Paimpont was converted into the quasi-mystical Brocéliande. The forest is still a profoundly mysterious place, especially in the mists of winter when, as the French author Michel Renouard says, it seems haunted by the ghosts of knights and fairies. It is said once to have housed a Druidic *bangor*, as well as a psychiatric clinic, and today is the site of an annual *Gorsedd*. Inevitably the region has its tomb of Arthur. It is a dolmen near Trébeurden.

One has an image of dispossessed and down at heel noble families gathered in their land of exile on winter's nights to listen as their bards told their stories. But it may well have been the lack of means to reward those bards which led them to seek employment elsewhere, providing the vehicle through which Celtic matter passed into the main body of European literature. Men like the Welsh storyteller Bledhri mastered French and, at one stage in his career, was employed at the brilliant Poitiers' court of Eleanor of Aquitaine. Here he joined renowned troubadours like Bernard de Ventadour, allegedly a paramour of Eleanor, said to be the most beautiful woman of her age, and Bertran de Born. He, a famous swordsman as well as poet, was as in love with warfare as Strabo's Celts. In one poem he writes:

> I tell you I have no such joy as when I hear the shout
> 'On! On!' from both sides and the neighing of riderless steeds,
> And the groans of 'Help me! Help me!' . . .
> And see the dead transfixed with spear shafts!
> Lords, mortgage your domains, castles, cities,
> But never give up war!

He typified an epoch in which, when there was no general war, there were either the perpetual territorial struggles of competing magnates or the tournaments which were nothing less than miniature battles in which men died or suffered appalling injuries. One can see how the Arthurian stories would mirror its ethos and, besides Poitiers, they were being told at other princely courts such as those of Champagne, Blois and Flanders. From the eleventh century there were also the Crusades, some say invented by the Church to divert ungovernable male aggression into religiously desirable channels. (As a rule, while men followed the True Cross, their womenfolk stayed behind, though not always. Louis VII, husband of Eleanor, had so little confidence in her fidelity – with good reason – that he insisted she accompany him. She seems not to have been reluctant, promptly kitting herself and her ladies-in-waiting out in armour. We have only rumour of their actual participation in battle, but we know that Eleanor evolved a scheme to offer herself to Saladin, the Saracen commander, but was waylaid just after she had left the palace at Tyre, where she and the king were staying.) It is likely that it was through the storytellers taken along by the crusaders to while away the long, tedious periods between battles that the tales were spread among the various European nations taking part, and probably among the native populations as well. It is certainly true that Arthur came to be associated with local heroes, so that in a Hebrew version he is partnered by King Solomon.

But there were, in my view, two other reasons for the ready acceptance of the stories by feudal society.

Literature always, in some degree, provides the ideological justification for the society in which it exists. Celtic was quite different from feudal society, the basis of which was a contract by which land and its revenues were granted in return for service, particularly of the military kind. The primary giver was the king who doled huge tracts of his realm out to his barons on these terms, while they, in turn, and under similar conditions, dealt it out in lesser parcels. At each level the contract was sealed by solemn vows of fealty, binding on both parties and regularly renewed.

For the Celts it was cattle and never land ownership which was the measure of status. Nonetheless, superficially the structure of Celtic society with its High King, provincial king and tribal chieftain might seem to parallel the pyramidal hierarchy of king-barons-vassals, making it possible to transform the mythology underpinning the Celtic into one underpinning feudal society. It is plain in the Medieval Arthurian stories that such a transformation has taken place.

The feudal land obsession had a second by-product. The unions whereby a lord enlarged his fiefdoms by marriage to an heiress were rarely contracted by the mutual agreement of principal parties, and usually in the infancy of future bride and groom. Some turned out well; others less so. The feudal lady, lacking the diversions of war or the tournament and indissolubly bound to a man she did not love satisfied her romantic cravings through the ritualised love game which came to be called *l'amour courtois*. She found a surrogate lover in her chosen 'champion' and in theory, though often only in theory, a strict code of morality governed their relations. To this the songs and lyrics of the troubadours, erotic even when their themes are religious, provided both a refrain and a stimulus. It was stimulated too by tales like those of Diarmait and Grainme, Tristan and Isoult, Lancelot and Guinevere in which the paramour risks all for love. It is not for nothing that they are called 'romances'.

One final question needs to be addressed. The Medieval retellings of the stories are full of mysteries. The incident of the Grail, the Wasteland and the Grail Castle can be explained as an attempt to convert originally pagan material into a Christian allegory. Other incidents sit less comfortably within this. We have the case of Merlin, for instance. Numerous attempts have been made to discover the historical Merlin and it is usually accepted that, if he existed, he was one of those figures who, like Taliesin, was part bard and part magician. Among those with whom he has been identified is the Lailoken, whose story strongly parallels that of Suibne, maddened, as in some accounts Merlin was said to have been maddened, by the slaughter of a terrible battle of which he feels himself to have been cause.

The Medieval Merlin plays the exact same role as the court Druids of the Irish stories. Yet there is a total discontinuity between the two. The eighth-century *Kulhwych and Olwen*, it is true, has two characters, Menw son of Teirwaedd and Gwrhyr Interpreter of Languages, probably originally Druids. Menw is able to cast spells of invisibility, while Gwrhyr can change his shape – at one point he takes on bird-form – and 'understands every tongue' including those of animals. That Menw and Gwrhyr are not actually called Druids is probably because such references were expunged to avert ecclesiastical disapproval.

Four hundred years elapsed between the putative eighth-century dating of *Kulhwych* and Geoffrey's *History of the Kings of Britain* in which Merlin first appears. However, even here he has not yet become a Druid. He is an orphan brought to the court of Vortigern to be the foundation sacrifice for the citadel the king plans to build at Eryri in north Wales. (The traditional spot, a few miles north of Bedd Gelert, is still marked by a roadside hillock.) He is not promoted to the post of magician-extraordinary until the time of Robert de Boron's prose continuators in the thirteenth century.

If Merlin is a mystery, he is not the only one. Marx has pointed out the similarity between the *geis*, the uniquely Celtic form of taboo, and the obligations the *amour courtois* imposed on the knight who had been chosen by a lady as her champion. Once so chosen, he is morally compelled, at no matter what cost or risk, to succour his 'domina' or her kin or go in quest of any object she has set her heart on. Refusal or failure will mean, not only the loss of her, but loss of face among his peers. One recalls Diarmait's choosing by Grainme and the advice given to him by his comrades of the Fianna. It was as if the obligations of the *geis* were fully understood in the Medieval courts.

Equally inexplicable are the sinister games which form the climax of both the *Mabinogion* story of *Gereint and Enide* and Chrétien's *Erec*. For all Tolstoy's suggestion that they represent a celebration of

Lugnasad, they are an incongruity. The setting is a tournament although, from the internal evidence, it takes place in the Otherworld against powerful Otherworld opponents. Yet, as the details of the incident have little real bearing on the plot, it is difficult to understand why Chrétien included them so conscientiously. One answer might be that they bore a meaning clear to himself and his audience, being part of a total context understood by both.

Could it be that there were at least some who knew exactly what the *geis* was and who and what Merlin was, perhaps because men very like him were still to be found, having escaped ecclesiastical proscription as Civilis's Druids escaped Roman proscription? And were they even to be found practising in the court circles?

The implication is that there existed a hidden cult keeping up the old pagan practices and for whom the Arthurian stories incorporated a kind of code.

Theories of secret esoteric cults have a long, if dubious, history. A great deal of scorn has been heaped on works like Margaret Murray's *God of the Witches* and *The Divine King of England*, with her argument for a royal connection with a witchcraft fertility cult. There are other more recent ones. In *The Holy Blood and the Holy Grail* Michael Baigent, Richard Leigh and Henry Lincoln have argued for a secret cult, still in existence, whose members included the brilliant French poet-artist Jean Cocteau. The cult's roots lay in the Knights Templar officially disbanded by Pope Clement V in 1312 after charges of heresy involving magic had been laid against them. The authors of *The Holy Blood* discuss Chrétien's version of the Grail legend and point out that there is evidence which links the poet with a school of esoteric studies established in Champagne by the eleventh-century Hebrew savant Rabbi Rashi, who was himself under the protection of the court.

There are a number of problems, not least among them that at the time he wrote his Grail romance *Perceval*, Chrétien, who died literally in mid-sentence before it was completed, was no longer under the patronage of the Champagne court, but under that of Flanders. However, whatever doubt may be cast on the existence of this or that cult, some certainly existed. Aristocrats, cloaked and masked against recognition, were to be found at the witches' sabbaths. Scrupulous security was maintained at these highly clandestine gatherings and their presence indicates that they were accepted by the other members.

Periodically, through its history, France has been shaken by a sensational exposure. In the fifteenth century there had been the group which coalesced round Gilles de Rais, Marshal of France and close associate of Joan of Arc, later to be revealed as practitioner of alchemy, sodomy and infanticide, and executed with his main collaborators after a sensational trial.

On 25 January 1680 came the Affair of the Poisons when six members of the court of Louis XIV were arrested on suspicion of ridding themselves of enemies by this means.

The purveyor was a woman known as Madame La Voisin, fortune-teller to the nobility, who at her trial was said to have been the leader of a cult of Satanists. It was alleged that she had in her employ reprobate priests who celebrated a Black Mass during the course of which babies were sacrificed. Among her followers was Athénaïs de Montespan, a mistress of the king who, finding he was tiring of her, was alleged to have offered her naked body as altar for these debaucheries, though it has to be said that Madame Lavoisin went to her execution without implicating anyone directly. Madame de Montespan, for her part, continued at the court but finally retired to a convent where, in the course of time, she became Mother Superior.

Gilles de Rais and the Affair of the Poisons demonstrated that such coteries could and did exist in the highest circles of society. Many must never have come to light, as Madame Lavoisin's might not have done despite its horrific practices, but for the malice of one royal mistress towards another who was displacing her.

Nevertheless, the question of a late, secret Druidic cult can only be a subject for speculation and must be left as such, though, in my view, it is one that merits investigation.

# Note

1 The derivation and meaning of the word 'grail' is disputed. According to some renderings it becomes the 'Sangreal'. This could mean 'Holy Grail', but it has been suggested that it derives from two French words of quite different meaning, viz *sang*, blood, and *réal*, which could mean either 'true' or 'royal'. So it is the *sang réal* or true blood and refers, not to the chalice, but to the phial with drops of Christ's blood which Joseph of Arimathea is supposed to have brought with him to Glastonbury.

# Chapter 13

# The Craving for Independence

In 1152 Louis VII obtained the annulment of his marriage to Eleanor of Aquitaine on the grounds of her misconduct with the nineteen-year-old Duke of Normandy, Henry Plantagenet. Within eight weeks the couple had married, uniting two hugely rich and powerful families. Besides Normandy, Henry was master of Maine, Touraine and Anjou, the last being the source of the name Angevin by which his dynasty was known. By his marriage, he added not only Aquitaine, but also Gascony, Poitou and the Auvergne to his estates, making their domains greater in area than those of the French king himself. What was more, Henry's mother, Matilda, was the daughter of Henry I of England and regarded herself as having a claim on the English crown superior to that of its present wearer, Stephen. A drawn-out civil war was left unresolved until the death of Stephen in 1154, whereupon Henry landed in England and, under the Treaty of Wallingford, was acknowledged as king.

The manner in which Henry II had ascended the throne inevitably meant that there were those who questioned his right to it. One way to make himself look less of an alien intruder was to persuade his subjects that he came of the same stock as they did – the one that had engendered Arthur. He commissioned Wace to write his verse translation of Geoffrey of Monmouth, *The Roman de Brut*. Whatever the mythological basis of his Round Table, it had the additional political one of showing that the new king intended to rule in the Arthurian tradition of *primus inter pares*. He further advanced his claim to be regarded as a High King by forcing Malcolm IV of Scotland to do homage to him.

At the same time Henry also saw to it that his grandson by his third son Geoffrey was named Arthur. This had to do with the very complicated succession arrangements behind which one can see the hand of Eleanor. The natural successor, his eldest son Henry, nicknamed Courtmantle, died of fever in 1183 putting the second son, Richard Coeur de Lion, in line. However, being homosexual he was unlikely to produce an heir and to avert the premature extinction of the Angevin name Geoffrey was nominated successor, an arrangement said to have had the full concurrence of Richard. In due course, Geoffrey's son would have become king and a substantial part of the old Celtic domains would be united under a second Arthur. The plan was thrown into disarray by Geoffrey's death in a tournament three years before his father died. John, youngest of Henry's sons, was unwilling to be denied a throne he regarded as rightly his by a nephew still a minor, especially since, in an earlier share-out of the family estates, he had been overlooked (hence his nickname 'John Lackland'). When the young Arthur accidentally fell into John's hands, he seized his opportunity and threw him into the dungeons of Rouen Castle where he was murdered, allegedly by John himself.

However, Henry II had two other reasons for his interest in King Arthur. The first sprang from his wider ambitions. Since the crowning of Charlemagne in AD 800 the chief temporal rulers of the Christian world had been the Holy Roman emperors, the descendants of the Franks. With the kingdom of England added to his great territories in France Henry saw himself in an imperial light and was anxious that the fact should be universally acknowledged.

The fame of Charlemagne and his heirs was commemorated in the *Chansons de Geste*, on the one hand, and on the other by the religious establishments they had endowed. The greatest of these, Cluny, incorporated a basilica which, until the building of St Peter's at Rome, was the biggest church in Christendom. Furthermore, the Holy Roman Emperor was the custodian of one of the most sacred of relics, the Spear of Longinus. One way for Henry to put himself at least on parity would be to show that England, too, had had a significant role in the genesis of Christianity and was also guardian of holy treasure.

Having decided that Glastonbury Abbey was to become a rival to Cluny, Henry invited Robert de Boron to England, entertained him liberally and, it is likely, packed him off to the abbey. There he would undoubtedly have heard of the legendary arrival of Joseph of Arimathea to establish the first Christian church in England, and of the objects he had brought with him, as well as tales of King Arthur and his association with the area. Through Robert's pen the chalice becomes the Holy Grail and as such identified with the procession in the Fisher-King's castle.

The second of Henry's reasons was a more pressing one. A Duke of Normandy, who had made himself William I of England a century earlier, had found the north west of his new domain so resistant to his rule that he had handed the task of subordinating it over to one of his most ruthless paladins, Hugh d'Avranches, Earl of Cheshire, who rejoiced in his nickname 'the Wolf'. He had invaded Wales, seized part of Flintshire, massacred men, women and children and divided the territory among friends and vassals. Resistance continued nonetheless. It continued even after William had concluded a secret deal with Rhys ap Tewdwr, king of south-west Wales, recognising his lordship. Though fresh attempts at pacification were made by William's immediate successors who created a heavily fortified March of Wales, the area remained prey to sudden, violent Welsh guerilla attacks.

As it happened the Welsh had found themselves a new ally. William had been shrewd enough to recognise the support to his power that could accrue from control of the religious establishments and Norman priests and monks had actually started coming to England during the reign of his predecessor, Edward the Confessor. After his accession William had continued and accelerated the process, even obtaining papal approval for his own nominee, Lanfranc, as archbishop of Canterbury. However, in Wales the Cistercian houses had identified themselves with the local population and its interests, thereby bringing about a closer union of Celtic and Catholic communions.

The monks' energies extended beyond the spiritual and their entrepreneurial talents helped to bring the backward and depressed local economy to the level of the surrounding ones. Largely underestimated at the time, this was to have long-term benefits for Wales, turning the yearning for independence from a dream into an economic feasibility. The monks were also patrons of the bards and among those they supported was one of the greatest of them all, Dafydd ap Gwilym (c. 1320–50). Hence they contributed to keeping alive a basic element of Welsh culture.

Thus it could be said that at the time Henry II came to the throne the menace from the west, far from having diminished, was potentially greater than in the days of his Norman predecessor. Nonetheless, where William had failed, Henry seems to have been determined to succeed once and for all, but beset by other problems, in particular the rebellion of his land-greedy sons, he needed to do so at minimal cost.

Welsh resistance had long been sustained by a myth: that of a king of their race who had defeated a foreign invader, held him at bay and, at least for a time, created a nation. He now lay sleeping in some secret place awaiting the summons of his people. While his precise resting place was disputed, every Welshman was convinced that it could be nowhere else but in their land. Henry saw that, if he could show that Arthur's body actually reposed on English soil, he would be delivering a considerable blow to the morale of the turbulent Welsh.

Visiting Glastonbury he mentioned over a dinner with the abbot that, through a chance meeting with a Welsh bard, he had learnt the body was buried within his abbey's precincts. Whether or not this was a royal invention we cannot be sure, but we do know that the monks, ever willing to oblige their generous benefactor, lost no time in beginning excavations and in 1191 made their momentous find – not one but two bodies, Arthur and his queen. Sadly by that time Henry himself was dead.

Such dismay as the Welsh may have felt did not long affect their aspirations to freedom. Llewelyn ap Iorwerth, surnamed the Great, led a rebellion against English rule during the reign of Henry's son, John (1199–1216). His grandson, Llewelyn ap Gruffydd, later to be called 'Llewelyn the Last', led another during the reign of Henry III (1216–72) which for a time was more successful. Llewelyn the Great had adopted the style of 'Prince of Wales', though he acquired only *de facto* recognition. By contrast, Llewelyn ap Gruffydd not only received the homage of the other Welsh princes, but even forced Henry III to sign a treaty acknowledging his overlordship. The political consequence was that Wales was now a principality, that is to say a federal state with an overlord rather than a disunited collection of often querulous, lesser princelings. For a time it looked as if it were returning to what it had been in an earlier age. The two Llewelyns revived many traditional customs, employing bards who were almost certainly those poet-prophets, the *awenyddion* described by Gerald of Wales, who was still alive when Henry III came to the throne.

However, relations cooled under his successor, Edward I. When Llewelyn began building a new castle the king ordered him to desist; Llewelyn defied him, was declared an outlaw and had his territories invaded by an English army. In the late winter of 1282 Llewelyn was caught in an ambush at a bridge and, in what is like an echo of Celtic custom, his enemies forthwith decapitated the body, washed the blood-stained head in a cottage well and sent it to the king. In due course it was crowned with ivy and paraded through the streets of London, then stuck on the Tower of London.

Even after this great blow, resistance continued for a time, finally to crumble in the summer of 1283. A revolt in south-west Wales under Rhys ap Maredudd four years later failed completely.

But it was not only in Wales that recourse was being made to the name of Arthur. In 1337, on the urging of his mother Queen Isabella, her fifteen-year-old son seized the crown from his father and proclaimed himself Edward III of England. Once more some form of reassurance to nobles and subjects seemed called for. By royal decree the Round Table was given tangible form. The 18-foot diameter wooden slab decorated with representations of king and knights was later assumed to be the original and is still to be seen at Winchester. At the same time, the new king founded his Order of the Garter as an attempt to revive the Arthurian knighthood. It was an idea which spread to France. After seeing the Garter Knights during a stay in England, Jean II of France went home and promptly founded his own Order of the Star.

The next fifty years saw the English crown imposing its own pattern of government on the principality while, as a sort of *quid pro quo*, the predacious Marcher Lords appointed by William I were brought under control, the worst abuses curbed and Welshmen brought into the administration of the nation. The policy proved so successful that Richard II ascended the throne in 1377 with a group of influential and well-educated Welshmen around him.

In 1400, at the beginning of the crisis which ended in his deposition by Henry Bolingbroke as Henry IV, Richard fled to Wales and from there tried to muster sufficient force to oust the usurper. It was actually at Flint Castle, where he had taken refuge, that the last scene of his drama – his abdication – was played out.

Among those with him was a member of his London Welsh circle. At that time in his mid-forties, Owain Glyndwyr is a good example of how far anglicisation of the Welsh upper classes had gone. Born in Wales – the location is disputed – he studied at the Inns of Court in London. This, plus the fact that he was described as an 'apprentice at law', has led to his being described as a barrister and his skill as negotiator suggests a legally-trained mind. However, at that time the

Inns were as much as anything a kind of university for the nobility and his main career seems to have been in the army, for in 1387 he was knighted apparently as a reward for his military services in France, Ireland and Scotland. Bardic lays were later to speak of his bravery and prowess in the field.

At about the same time he contracted an English marriage with Margaret, daughter of Sir David Hamner, an eminent judge. The degree of intimacy in his relations with the king is uncertain, though his presence at Flint suggests a certain closeness between them and later, when Glyndwyr was credited with magical skill, it was said that Richard had been one of his initiates.

On the king's word he was allowed to leave Flint Castle and retired to manage his Welsh estates and farms. However, with the deposition of the pro-Welsh Richard, the Marcher Lords of which Henry, by virtue of his title of Duke of Hereford, was one, felt constraints had been lifted and began casting round for pretexts which would allow them to extend their domains at the expense of their Welsh neighbours. There is some evidence that Glyndwyr did his best to avoid embroilment until provoked beyond endurance. The precise cause of his quarrel with Reginald Grey de Ruthyn is not known. One version is that Grey had kept back a royal command so as to present his neighbour as a rebel, liable to forfeiture of his property. Another version has it that the dispute involved lands Glyndwyr claimed as his but which Grey refused to disgorge. When appeals to the courts and directly to the king brought no redress, Glyndwyr, sharing in the general conviction that no Welshman could expect justice from England, raised the stakes by declaring himself the rightful Prince of Wales, basing his claim on his descent on his mother's side from Llewelyn the Last.

The spark of rebellion took spontaneous fire across the Principality with even expatriate Welshmen rushing home to fight for what quickly came to be seen as a struggle for national independence. Glyndwyr himself was now in fact an outlaw with his estates forfeit, while his person was liable to seizure. Yet he seemed to live a charmed life as he avoided trap after trap set for him, often just at it was about to be sprung.

At the same time, he bore all before him in battle. The English troops blamed failure, partly on the difficult terrain, but mainly on the spells cast against them by Glyndwyr and his bards. He was said to possess the Druidic mastery of the elements and to be able to raise fogs and storms to confound them. He was rumoured by both sides to have as refuge his secret palace beneath the waters of a lake and an enchanted stone which could make him invisible. His banners possessed such potent properties they were repeatedly torn to shreds by followers who used them as talismans. Many contemporary accounts of his battles read like recapitulations of Tacitus's description of the assault on Môn when the Roman veterans were so numbed with terror they appeared paralysed.

In the early spring of 1402, when a blazing comet scarred the heavens, his bards immediately brought it into their song as evidence that he was the fulfilment of the ancient prophecies. This, and the heavenly auguries attending his birth, of which Shakespeare's 'Glendower' was so fiercely proud, were portents of his ultimate success. To his enemies they were yet further confirmation that he was in league with dark forces.

Soon afterwards Grey de Ruthyn was captured and in a battle at Bryn Glas hundreds of English troops were slain and many prisoners taken. (Four tall redwoods on a hillside at Pilleth in Powys still mark the burial place of the Welsh dead.) For the king there were further blows. Henry Percy, nicknamed 'Harry Hotspur', Earl of Denbigh, commissioned by the king to put down the rebellion, defected. Then Percy's brother-in-law Edmund Mortimer, captured at Bryn Glas, fell for one of Glyndwyr's daughters, married her and threw in his lot with her father.

In the summer of 1404 a Welsh parliament sitting at Machynlleth formalised his title of Prince of Wales. (The site of his supposed Parliament House remains a popular tourist attraction at Machynlleth.) At Harlech Castle, captured from the English the previous spring, he was crowned undisputed ruler of some 150,000 Welshmen, in the presence of envoys from Scotland, France and Spain. From his palace embassies were soon travelling to the Papal court, to those of France, Spain, Scotland and to the chieftaincies of Ireland. Troops from France and Brittany, transported in the French men-o'-war which could often be seen anchored in the Harlech roadsteads, came to augment his own forces. The French, with whom England was at war, were even considering a formal alliance.

That was the climax which was to be followed by the inevitable decline. His forces suffered two serious defeats, in the second of which his eldest son, Gruffydd, was captured and died of the plague in the Tower of London. Hope dawned briefly as more French troops began to arrive and the forces which Henry, quick to smell the danger, rushed to meet them were impeded by bad weather. But ironically, he who had a reputation for being able to bend the elements to his will, now found them conspiring against him. Expected to fight in such uncomfortable and unfamiliar conditions, the largely mercenary troops of his French ally began deserting. At the same time internal crises prevented the French king from giving further aid. Left with only lightly-armed infantry and some crossbow men, Owain Glyndwyr was forced into retreat. Aberystwyth and Harlech were lost, the latter with all his family and possessions falling into enemy hands. He was once more a fugitive outlaw. An attempt to extend the revolt to northern England failed with a defeat at Bramham Moor. By 1409, save for sporadic guerilla actions, one more struggle for Welsh independence was over.

The great rebel ended his life in obscurity, possibly at the home of one of his daughters. As is so often the case with Celtic heroes, even his burial place is uncertain, a fact which gave rise to the usual spate of stories that he was not dead or that, if he was, he would return.

These tales were of a piece with his lifetime reputation as a wonder-worker. Much of this was obviously fantasy and hearsay embellished and exploited for propaganda purposes. Yet there is no doubt that Glyndwyr himself implicitly believed in magic – one whose ultimate source was Druidic. He consulted seers such as Hopkin ap Thomas ab Einon, lauded in surviving poems. In later ages a poet, the vicar of Grosmont in Gwent, reputed to be a spell-caster and conjuror of spirits, was spoken of as Owain Glyndwyr's reincarnation. One is again reminded of his delineation by Shakespeare and of his boast to Harry Hotspur: 'I can call spirits from the vasty deep'.

In the traditional fashion of a Celtic prince, he also fulfilled the expectation in his liberality towards his bards. All in all, it was perhaps hardly surprising if Henry placed a ban on their activities. Henceforth no 'waster, rhymer, minstrel or vagabond' was to make a 'commortha' (an anglicism of the Welsh *cymhortha* or gathering).

Nonetheless, as with Dr Ross's Derbyshire and Cheshire families, Owain Glyndwyr, too, managed to combine magical practice with a devout Christianity. Priests formed a permanent part of his retinue and he had as chancellor an archdeacon. One highly significant aspect of the rebellion is the support given him by the Franciscan monasteries, in some cases it seems, those of England as well as those of Wales. English campfire gossip had it that one form of penance imposed by Franciscan confessors was to go to Wales to fight for Glyndwyr. Such was the fury at their partiality that at least one monastery was razed. The troops' frustration was understandable. The English Franciscans, who produced some of the leading minds of the Middle Ages, were in a position to exercise a considerable influence on opinion.

Glyndwyr's rebellion as one manifestation of the unquenchable thirst for independence epitomises the Celtic sense of cultural separateness sustained, among other ways, through belief in what can only be called the occult. As we know, in this respect his struggle was not unique. In 1885, two preoccupations, national independence and psychical research, began to dominate the horizons of the Irish poet and Nobel Laureate W.B. Yeats (1865–1939). It was at about this same time that he was coming under the influence of the nationalist John O'Leary, who had just returned after five years' imprisonment in England for participation in an armed rebellion. From 1889 with the publication of *The Wanderings of Oisin* Yeats began his retellings of the myths, consciously using them as the means of advancing the independence cause.

Shortly before, gathering together a group of like-minded friends, he had founded the Dublin Hermetic Society. It was not long afterwards that he met Helena Blavatsky, and for about a year, until his constant indulgence in unsuccessful occult experiments irritated its founder beyond endurance, was a member of her Theosophical Society. A month or two after leaving the Theosophists, he joined the ten-year-old Hermetic Students of the Golden Dawn, yet another of the bodies which had been spawned out of the European intellectual fad for the paranormal.

The Theosophists were preoccupied with the eastern magical tradition. The Golden Dawn, by contrast, basing much of its teaching on those of the Abbé Constant, who wrote under the name of Eliphas Lévi, stressed the western one. Its models included, not only figures like Orpheus and Pythagoras, but the Druids themselves. The Golden Dawn Hermeticists also toyed with spiritual alchemy, the object of which is to transmute the alchemist's personality, as well as with the Kabbalah, the ancient Hebrew esoteric system, which could be said to have a similar objective. The cosmology of the Kabbalah closely resembled that of Neoplatonism, but what is no less striking is that in many ways it also resembled the *Barddas*. Eccentric as these ideas may appear to us, at that time the group attracted a number of celebrated members, among them the Astronomer-Royal for Scotland and writers like Arthur Machen and Algernon Blackwood.

The Golden Dawn Hermeticists practised rituals supposedly magical in character which Yeats, according to his biographer Richard Ellman, found particularly beautiful. He was much taken with the central myth which involved the mystical death and rebirth of the adept, the shamanistic and Druidic overtones of which hardly need stressing.

None of this caused him to lose sight of either his nationalist or literary aspirations. He founded a literary society in Dublin and another for Irish expatriates in London, both having the aim of publicising the literature, folklore and legends of Ireland.

Since 1896 he had been a member of the Irish Republican Brotherhood, formed to overthrow British rule, if necessary by violence, but sickened by its internal feuding and the intolerance towards one another shown by its constituent groups, he soon ceased to take an active interest in politics. Thereafter his nationalism was, as Ellman says, restricted to the literary.

Nevertheless, he had been thinking for some time of founding a national cult, a sort of Irish Celtic 'Golden Dawn' which was to revive the 'Druidic mysteries'. In a letter to his friend George Russell, an enthusiast for the scheme, Yeats wrote that the 'gods had returned to Eri', had taken up residence in the 'sacred mountains' and 'had been seen by several in vision'.

An uninhabited castle on an island was taken over as its headquarters and planning of such things as rites began. As to teachings, these resemble those of the Theosophists and the Golden Dawn, but were given a vivid Irish and Celtic hue. 'The radical truths of Christianity', it was claimed, were to be united with those of the ancient world. To further the scheme, Yeats enlisted support among the London Irish who were to exert a kind of spiritual power to will the cult into existence. At one of its meetings Yeats himself performed what was claimed, though on unspecified grounds, as 'a Celtic invocation ceremony'. According to records of the occasion, those taking part felt themselves transported to a mountainous region where they found themselves by an ancient well overshadowed by a rowan tree. The 'transportation' may, of course, have been a kind of group vision, though more probably it was simply a high-flown epithet to express Yeats's graphic description of the typical mythological scenes in which wells and rowans figure. These include *Diarmait and Grainme*, a story well known to the poet who had used it as the basis of a play.

In the end his cult came to nothing, though Yeats himself claimed to be having visions at this time. In one of these he saw a book containing the lost poems of William Blake, and it is noticeable that for some time thereafter mystical themes figured in his plays.

Attempts have been made to explain Yeats's interest in things occult by reference to his unrequited love for Maud Gonne. Reputedly the most beautiful woman in Ireland, her rejection of his proposals was said to have been because her sole abiding passion was for Irish independence. Her marriage in 1893 to Major John MacBride, one of the rebels executed by the British after the rising of Easter 1916, was undoubtedly a bitter blow to Yeats. He himself later married Georgie Hyde-Lees, a member of the Golden Dawn.

The next few years saw Yeats toying with symbolism, much as the Renaissance and Elizabethan mages had done, as well as doing psychical research, some of which helped to reinforce his belief in paranormal phenomena. For a period he left Ireland to live in Britain. When he returned in 1922, independence had been achieved and that same year President Cosgrove appointed him to the Senate of the newly formed Free State.

In 1938, Yeats wrote his last play, *The Death of Cu Chulainn*. There is a significant passage in Ellman's biography: 'Cu Chulainn . . . recognises that to go forth to battle will probably be fatal . . . yet, though he could avoid the combat, he goes forward . . . All that is known fights with all that is unknown; God is Himself man's opponent, and the final struggle is with Him, whether He keeps His own shape or takes that of death or destiny . . . The war on God is the ultimate heroism, and like all heroism in Yeats ends in defeat.' But it is not just for Yeats that all heroism ends in defeat. It is intrinsic to much Celtic mythology and, indeed, history. The object being not to win or lose, but to act heroically.

# Chapter 14
# Religion and the Celts

Welsh hopes which had sunk so low with the collapse of Owain Glyndwyr's bid for independence in 1409 began to revive seventy-six years later when the crown of England, rolling from the head of the slaughtered Richard III, was picked out of the mire of Bosworth Field. Still bloody, it was clapped on the head of Henry Tudor, there and then proclaimed Henry VII. The Tudors were an ancient Welsh family. It had been with one of Henry's ancestors, Rhys ap Tewdwr, king of south-west Wales, that William of Normandy had been forced to conclude a secret concord recognising his kingdom. Henry was well indoctrinated in Celtic ways for he had spent much of his boyhood in Brittany, where his uncle and guardian, Jasper Tudor, Earl of Pembroke, had lived in exile.

Welsh optimism in 1485 was based on more than the accident of birth, for it had been they who first rallied to Henry's support when he landed with a small army at Milford Haven. It continued to rise, therefore, when the new king named his first son Arthur and had the Round Table repainted and refurbished. The Welsh people began to look Londonwards once again and flocked to the city as they not done since the reign of Richard II. The Venetian ambassador told his masters that the Welsh 'may now be said to have recovered their former independence'.

To the English population at large, Henry's accession was welcome for another reason. In contrast with the deep-dyed villain presented by Shakespeare, among the generality of his subjects Richard III was an extremely popular monarch. His portrait by an anonymous artist, now in the Mansell Collection, shows a sensitive and intelligent face and no hint of the crooked back later attributed to him. He was responsible for a number of measures which ameliorated his subjects' situation and raised their standard of living. For all this, Henry represented the end of the Wars of Roses which, like all the wars of the feudal nobility, had imposed hideous sufferings upon the common people. However, its protraction over some forty years had not only drained the resources of the aristocracy itself but had witnessed the extinction on the battlefield of many of its greatest families, in this way delivering a death blow to feudalism itself. What was now hoped for was a period of peace and stability with the opportunity to rebuild the nation's prosperity.

The war and its effects had delayed the country's participation in the great movement then sweeping through Europe – the Renaissance – and it now wished to make up the leeway. It has become habitual to treat the Renaissance and the Reformation as separate phenomena, though it was the respectability the Renaissance gave to classical learning and the freedom of thought that sprang from this that caused men and women to reconsider religious attitudes. The intellectual roots of the Renaissance lay in Christian Humanism with its emphasis on a view of the human as a creature 'made in the image of God' rather than as an incorrigible sinner. The desire to explore the relationship with the divine based on this foundation led to the formation of various movements, some, perhaps inevitably, of a distinctly wayward and mystical bent. By the sixteenth century, with improving education and the printing press, the ideas informing these movements were reaching England and knowledge of a kind, hitherto restricted to the cloister, began spreading to an intellectual elite among the laity.

This evolution from what one might call esoteric to exoteric was in many ways not new. Christianity, especially when its followers were secret members of a persecuted cult, could itself be said to have been an esoteric movement. Almost from its inception it had had its mystics. Indeed, in the early Church visions and trance states were taken as a matter of course. St Paul writes of those in which 'he heard things that cannot be told, which men may not utter'. Such movements continued after the Church had become tolerated, but tended to be regarded by its leadership with an increasing suspicion which could intensify into hostility. The esoteric elements which emerged among the Gnostics and Cathars, the Paulicians and Bogomils, as well as among the Knights Templar, were significant in bringing about their condemnation as heretics.

Insofar as shamanistic elements can usually be detected in such movements, and Druidism was itself shamanistic, one might be tempted to speak of Druidic influences at work. In the case of the Cathars, whose centre was in southern France, the ancient Gaul, there is some justification for supposing that such elements had been preserved or revived, but so many other influences had been at work it is impossible to separate one from another with any confidence.

Nonetheless, there was one element in the thought of the time which, while it may not have developed out of the Druidic past, found fertile soil because of the legacy of that past. This was Neoplatonism. Initially it had consisted of two separate strands. One was Neopythagoreanism, a philosophical school founded by the first century AD mystic Apollonius of Tyana, who believed himself to be a reincarnation of Pythagoras and sought to revive his teachings. The other comprised those interpreters of Plato who laid stress on the elements of Pythagorean mysticism which it undoubtedly contained. The teachings of both were so close that their final amalgamation was inevitable and thus Neoplatonism came into being heavily charged with ideas which, as we have seen, were regarded as sufficiently close to what was thought to be Druidic doctrine to give rise to the legend that Pythagoras had been instructed by them. (In an alternative form it was said that it was he who had instructed the Druids!) This included – though with what success we do not know – the cultivation of what was called 'flight from the body', analogous to the shaman's 'spirit flight' which Pythagoras is reputed to have practised and with which, from the accounts of Mag Roth's activities, the Druids were acquainted.

Neoplatonism had been embraced by several of the later Greek philosophical schools, among them the Stoics, one of whose exponents was Posidonius, possibly the greatest expert on the Celts and Druidism of all time.

Among those who later adopted it were the Renaissance mages, figures typified by the magician Prospero in Shakespeare's *The Tempest*, who is said to have been modelled on the Welshman John Dee. A necromancer, alchemist and astrologer, besides setting a propitious date for the coronation of Elizabeth I, he provided accurate star charts for navigators and is generally believed to have been the author of a translation of Euclid, though it was officially credited to Sir Henry Billingsley, later sheriff and lord mayor of London.

Besides dabbling in the Kabbalah, some of the Renaissance mages, like the Neapolitan Giordano Bruno, claimed to be able to induce trances in which they could visit the 'Celestial Spheres'. Dee, lacking this ability, employed a fellow Celt, the Irishman Edward Kelley, to do it for him, carefully recording in his beautiful script the dialogues between the medium and an angel, Ophiel. In Dee we can see the continuation of a tradition which could well have gone back, if not to the Druids, at least to the bards who claimed to be the heirs of so much of their knowledge.

The terror of heresy which lay behind the Church's distaste for the esoteric can be detected in the attacks on the Celtic bards by Henry II and by the earlier edicts against stones, tree and water worship of Canute and Charlemagne and the various Church councils. But given their considerable divergence from the Catholic mainstream and the Christianity of the Celtic countries, especially of those countries where the missionaries had come into direct contact with Druidism, one might expect esotericism to produce thinkers and theologians whose ideas were at odds with those of Rome and who prepared the ground for the Reformation.

The case of Pelagius has been discussed and there is an obvious similarity between his teachings and those of the Renaissance Christian Humanists. He was not unique. The Breton teacher Peter Abelard (1079–1144) was twice condemned for heresy and it could be said that his contention that words were inadequate for demonstrating inner truths was markedly Druidic even if we have no evidence that he drew directly on their teachings.

Among the Franciscans of the British Isles, who were to give such support for Owain Glyndwyr, was Roger Bacon (1220–92), the 'Wonderful Doctor'. Mostly known for the recipe for gunpowder, he also proposed mechanically propelled ships and carriages and suggested designs for lenses to improve vision resulting in the first spectacles. At some time between 1277 and 1279 he was imprisoned by his fellow Franciscans on the charge of introducing certain 'suspected novelties' into his teaching. Exactly what these were is obscure, but he is known to have acquired a personal library of 'secret books'.

The Franciscan schools of theology at Paris and Oxford became among the most celebrated in Christendom. Markale reminds us that one of the most famous of the French Franciscans, François Rabelais (c. 1483–1553), as well as being one of the most eminent physicians of his day, was the author of the world's greatest masterpiece of ribaldry. His giant-hero, Gargantua, may well descend from Celtic giants like Gwrgant Varyf Twrch or Gwrgant of the Boar-beard in *Kulhwych and Olwen*.

The products of Oxford numbered William of Ockham, who gave his name to 'Ockham's Razor', the principal that all hypotheses should be reduced to the minimum necessary to explain a particular phenomenon, which is still the basis of scientific speculation. Like Roger Bacon, his views brought him into collision with his Church and similar disapproval fell on the head of the Christian Neoplatonist John Duns Scotus Erigena whose teachings on natural law at the University of Paris were, in many ways, markedly Celtic and Druidic. Both these and his book *De divisione naturae* were denounced, though his ideas continued to circulate in the form of annotations to other works.

The inadequacy of language to express things divine which characterised the teachings of Peter Abelard could also be said to be implicit in those of John Wycliffe (born *c.* 1330, died 1384) which were later to be absorbed into what became the greatest of all the heresies – Protestantism. His argument, expounded in *De domino divino libri tres* and *Tractatus civili dominio*, that authority came directly from God, seems to re-echo Celtic belief in the king as ruler only through the sanction of the Otherworld. The concern to make scripture generally available, which led him to translate the Bible, also brings to mind the severely scriptural Christianity of the early Celtic fathers and was again to form the basis of Protestant fundamentalism.

It is plain that the reform movement had a long history, gathering momentum with the Renaissance. It could be said to have been compounded of two elements. On the one hand, there were the critiques of theologians from Pelagius to Wycliffe, and on the other, the attitudes towards and the grievances against the organised church on the part of the laity. For them, the theological arguments may well have seemed unimportant, but the greed, rapacity and arrogance of many of the bishops and religious houses was something of which they had had painful experience. Their sentiments could be said to have been summed up by a contemporary of Wycliffe's, the poet William Langland in the lines:

When the kindness of Constantine gave the Holy Church endowments
In lands and leases, lordships and servants,
The Romans heard an angel cry on high above them,
'This day *dos ecclesiae* has drunk venom
And all who have Peter's power are poisoned forever . . .'

The discontent to which Langland gives voice, that the clergy, especially at its higher echelons, had been made equally and often more oppressive overlords than their secular counterparts, had been active ever since the Celtic Church had been suppressed. Unfavourable comparisons were repeatedly drawn between the wealth of the Church of the day and the humble simplicity and poverty of the Celtic monks.

Of the reformers themselves it could be said that they fell into two camps. There were the conservatives, out to correct the abuses of the past, but otherwise leave the Church as intact as possible; and those who favoured root and branch change.

Members of the first included the German cardinal Nicholas de Cusa (1401–64) who, like John Duns Scotus, was a Neoplatonist. In England they were represented, among others, by Sir Thomas More and his master, Henry VIII. Thomas More demonstrated a marked radicalism of approach. He translated a biography of the Florentine mage Pico de la Mirandola in which the mysteries of the Hebrews, Chaldeans and Arabs are favourably described. In his own *Utopia* the lives and customs of the inhabitants in his fictional country are very different from those of most Christian societies of his day. There is total religious freedom, for example. 'Some worship for God the sonne: some the mone: some, some other of the planettes . . . But the moste and wysest parte believe that there is a certayne Godlie powre unknowen, everlastinge, incomprehensible . . . Him they call the father of al.' The only man his hero Raphael Hythloday sees punished is one who, newly converted to Christianity, shows such intolerance towards the beliefs of others that he is seen as a 'sedicious person and raiser up of dissension amonge the people.' Nor can the Utopian custom whereby lovers, under proper safeguards, inspect each other naked, be said to concur with accepted morality.

Despite the fact that divorce is permitted in his Utopia, More proved so uncompromising over the question of the royal divorce as to antagonise Henry to the point where his vengeance was inevitable. Forced by the issue to break with Rome, the king then tried by every possible means to create a national church which was as much like the original as possible. This was a bitter disappointment to those who wanted to see one with a radical and individual character of its own, perhaps reviving that of the past.

Discontents of a similar kind in France led to periodic demands for the revival of the Gallican Church. This had been strongest in

Brittany where a kind of guerilla struggle with Rome had been carried on since the ninth century when Duke Nominoë, having freed his realm of Frankish dominance, also sought to establish the independence of the church. He abolished the jurisdiction of the archbishops of Tours, in practice accepted only in the Gallo-Roman sees of Rennes, Nantes and Vannes, and inaugurated two new dioceses, making a total of seven. Overall jurisdiction was given to St Samson's old diocese of Dol which, translated to an archepiscopal see, survived for 300 years in the teeth of strenuous opposition from Church and Pope. From time to time its opponents were able to find temporal allies. In the eleventh century William of Normandy, who had his eyes on Brittany, intervened when the Bretons drove out the then archbishop of Dol, Juthael, whom they accused of expropriating ecclesiastical properties to his own benefit. When Duke Alain III refused to withdraw his support from Juthael, William sent troops to the area, plundering and burning villages.

In the meantime imprudence on the Breton side gave the Pope an opening. In an ironical gesture of defiance they had elected in Juthael's stead the sixteen-year-old brother of the powerful Count of Combourg, and sent him to Rome with a tutor to be consecrated. Refusing to grant the crozier to a mere lad, the Pope instead offered it to the tutor after first obtaining his agreement to surrender the independence and all liberties of the see. The people of Dol accepted the situation, but gradually reinstated their traditional rights and only in 1199 did Innocent III, backed by the French crown, succeed in crushing the see which thereafter ceased to be metropolitan. Yet the Breton dioceses continued to maintain their special rites and ceased to use the Gallican Breviary only in 1848.

The last serious attempt to revive the Gallican Church occurred during the early phases of the Revolution, but a government with more pressing problems and little interest in religion postponed consideration of a question which was made irrelevant when, in its later phases, the Revolution became militantly atheistic. With the Revolution Dol ceased even to be a bishopric.

In the final analysis, Henry VIII's attempt to maintain a Church in England as a kind of replica of the Roman one, with the sole difference that he, rather than the Bishop of Rome, was head, proved impossible. The seeds planted in the past, slow in germination, proved themselves extremely hardy with an uncontrollable tendency to self-propagation. The truth was that there had grown up among men and women a desire to free themselves from the system in which redemption was gained partly, it is true, through their own merits, but mainly through the mediation of the Church's functionaries, doctrines and sacraments. As the Protestant reformers saw it, it had interposed its authority too much between God and mortals. The divine grace was only conditionally and not readily available. One can obviously see in this a similarity to the Celtic and Druidic view of an Otherworld omnipresent and close at hand.

Yet the more radical of the new ideas soon found themselves confronting a diehard conservatism. Within the Roman Catholic Church, the ideas of the Neoplatonists were discarded, the mages with their flights from the body were arraigned before the Inquisition at the first opportunity. Giordano Bruno died at the stake with an iron gag in his mouth to stop him proclaiming his beliefs from the flames. Nor was there greater tolerance in the reformed churches.

However, in most of the Celtic lands there was a tendency to go much further than the original reformers can ever have envisaged. In Bohemia, which took its name from the Boii tribe, there was Jan Hus; in Switzerland, the land of the Helvetii, Huldrych Zwingli and John Calvin. The elements of predestination and the Elect of the Saved to be found in their doctrines were taken up by John Knox in Scotland, where the church had remained independent of Rome until late times.

In Wales, the Isle of Man and the Channel Islands, the bland respectability of Anglicanism gave way to chapel-going nonconformity; in Northern Ireland, to fundamentalism. If the Southern Irish and the Bretons stuck loyally to Catholicism, it was a Catholicism of a highly individual kind. It is ironical that all these, in essence attempts to produce a 'purer' Christianity, were in many ways a harking ever deeper into the pagan past. Indeed, the very belief in religious purity brings to mind the laughter at Delphi.

Out of these drastic reforms was born a new zeal. Jan Morris writes: 'The Christian faith took centuries to root itself in Wales; Catholicism spread slowly . . . Anglicanism was imposed by writ of law; but the Methodist Revival, *Y Diwygiad*, hurled everything topsy-turvy, demolishing the social structure, transforming the culture, shifting the self-image and the reputation of the people, and eventually giving rise to a great convulsion of power that was a truly a revolution.'

One manifestation of that revolution was a reversion to the Biblical theology of those early missionaries who first set foot on Celtic shores. Another was a strong distaste for imagery, reminding one of the Druidic reluctance to give human representation to the gods. A third and more striking one was the open-air preaching session, the *Cymanfa Pregethu*, originated by the Wesley brothers, John and Charles, but continued by their successors. Jan Morris again:

> Thousands of people often assembled on a hillside or beside a lake for these marathon festivals . . . Hour after hour the meeting would proceed, successions of preachers standing on makeshift platforms, shouting hoarsely against the wind as often as not or bright-eyed and bareheaded in the rain. The vast crowd listened intently, weighing every word, pressing ever more closely, and when all was over the meeting ended with some vast, grand and melancholy hymn, its theme rolling all round the empty countryside, echoing through the mountains, its last refrain repeated again and again, ever more emotionally, by the weeping, laughing, Hallelujahing and richly singing multitude.

The phenomenon was not restricted to Wales. Similar meetings were taking place in Cornwall, in Jersey and Guernsey, and it is hard not to compare them with the accounts of the Druidic festivals, the great mass sacrifices as we have them in Caesar and other authors. The reference to lakesides, in particular, brings to mind the lakeside festivals of pagan times of which we have evidence in the ritual deposits in Lakes Neuchâtel, Toulouse and Cerrig Bach in Anglesey.

Baring-Gould draws a parallel with the *pardon* of which he writes that it 'is to the Breton what a revival is to the Cornish Methodist and a camp-meeting to a Yorkshire Nonconformist'.

One must not lose sight of another Druidic element: that of rebirth with which revivalism, almost by definition, was deeply imbued. In his *Battle for the Mind* the psychologist William Sargant has discussed this in detail. Emphasised in all forms of fundamentalism, it was also of course the climax of the shamanic crisis as well as central to Druidism and the Mystery Religions whose similarities with the Breton *pardons* have been noted.

Associated with rebirth was the idea of baptism. Among the first Christian converts this was, of necessity, carried out in adulthood and by total immersion. From the adult, fully aware of the relevance of the rite he or she was undergoing, the orthodox Christian denominations adopted infant baptism, where there could be no conscious participation. Indeed, baptism receives little more than lip service from most denominations. By contrast, several of the more fundamental Protestant churches reintroduced adult baptism by total immersion.

It was another paradox that the epoch which saw the development of Christian Nonconformity and revivalism also witnessed a growing interest in the pagan past. It had, of course, begun earlier. For Michael Drayton whose *Polyolbion* was published in 1622, the Druids were sacred bards and philosophers unrivalled in their knowledge of 'great Nature's depth'. Through the ensuing decades books on the Celts and Druidism, often works of pure imagination, poured from the presses at an ever-increasing rate. At the same time the Druids were subjected to a romantic idealisation in which the decapitation of enemies, human sacrifice, the horrors depicted with Lucan and Tacitus, were more and more obscured. To all intents and purposes the Druids became indistinguishable from Goldsmith's sentimental portrayal of the Anglican parson in *The Deserted Village* or *The Vicar of Wakefield*. Even Scripture itself was dragged in: Noah and Abraham were both Druids; Biblical Judaism, virtually a British invention. The megaliths, and above all Stonehenge, were Druidic monuments and, in the public mind, have so remained to this day.

The century witnessed a revival of interest in many of the preoccupations of the Renaissance mages. Neoplatonists like Thomas Taylor were experimenting with Kabbalism, Pythagorean number mysticism and what was closely allied to it, *gematria*, the complex system of Biblical exegesis which involved resolving text to numerical form[1].

What was happening should not be dismissed merely as a fashionable fad. The eighteenth century and early nineteenth centuries coincided with the Industrial Revolution and those 'dark, Satanic mills' against which the poet and engraver William Blake (1757–1827) inveighed. As in all such periods, there was a desire to rediscover a past in which humans were thought to live in more natural and idyllic conditions. This may well have been one of the attractions of the Celts, for whatever lacunae there may be in our knowledge of them we do know they had an intense feeling for the beauties of landscape and environment. It was through the Welshman Owen Pughe, one of the Twenty-four Elders of the millenarian Joanna Southcott, that Blake was introduced to the Druids. They soon found a place in his *Prophetic Books* and their megaliths in his art.

However, critics of the Industrial Revolution like Blake were not concerned only for the desecration of the countryside. They recognised it as turning a peasantry into the serfs of the manufacturing process and were deeply moved by their plight and by the human degradation involved. The orthodox church, on the other hand, appeared indifferent. Its clergy were either unable to abandon the pleasures of hunting field or ballroom or were lost in the aridities of debate on such questions as whether it was scripturally permissible for widows or widowers to remarry.

For a short time after 1789 the French Revolution was seen as a possible hope for humanity caught in the trap of industrialism. This perished with the Terror and the dictatorship of Bonaparte.

# Notes

1 In the Hebrew form for which *gematria* was originally invented this presented no problem, as the letters of the Hebrew alphabet were also used to represent numbers. With other alphabets, such as the Greek or Roman, where numbers are written with different characters, tables of equivalents had to be evolved.

# Chapter 15
# The Gods Dethroned

There is nothing in Celtic myth comparable with the Christian Judgment Day or the Germanic *Götterdämerung*. The end will come at that unheralded moment when the skies fall and the seas engulf the land. Far from perishing spectacularly amid the flames and ruination of a collapsing Valhalla the Celtic gods were disfranchised. The Christian priests insisted that their God had assumed – in reality had always possessed – mastery over life and death, health and sickness, the storm, the passage of sun and stars, the yield of field and byre.

If one believes the Irish transition stories, that is to say those which came into existence at the time when the island was undergoing conversion, not all the Tuatha clung obstinately to the old faith. Some embraced the new, though never with total enthusiasm. The lovely Ethne, brought up at the court of Manannan mac Lir, is forced to wander disconsolately when she loses her veil of invisibility while bathing. Finding herself in a monastery garden she is befriended by the monks and received into the Church. Pious as she becomes, there are still times when her prayer is distracted by a flurry and soft, sad voices calling her name. The loss is too great and she dies in the arms of St Patrick.

As we know, not all died. The Welsh expression *Tylwyth Teg* means 'the fair folk', the fairies. The word *tylwyth* is cognate with the Irish *tuatha* and identifies them with the Tuatha De Danann of Ireland. The Tuatha, we know, took over the megalithic tumuli, the *sidhs*. The Cornish piskies, the Breton *bonnes dames* and Channel Island *faitiaux* favoured similar accommodation, on which account they must be left undisturbed. In Jersey in 1912, a furious old man, brandishing his walking-stick, descended on the members of the local archaeological society who were excavating a dolmen, and warned them, 'If you disturb the fairies you will bring trouble on the neighbourhood'. On a later occasion workmen refused to dig near the same spot.

Perhaps such caution was understandable. The woman from the *sidh*, the *banshee*, palely beautiful and with her tresses of flowing hair, was an omen of disaster whose dirge could be heard among the glens and lochs of Ireland and Scotland. Some clans, like the Dalcassians and MacCarthys even had their own *banshee*. She was certainly a surviving aspect of the triple Macha and it is significant that in Ireland she was often called the Babd and believed to be able to appear as a trio of death-presaging hooded crows. In April 1014 they were seen revelling in the slaughter at Clontarf where the Irish fought a terrible battle with the Danish invaders. It was just before that battle that a woman of the Tuatha begged one of the Irish commanders not to fight because he and his fellows were destined to fall.

The Macha could also manifest herself, as she did to Cu Chulainn and King Cormac, in the guise of Washer-at-the-Ford. The twelfth-century Norman leader Richard de Clare, known as Strongbow, was warned of the defeat of his troops by the apparition of a hag washing at a ford 'till the red gore churned in her hands'. In Scotland she was the web-footed *ban nighechain*; in Brittany, the *cannered noz* washing the shroud which would shortly be worn by whoever had the misfortune to encounter her. In Wales she was the black *Gwrach y Rhibyn* stirring the waters with her bat-like wings and foretelling misfortune or death with her blood-curdling shriek.

Not all the *sidh*-dwellers were so menacing. Some were merely playful. The word *pouque*, especially connected with Channel Island megalithic monuments, is obviously related to the Irish *puca*, the Welsh *pwca*, the Cornish *bucca* and the English Puck. Besides manifesting themselves as the will-o'-the-wisp or as poltergeists, they had a whole repertoire of tricks, sometimes cruel, which they played on mortals. A traveller could find himself led astray by a false light, a cow would be secretly robbed of her milk or, if its rightful owner managed to save it, it would refuse to turn to butter in the churn. Worse still was their habit of exchanging their own for human babies. Many of these were tricks which, according to the twelfth-century *Book of Leinster*, the Tuathan gods employed against the Milesian invaders. Some would cease their mischief if suitably propitiated. The Newlyn *bucca*, for example, could be bribed with gifts of fish. The Breton *corrigans*, so given to exchanging babies that the term 'Little Corrigan' was applied to any infant whose parentage was dubious, could be placated by those willing to join their dance among the dolmens and menhirs, reciting the days of the week.

Some could be positively beneficent. If so disposed a Cornish pisky might thresh a farmer's corn for him during the night or, by knocking, warn tin miners of imminent danger. The *bonnes dames* have even been known to help a weary housewife or skivvy. One thinks of the Breton woman singing the praises of Viviane. Aine, probably derived from Ana, lives on the slopes of Knockainy, County Limerick, with her two sisters and so is the typical, triple-aspected Celtic goddess. She is credited with warding off disease and curing the sick.

Just as the gods could revert to the forms they had as tribal totems, so the fairies could change themselves into animals. In Ireland, Scotland, Wales and the Isle of Man one finds the dangerous water horse which emerges from a lake, taking on human shape in the process. In a Highland story, a crofter's daughter is wooed by a tall, handsome young man. It is only when she finds strands of waterweed on the comb she is using on his hair that she realises what he is. She escapes in the manner the Druids prescribed to Pliny, by setting a stream between herself and him.

The Irish and Manx water horses were less sinister. Like the *bonnes dames* they could help with household chores, though, if ill-rewarded they would take offence and vanish. Or, perhaps recalling their former divinity, if a task was too menial they would drag whoever had set it back to their lake.

The water horse's feminine counterpart could sometimes choose a mortal mate, as the Irish Macha chose to make herself mistress-housekeeper to Crunniuc mac Agnomain. Jean Markale records a story from the Vosges in which a young man is given crucial aid in his love affair by a mare. After the animal has saved him from a lingering and painful death, she turns into a beautiful girl whom the young man chooses in preference to the original object of his desire.

The husbands of these mare-wives are invariably placed under the *geis* never to exploit their equine nature. The Macha curses the Ulstermen when forced to race against Conchobhar's horses. In two tales recorded by Rhys, young Welsh farmers each lose their fairy-wives when a bridle they are trying to fit on an unbroken horse accidentally falls on the girl instead and she vanishes, never again to be seen.

Just as Macha, besides being Crunniuc's housekeeper and lover, also provides food and clothing, often these ladies would bring dowries from their watery homes and the wealth of some Welsh families was attributed to such a union in its past. Some families claimed descent from such mothers. One of them, in a version from Llyn y Fan Fach in Brecknockshire, deserted husband and sons, but was said to have revisited and taught them the lore of healing herbs so that they became famous physicians. As late as the nineteenth century it was believed that the fairy herself reappeared on the first Sunday in August and country folk would climb a local mountain in the hope of glimpsing her.

Traces of horse lore survive in such customs as the Hallowe'en 'White Mare' in County Cork, where a procession was led by a man in white, carrying a representation of a horse's head. This is very similar to the Christmas *Mari Llwyd*, or Grey Mare, found especially in South Wales. There is also the Padstow 'Obby 'Oss, while the decorating, particularly of wagon horses, with brass knickknacks on a leather strap may have Celtic origins. Even the use of horses' skulls seems to have persisted. Merrifield mentions a number of cases where they have been found beneath floorboards, in some cases put there as late as the nineteenth century. The excuse was that it improved a room's acoustics; a belief, needless to say, without scientific basis. This can hardly have applied to a custom recorded in the 1880s in the unlikely milieu of a Primitive Baptist chapel in the Cambridgeshire fens. When its foundations were being laid, the builder sent one of his workmen to a knacker's yard to procure a horse's head which was then placed on a stake in the centre of the trench and libated with beer!

Horses are not the only creatures to emerge from the waters. *Fuwch Frech*, the Brindled Cow of Ireland, who could fill the biggest milk pails, lived in a lake and, when threatened with slaughter by a farmer, returned to it for good. Another bovine provider, the Grey Cow of Goibniu, which once supplied free milk to every home, was offended by a woman who sold some of it, and swam across the sea to Wales and Scotland.

Besides cows and horses, there are also water bulls. The antiquity of these creatures is archaeologically attested. The stone slab, dated to the first century AD , found at Nôtre Dame Cathedral with its the left-handed woodcutter and its inscription Esus, has already been mentioned. On its reverse side is a bull with three water birds on its back and the inscription *Tarvos Trigaranos*, which means 'The Bull with Three Cranes'. Esus is also shown on a relief discovered at Trèves in 1895. Here the tree is identifiable as the willow, a tree that thrives near water, and among its foliage the head of a bull and three wading birds can be made out. A silvered bronze bull from Maiden Castle, Dorset, has on its back, not water birds, but three goddesses with notably bird-like bodies. A bull with a back broad enough to provide a dancing floor for goddesses is not exceptional. The back of the Great Bull of Donn was broad enough for fifty lads to play hurley on it!

Of course, it was not always the Otherworld creatures who crossed into the world of mortals. As we have seen, mortals could themselves stray into the fairy realm. Gerald of Wales, with his usual straight face, tells of a priest who, in boyhood, was taken on a visit to an underground country where the people spoke a language like Greek. A Scottish Presbyterian minister told Evans Wentz he was 'very certain' fairies existed as he had 'states of ecstasy' in which he had seen them – echoes of Gerald's *awenyddion*.

Tales of young men tempted into crossing the frontier by some ravishing creature – Hallowe'en was a specially dangerous season – were being told in Wales, the Isle of Man and Ireland until recently. Even today many Irish people will avoid churchyards at this time. In a story from the Isle of Man, a pair of ploughmen are lured by beautiful women into a house where feasting and wild dancing are in progress. One of them breaks the taboo on accepting the Otherworld hospitality by drinking from the cup offered him. His wiser companion refuses and leaves. Returning next day he finds that his companion, the women and the house have vanished, not to reappear until the following Hallowe'en when his friend is seen, still dancing with the house's seductive occupants.

All these examples only go to show how the Druidic tradition of an Otherworld coexistent with our own has survived. The travel writer Jan Morris, herself a Welshwoman, writes that 'the conviction that some other state of being exists, invisible but sensible, outside our own windows' has remained embedded in the psyche of her compatriots.

The same author mentions the high incidence of Unidentified Flying Object sightings in Wales and how long their history is. The Welsh *Tanwedd*, or Fiery One, appears from nowhere in the night sky, flashes from one point to another then vanishes. An eighteenth-century farmer from Monmouthshire testified to seeing a fully-rigged sailing ship, surrounded by birds, emerge from the Eryri mountains. The phenomenon, also witnessed by his wife and a farmhand, occurred three times at precisely ten-year intervals and nothing could shake their testimony. In the mid-nineteenth century another family claimed to have watched the aerobatics of some kind of flying machine in the same area. In 1977 a whole class of Dyfed primary school children reported watching a UFO land in a field and drew pictures similar in all basic essentials which now hang in the school hall. Other witnesses of UFO activity include policemen, clergymen, schoolteachers and farmers.

The Otherworld may intrude upon our own, but is, nonetheless, akin to a dream world. As in the shaman's Otherworld, time is different there. An Irish bridegroom, who visits fairyland on his wedding day, returns thinking he has been absent for a single night, to find it was actually several generations and that his bride had died long ago. Rhys tells of a young Welshman who spends what seems to be a mere evening in this land only to find when he returns that seven years have passed, his parents are dead and the sweetheart he left, as it seemed, such a short time ago, has married someone else. Guinamor, hero of a Breton story, is granted the favours of the beauty he has seen bathing and is taken to her palace. When he wants to leave he finds three hundred years have passed.

Markale, who is a Breton, draws attention to the opening formula used by local storytellers until recently: 'Once upon a time there was no time . . .' and to the tense-jumbling often found even in Celtic literature. This could be said have re-emerged in recent decades with the French *Roman Nouveau* whose founder, Alain Robbe-Grillet, was also a Breton.

Literature and dream are related insofar as both are products of the unconscious. The greatest literature is that which seems to strike chords deep in the unconscious. Mythologies are particularly potent in this respect and we have seen how true this is of Celtic mythology. One of the enduring fascinations of the Arthurian legends is the air of mystery which pervades them: those castles which loom out of the primeval mist or which stand as dark silhouettes on promontories overlooking a grey sea; the arm which emerges from the midst of a lake bearing the sword; the ambivalent character of Merlin; the forests, teeming with an innate, ever-watchful life and where the only human to appear is likely to be some weird old man, an ancient half-mad hermit or a Druid.

Mythologies are the imprint of the earliest experiences of our species couched in the language of metaphor. The Celts understood this, for they understood that these were supernatural truths and, as Peter Abelard found and as Lao-Tzu declared some 1,500 years before him, these are beyond articulation in direct language. Celtic art makes its affirmations in symbolic terms, by clues to be assembled, which may underlie the Druids' reluctance to portray the gods realistically. Diogenes Laertius mentions their preference for 'riddles and dark sayings' and Pomponius Mela claims that statements were half expressed, the listener being expected to fill the gaps.

As Jan Morris points out, the mystery story is a typical product of the Celtic imagination and it is not surprising that its founder, Arthur Conan Doyle, should have been a Celt.

Their very antiquity may go some way towards explaining the survival of many beliefs. The Neolithic farmers, the builders of impressive henge monuments, date back to something like 3000 BC. The Indo-European root race goes back at least 2,500 years before that and probably earlier. Even that is hardly more than the beginning. Human beings have walked the earth for something like two million years. *Homo erectus*, that is to say a creature walking on two legs, building some kind of shelter and hunting with stone weapons, appeared about 800,000 years ago; the first *Homo sapiens neanderthalensis* about 100,000 years ago, and the ancestors most like ourselves anatomically and intellectually, *Homo sapiens sapiens*, about 33,000 years ago. The first traces of shamanism date to round about the same time, but it is likely that they go back much further.

It is here that we can find the ancestry of the countless phantom hunters embedded in folklore. Gwynn's Hunt flourished in Wales until recent times where, dressed in grey, he would lead the *cwn Annwn* (Annwn is a variant for Annwvyn), the hounds of Hell and a string of dead souls who could be heard and seen on nights when midwinter gales howled their most boisterously. The white bodies and red ears of his pack match those of the hounds of Arawn in *Pwyll Lord of Dyved*, the name Arawn itself possibly resulting from a misreading for Annwn. It is the same pack which, in one version of the Perceval story, the hero encounters in a forest, and who are here described as the hunters of the Fisher-King.

Phantom hunt stories were being told in Scotland at least until the sixteenth century and the belief that Arthur and his knights took part in one on certain moonlit nights was still current in France three centuries later.

In some localities the huntsman is not the British king, but none other than the devil mounted on a black horse with fiery eyes. He it was who led the Wild Hunt across the Cornish moors, his Dandy Dogs overtaking the struggling wayfarer on a windy night. The only means of escape was devout prayer. It was these same hounds who, in local lore, were the instrument of Nemesis for a certain notoriously wicked seventeenth-century steward. Pursued to his death, his spectre can be heard moaning and cursing as it carries out its posthumous ordeal of trying to empty a pond with a leaky shell.

Nor was belief in the hunt limited to Celtdom. Tolstoy mentions an entry in the *Anglo-Saxon Chronicle* for 1127 in which it was seen and – as blasts from a hunting horn – heard by the terrified citizens of Peterborough. The English tradition actually also includes Herne whose name, derived from the word 'horn', is plainly identifiable as Cernunnos and is commemorated in the place name Herne Bay in Kent. However, his main link is with Windsor Great Park. In Shakespeare's *Merry Wives of Windsor* one of the characters disguises himself as Herne to add to the torments of the unhappy John Falstaff. Dressed in deer-skins and wearing horned headgear Herne also features in Harrison Ainsworth's *Windsor Castle* and Tolstoy relates the recollection of an old gamekeeper who claimed to have seen him.

There are, of course, a great many more phantom hunters. One, connected with the Buckinghamshire village of Fingest, is said to be a fourteenth-century Bishop of Lincoln, Henry Burghersh, who caused hardship to the people of the area when he annexed 300 acres of common land to his own estates. The fact that the bishop was a keen huntsman and that his ghost is described as dressed in green seems to place him firmly among the Lords of the Forest. 'Green Man' sightings from another part of Buckinghamshire, Hughenden, as well as from Leeds and Swindon, were recorded in 1986 and 1987.

If C.G. Jung's theory of a Collective Unconscious has any validity – and it is hard to account for much in folk custom without invoking something of the sort – it is only to be expected that these age-long experiences would have left an imprint. Why do we celebrate a failed attempt to blow up the Houses of Parliament when we leave so many far more important occasions unmarked? Why was it found necessary to revive May Day as a public holiday? What urge was it that led Victorian and Edwardian builders to use representations of human heads as decoration?

All the same, to attempt to explain a phenomenon as complex as Celtic belief by reference to history and influences is to lose sight of the wood by concentration on the trees. The Scythians provided them with the models for their plastic art, yet they made it individually, definably, unmistakably their own. And whatever influence one can isolate as having shaped the Celts one finds they have remoulded it in unique form. Originally ignorant of classical literature, once they discovered it they were quick to spot the similarity between heroes like Cu Chulainn and the Homeric ones. In an anonymous thirteenth-century Irish version of the *Odyssey*, for example, Ulysses' return to Ithaca and his recognition by his dog is treated exactly as such an event might be treated in native epic.

His wife, Penelope, refusing to believe it is her husband returned after so long, tells him,

'If you were Ulysses you'd ask after your dog.'
'I'd not thought it'd be alive at all,' he says.
'It made broth of a long life,' she says. 'And what sort of a dog at all is that dog?'
'It has white sides and a light crimson back and a jet-black belly and green tail.'

Even Christianity could make no headway until its missionaries imitated the Druids. As Toynbee says, the Celts reshaped it to fit their own heritage.

This helps to explain what made them so incomprehensible to outsiders, particularly the Romans, a severely practical, even materialistic people. Their national bent was for organisation and technology. It was the former that enabled them to conquer and build cities, connected by fine roads and bridges. The latter which enabled them to build houses of a luxury previously unimaginable. They knew how to heat them. They had amenities like baths. But their religion was scarcely more than a formality; their gods members of a remote state pantheon. Toward anything redolent of the mystical or the occult, they were profoundly hostile. In Rome even fortune-telling was forbidden under pain of awesome sanctions. There could certainly be no question of the gods dropping in on mortals or mortals making trips to their world.

For the Celts, a ubiquitous, omnipresent Otherworld exerted a ceaseless, irresistible fascination. Bran Mac Febail and Mael Duin all make their magical journeys to it. Even St Brendan's was not entirely a physical one. Welsh shepherds whiled away the hours tending their flocks by cutting 'Caerau Droia' mazes in the turf of pastures. There is one still to be seen on a rock near Llanfairfechan, on the Gwynedd coast, and as we have seen they have an antiquity going back to the Neolithic megalith builders. Threading a maze, like Bradley's trance-inducing patterns in the passage graves, was supposed to lead to a heightened state of consciousness, to put one in touch with the Otherworld forces.

It is, of course, the place sought with such pain and difficulty by knights like Sir Galahad. Yet it is not the place alone which matters. It is what is to be found there: the magic power-imbuing and life-transforming object. The Bull of Donn is such an object. That is why Mebd desires it so avidly and why, when she tries to seize it, the Ulstermen wage a war to defend it. The cauldrons, ultimately transmuted into the Grail, are another such magic object.

But they can be acquired and retained only by the worthy. The Ulstermen have shown themselves unworthy guardians of the Bull of Donn by their heartless treatment of the pregnant Macha. Paralysed in their hour of need, the task falls on shoulders of the boy-hero Cu Chulainn, spiritual son of Lugh. In Grail legend it is Sir Galahad alone who proves himself worthy of succeeding in the quest. Cu Chulainn possesses the merits of the pagan hero: bravery, loyalty, 'truth in his heart'. Sir Galahad adds to these the Christian virtue of chastity. The nature of the object and the qualities of the seeker are so intimately interwoven that the Celtic quest resembles that of the alchemist for the Philosopher's Stone. The alchemist will discover the means whereby base metal is to be transmuted into gold only if he also transmutes the base metal of his soul in the process.

In this way the quest is itself a species of rebirth. Peredur undergoes such a rebirth before he sees the fields with the white and black sheep. It is symbolised by his successful struggle with the lion guarding a pit filled with bones of men and of animals, a dim recollection perhaps of the ritual shafts.

To the Celts, rebirth was first and foremost a reawakening to the great cosmic mystery and it is scarcely necessary to remind ourselves that the concept of rebirth and, essentially, rebirth to the great cosmic mystery is very much with us. Obviously it is seen at its plainest in the 'born again' Christian sects, but 'rebirthing' is the *raison d'être* for all manner of cults. In fact, it is as if many in our society feel the need to be born anew, if not to a different life, at any rate to a different kind of life. Underlying this may be our growing disenchantment with the rationalistic and mechanistic view of the universe which has grown increasingly dominant since the time of Isaac Newton and which has combined with a critique, often unjust, of orthodox religion.

This book has been an attempt to show that the legacy of the past has been preserved, not just in a collection of superstitions or quaint folk customs, but as a basic mind-set.

Like most Europeans, we have been indoctrinated with the belief that Greece and Rome were the twin founts of our civilisation. That, indeed, for us, it began only with the Romans' arrival. Of course, in many ways, we are still surrounded by much that is modelled on that past: our public architecture, for example, as manifest in town halls up and down the land. Furthermore, like our own, the Romans' was an urban society and, in that sense, is familiar to us.

All the same, we are now beginning to realise that there are patterns of civilisation other than the Roman one. 'The contribution made by the classical world has not been doubted since the Renaissance, and has sometimes been exaggerated', writes J.X.W.P. Corcoran in his introductory chapter to Nora Chadwick's *The Celts*. 'It is time that the contribution of prehistoric Europe, and more particularly that of the Celts and their forebears, was recognised adequately.' Nora Chadwick in the same book speaks of them as the 'heralds of modern civilisation'.

She is right. And the truth is that rough and tough as we should find the pagan Celtic world, there are many aspects of it with which we should today find ourselves in greater harmony than some of the things we might find in Rome or Athens.

For example there is their attitude to women. Obviously it is now impossible to know exactly how they fared in Celtic society or what was the real attitude of the Celtic male towards them. Nonetheless, as we saw, law and custom gave women privileges unknown elsewhere. In any event, one can imagine the Celtic woman throwing herself wholeheartedly – and militantly – behind the feminist movement.

There is also the strong consciousness of the natural environment which probably goes a long way towards explaining the Celts' success as farmers. The shaman was the environmentalist *par excellence*. What little we know of the Druids' tree lore suggests that the shamanistic sense of participation in and partnership with the natural world was something that they preserved. An identification with the natural world in all its seasonal facets comes across forcibly from even the most superficial acquaintance with Celtic poetry. In their art, besides the remarkably sensitive and vivid representations of animals, there are those patterns of leaves and swirling tendrils which seem charged with the very energies of nature. Obviously one thinks, too, of Lucan's forest-dwelling Druids and the hermits of the Arthurian stories, or the wizards and magicians of fairy tale who so often live in such surroundings.

There is also the Celtic belief in maximum freedom within a set of commonly accepted laws. This is in opposition to what could be called the Romanising spirit, one which believes in organising, documenting and devising laws which attempt to cover every eventuality.

When the British monarch takes his or her place on the coronation chair to receive the insignia of royalty, they are not simply sitting on a well-worn slab of stone which just might have been the one the ancient Irish High Kings sat on. They are actually binding themselves to rule as they ruled, as sovereigns subject to the Law, a law ultimately of divine origin, to rule as 'constitutional monarchs'.

It is not so long ago that, for many, the very idea of constitutional monarchy was unthinkable, even ludicrous. 'I can understand a republic. I can understand an absolute monarchy', said Tsar Nicholas I who ruled Russia from 1825 to 1855. 'What I cannot understand is a constitutional monarchy . . . Rather than adopt it I'd withdraw to China.' Today, almost without exception, the world's remaining kings and queen are constitutional ones and the day may not be far off when Russia herself has one. There is something symbolic in that. The Russian word, tsar, like the German Kaiser, comes from the word 'Caesar' and, as such, is a linguistic tribute to the Roman past and the Roman concept of government, a concept now in the process of supersession.

The Celts' sojourn in Delphi may have been brief, but it could be said that in the sanctuary of Apollo their commander had the last laugh.

# Select Bibliography

Ashe, Geoffrey, *King Arthur's Avalon*, London, 1973.

Baring-Gould, S., *A Book of Brittany*, London, 1909.

Bradley, Richard, *The Passage of Arms*, Cambridge, 1990.

Brothwell, Don, *The Bog Man and the Archaeology of People*, London, 1986.

Campbell, Joseph, *Primitive Mythology*, London, 1960.

Campbell, J.F., *Popular Tales of the West Highlands*, Edinburgh, 1860-2.

Chadwick, Nora, *The Celts*, Harmondsworth, 1977.

Chrétien de Troyes, *Arthurian Romances*, trans. W.W. Comfort, London, 1975.

——, *Arthurian Romances*, trans. W.W. Kibler, Harmondsworth, 1991.

Clark, W. Fordyce, *The Shetland Sketch Book*, Edinburgh, 1930.

Curtin, Jeremiah, *Hero-Tales of Ireland*, London, 1894.

——, *Myths and Folklore of Ireland*, Boston,1890.

De Vries, Jan, *La Réligion des Celtes*, Paris, 1963.

Dillon, Myles, *Early Irish Literature*, Chicago, London, 1972.

Edwards, David L., *Christian England*, London, 1981.

Eliade, Mircea, *Shamanism: Archaic Techniques of Ecstasy*, trans. Willard R. Trask, New Jersey, 1974.

——, *Images and Symbols*, trans. Philip Mairet, New York, 1969.

Ellman, Richard, *Yeats: The Man and the Masks*, Harmondsworth, 1987.

Evans, William, *The Bards of the Isle of Britain*, Anglesey, undated.

Fawtier, Robert, *La Vie de Saint Samson*, Paris, 1912.

Frazer, J.G., *The Golden Bough*, London, 1978.

Gimbutas, Marija, *The Gods and Goddesses of Old Europe*, London, 1974.

Gantz, Jeffrey, trans., *The Mabinogion*, Harmondsworth, 1976.

——, trans., *Early Irish Myths and Sagas*, Harmondsworth, 1984.

Geoffrey of Monmouth, *The History of the Kings of Britain*, trans. L. Thorpe, Harmondsworth, 1976.

Gerald of Wales, *The History and Topography of Ireland*, trans. John O'Meara, Harmondsworth, 1982.

Green, Miranda, *The Gods of the Celts*, Gloucester, 1986.

Gregory of Tours, trans: Lewis Thorpe, *The History of the Franks*, Harmondsworth, 1988.

Guest, Lady Charlotte, trans., *The Mabinogion*, London, 1980.

Halifax, Joan, *Shaman: The Wounded Healer*, London, 1982.

Henderson, George, *Survivals in Belief among the Celts*, Glasgow, 1911.

Herm, Gerhard, *The Celts*, London, 1976.

Hull, Eleanor, *Folklore of the British Isles*, London, 1928.

Hunt, Robert, *Popular Romances of the West of England, or the Drolls, Traditions and Superstitions of Old Cornwall*, 3rd ed., London, 1896.

Johnson, W. Branch, *Folktales of Brittany*, London, 1927.

Jones, T. Gwynn, *Welsh Folklore and Folk-custom*, London, 1966.

Jones, T. Gwynn, *Welsh Folklore and Custom*, Cardiff, 1979.

Jones, Gwynn and Thomas, trans., *The Mabinogion*, London, 1963.

Kendrick, T.D., *The Druids: A Study of Celtic Prehistory*, London, 1966.

Kennedy, Patrick, *Legendary Fictions of the Irish Celts*, London, 1866.

Le Braz, Anatole, *Le Légende de la Mort chez les Bretons Armoriques*, 3rd ed, Paris, 1912.

Lethbridge, T.C., *Gogmagog*, London, 1975.

Lloyd, J.E., *Owen Glendower*, London, 1931.

Lucan (Marcus Annaeus Lucanus), *Pharsalia*, 1962.

Luzel, F.M., *Contes Populaires de Basse-Bretagne*, Paris, 1887.

McKay, John G., *West Highland Tales*, Edinburgh, 1930.

Mallory, J.P., *In Search of the Indo-Europeans*, London, 1991.

Malory, Sir Thomas, *Le Morte d'Arthur*, 2 vols., Harmondsworth, 1984.

Marie de France, *The Lais*, trans. Glyn S. Burgess and Keith Busby, Harmondsworth, 1986.

Markale, Jean, *La femme celte*, Paris, 1973.

——, *Le roi Arthur*, Paris, 1976.

——, *Les Celtes*, Paris, 1975.

——, *Le Druidisme*, Paris, 1985.

Marx, Jean, *La Légende arthurienne et le Graal*, Paris, 1952.

Mattaraso, P.M., (ed.), *The Quest of the Holy Grail*, Harmondsworth, 1976.

Merrifield, Ralph, *The Archaeology of Ritual and Magic*, London, 1987.

Michelet, Jules, *Satanism and Witchcraft: A Study of Medieval Superstition*, New York, 1946 (originally published as *La Sorcière*, Paris, 1862).

Moore, A.W., *The Folklore of the Isle of Man*, London, 1891.

More, Sir Thomas, *Utopia*, London, 1931.

Morganwg, Iolo, *The Triads of Britain*, trans. W. Probert, London, 1977.

Morris, Jan, *The Matter of Wales*, Harmondsworth, 1986.

Nelli, René, *Les Cathares*, Paris, 1972.

O'Flaherty, Wendy Doniger, trans., *Hindu Myths*, Harmondsworth, 1972.

Onians, R.B., *The Origin of European Thought about the Body, the Mind, the Soul, the World, Time and Fate*, Cambridge, 1951.

O Suilleabhain, Sean, *A Handbook of Irish Folklore*, Dublin, 1942.

Owen, Ellis, *Welsh Folklore, a Collection of Folktales and Legends of Northern Wales*, Oswestry and Wrexham, 1896.

Piggott, Stuart, *The Druids*, Harmondsworth, 1975.

—, *Ancient Europe*, Edinburgh, 1973.

Rasmussen, Knud, *The Intellectual Culture of the Igulik Eskimo*, Copenhagen, 1928.

Renfrew, Colin, *Archaeology and Language: The Puzzle of Indo-European Origins*, London, 1987.

Rhys, John, *Celtic Folklore, Welsh and Manx*, Oxford, 1901.

Richardson, Emeline Hill, *The Etruscans*, Chicago, 1976.

Rolleston, T.W., *Myths and Legends of the Celtic Race*, London, 1929.

Ross, Anne, *Pagan Celtic Britain*, London, 1974.

Rutherford, Ward, *Celtic Mythology*, Wellingborough, 1987.

—, *Shamanism: The Foundations of Magic*, Wellingborough, 1986.

—, *The Druids*, Wellingborough, 1985.

—, *Pythagoras*, Wellingborough, 1984.

—, *Hitler's Propaganda Machine*, London, 1985.

—, *The Untimely Silence*, London, 1973.

Sayers, Dorothy L., *The Song of Roland*, Harmondsworth, 1984.

Sébillot, Paul, *Le Folklore de France*, Paris, 1905

—, *Légendes Locales de la Haute Bretagne*, Nantes, 1899.

—, *Contes Populaires de la Haute Bretagne*, Paris, 1880–2

Sen, K.M., *Hinduism*, Harmondsworth, 1975.

Spence, Lewis, *Legends and Romances of Brittany*, New York, undated.

Squire, Charles, *Celtic Myth and Legend*, California, 1975.

Tacitus, *The Agricola and the Germania*, trans. H. Mattingly, Harmondsworth, 1976.

——, *The Annals of Imperial Rome*, trans. Michael Grant, Harmondsworth, 1989.

Taylor, Thomas, trans., *The Life of St Samson of Dol*, London, 1925.

Thomas, W. Jenkyn, *The Welsh Fairy Book*, Cardiff, 1979.

Toynbee, Arnold, *The Study of History*, London, 1961.

Tolstoy, Nikolai, *The Quest for Merlin*, London, 1985.

Trevelyan, Marie, *Folklore and Folk-stories of Wales*, London, 1909.

Van Gennep, Arnold, *Manuel de Folklore Français Contemporain*, Vols 3 and 4, Paris, 1937–8.

Watkin, M., *La civilisation française dans les Mabinogion*, Paris, 1963.

Wentz, W.Y. Evans, *The Fairy Faith in Celtic Countries*, London, New York, 1911.

Wilde, Francesca Speranza, Lady, *Ancient Legends Mystic Charms and Superstitions of Ireland*, London, 1888.

Wilson, Barbara Ker, *Scottish Folk-Tales and Legends*, Oxford, 1955.

Wolfram von Eschenbach, *Parzival*, trans. A.T. Hatto, Harmondsworth, 1980.

Wood-Martin, W.G., *Traces of the Elder Faiths in Ireland*, London, New York, 1902.

Yeats, William Butler, *Irish Fairy and Folk Tales*, New York, undated.

# Index